BREAKDOWN

All the best —

Bob Halloran

ALSO BY BOB HALLORAN
Irish Thunder: The Hard Life and Times of Micky Ward

BREAKDOWN

A Season of Gang Warfare, High School Football,
and the Coach Who Policed the Streets

BOB HALLORAN

LYONS PRESS
Guilford, Connecticut
An imprint of Globe Pequot Press

To my parents, who took care of me as a child.
To my wife, who takes care of me now.
And to my children, who better take care of me when I'm old.

Lyons Press is an imprint of Globe Pequot Press.

Project editor: Gregory Hyman
Text design: Sheryl P. Kober
Layout: Melissa Evarts

Library of Congress Cataloging-in-Publication data is available on file.

ISBN 978-1-59921-904-2

Printed in the United States of America

10 9 8 7 6 5 4 3 2 1

CONTENTS

PREFACE

The best part about writing is learning. You take on a project with a certain focus, and then watch the story morph into something different. It almost always happens, and it almost always needs to happen. In the case of *Breakdown,* the change came when I realized I wasn't writing about a bunch of violent gang kids living in a troubled city; I was actually writing a book *for* readers in the suburbs.

Parents like me who stand around soccer fields in affluent communities wondering if little Tommy is under too much stress because he has so many after-school activities have no idea what the kids in Chelsea, Massachusetts, have had to deal with. Hypothetical Tommy has soccer, piano, and the Boy Scouts, but the real-life Danny Cortez had to step over a dead body to get into his home. Mario Hernandez crawled on the floor of his apartment for a week in fear of gunshots coming through the window. This kid's dad is in jail. That kid's mom is on drugs. That's Chelsea. And it was a fulfilling learning experience for this suburban dad.

The story of James Atkins and the Chelsea High School football program began to be told in the *Boston Globe* in December of 2005. It was brought to my attention by a friend, Gene Miller, who was greatly moved by the details of how a police officer coaching a football team was willing and able to take gang kids off the streets and put them on his squad. He was turning troubled kids into promising young men. Gene thought it would make a great book, and I think she was right.

I sat on the idea for about eight months while I completed the manuscript for *Irish Thunder: The Hard Life and Times of Micky Ward.* I first met Jimmy Atkins at the end of the summer in 2006. He was getting the Red Devils ready for practice, still wearing his policeman's uniform. His voice boomed down the school corridors. I stood off to the side waiting for the right moment to approach him. It never really came. Jimmy disappeared into the locker room, and when he finally bounded out, he came directly toward me wanting to know who I was and why I was there.

I referred to the *Globe* article and told him I was interested in the possibility of writing a book about him, the Red Devils, and the upcoming season. He was immediately interested.

"It sure would help if you guys win the Super Bowl this year," I said.

"We might be able to," he said. "If we can find a quarterback."

Our first meeting couldn't have lasted more than five minutes. I wanted him to know that I didn't have a contract with a publisher yet, so there were no guarantees a book would ever be released. Also, I needed to have total access to the team. That meant that I'd be allowed into the locker room before, during, and after every game. I'd be on the sidelines during games. I'd be in the time-out huddles, on the bench, and in team meetings. For any football-related activity, I could come and go as I pleased, carrying a tape recorder everywhere I went. That was very important. And I told Jimmy he wouldn't be able to see anything I wrote before the book came out, and he wouldn't have any editorial authority. Anything I saw or heard was fair game.

"I'm the writer. So, I decide what does or doesn't go in the book." He agreed.

I'm not sure when Coach told the kids I was writing a book, because it appeared he had forgotten all about it a few days later. I returned to practice on Thursday before the Red Devils' first game. I was sitting in the grass about 30 yards away from the defensive drills when Coach sent an assistant over to find out who I was. I told the assistant about the book, and shouted toward Jimmy.

"It's me, Bob Halloran, the guy writing the book."

"Oh, yeah! Right," Jimmy said. "I didn't recognize you at first."

Practice continued and I quickly developed an understanding of how Coach handled his team. He ruled through multiple personalities. One minute he was a drill sergeant angrily shouting swear words at any player who didn't listen or perform up to standards, and the next minute he was Don Rickles, making jokes, poking fun, and trying to get the kids to relax. Several people I would interview later told me these kids feared Jimmy, but I never got that sense. I think they loved him, and the only thing they were afraid of was disappointing him. Even though he was often verbally abusive, his actions told them how much he cared about them. For many of the players, the relationship they had with Jimmy was the closest and most honest one in their lives.

While watching Jimmy on that first day, seeing him coach at such a frenetic pace, always talking, always teaching, I knew then that I had a great main character. It wasn't until a month or so later that I realized that while Jimmy's life and efforts would certainly be the heart of the book, the soul of the story belonged to the kids.

My regular job as a news and sports anchor for a Boston television station was going to pose a problem for me. I could leave for Chelsea after the 6:00 news on Friday nights, and get there in time for the start of their 7:00 games, but I would have to leave by 9:00 to get back for our 11:00 news. That would preclude me from getting the pre- and postgame locker room material I needed.

This is where I single out Drew Crea for high praise and appreciation. Drew was a student of mine when I taught a class at Curry College in Milton, Massachusetts. Drew received college credit for interning for me as I wrote and researched this book. Equipped with only a tape recorder and his wits, Drew walked the sidelines, conducted interviews, and talked to players as they came off the field. When I couldn't be there, Drew was. And when I was there, we had four eyes and two tape recorders gathering material.

We had total access to the team, but I was looking for much more than the story of a football season. I had to know more about the city of Chelsea, the origins and current state of its gang problem, and what was being done, above and beyond what Coach was doing, to protect the children of Chelsea and to provide for their futures. So, I conducted interviews with Jimmy's colleagues in the Gang Unit, the chief of police, the city manager, the school superintendent, the high school principal, teachers, parents, past football coaches in Chelsea, gang members, and the good people at ROCA, a youth center in Chelsea whose goals coincide with Jimmy's, but whose methods conflict with his.

Each person I interviewed added another perspective to the city's problems. And it's important to note, I was never denied an interview request. The only thing I asked for that wasn't granted was the opportunity to shadow a player during a school day. The principal, Morton Orlov, thought I would be too much of a disruption. Otherwise, everyone was willing to give me as much time as I needed. That surprised me, because while the focus of the story and my questions centered on the good things people were doing and the progress that was being made, there is little doubt that to portray Chelsea accurately is to admit it is a city with an embarrassing and corrupt past and a troubled and potentially violent present. Some of the people charged with fixing Chelsea were willing to admit that. Others tried to paint with an overly optimistic brush. You'll be able to recognize who's who.

Being in the locker room for Jimmy's pre- and postgame speeches, walking the sidelines with the team, and riding in a patrol car with the Gang Unit on Halloween night were incredible opportunities to get an inside look at the story I was trying to write. But it wasn't until I began conducting interviews with the kids and going into their homes that I fully realized how deep the story was and how important the work was that Jimmy was doing. I don't know why the kids opened up so much to me about their personal lives, but they did. These troubled teens were intelligent, insightful, and honest. They were good kids in a bad situation. And their stories are often shocking and tragic, yet surprisingly hopeful. As it turns out, their futures are even more hopeful than their coach's.

Chelsea Red Devils Roster

Name	Number*	Grade	Position
Joshua Rubiera	5	12	QB/S
Cody Verge	7	11	QB/DE
Anthony Morales	11	10	QB/S
Hector Jiminian	13	9	RB
Melvin Ramirez	14	10	RB/LB
Juan Carrasuillo	15	12	TE/DE
Miguel Medina	17	12	QB/C
Cesar Camacho	19	11	K
Ian Martin	20	11	RB
Yves Casseus	22	11	RB/C
Carrington Guillaume	24	11	LB/TE
Alex Caraballo	26	11	RB
Daniel Cortez (Cpt.)	28	12	FB/LB
Rene Olivera	29	11	RB/C
Richard Oliveras	30	12	RB/C
Orlando Echevarria (Cpt.)	32	12	TE/DE
Sabahudin Omeragic	33	10	RB
Jonathan Barbosa	35	11	RB/LB
Arnold Chaves	36	10	RB/C
Brandon Trainito	38	12	RB
Andrew Colon	40	9	RB
Mario Hernandez (Cpt.)	42	12	RB/S
Christian Perez	43	9	RB
Joseph Barbosa	44	12	RB/S
Frankie Quiles (Cpt.)	45	12	RB/LB
Lorenzo Recupero	46	11	RB
Juan Rosa	50	12	OL
Michael Augustine	52	10	OL/DL
David Claudio	53	10	OL/LB
Malcolm Neverson	54	11	OL/DL

* Some uniform numbers are shared by more than one player.

Oscar Rodriguez	55	10	OL/DL
Jorge Figueroa	55	9	LB
Dont'e Wilson	56	11	OL/LB
Jonathan Luna	58	12	OL/DL
Armando Blanco	59	10	OL/DL
Jonathan Santiago	60	12	OL/LB
Hector Morales	61	12	DL
Nelson Maldanado	61	9	OL/DL
Carlos Rodriguez	62	10	C/DL
David Flores	63	12	OL/LB
Angel Rodriguez	64	9	OL
Jose Ponce	67	11	C/DL
Josue Hernandez	68	10	OL/DL
Margarito Canales	70	11	OL/DL
Guillermo Guillen	71	11	OL/DL
Christian Orellana	72	11	OL/DL
Ivan Romero	73	11	OL/DL
Antuan Jagne	74	12	OL/DL
Erik Flores	75	11	OL/DL
Darius Corchado	75	9	OL/DL
Austin Hightower	77	10	OL/DL
Ahmed Gohari	78	10	OL/DL
Alex Cabasa	79	9	OL/DL
Wayne Sheets	82	10	WR
Abdul Hamza	84	11	WR
Daniel Baptista	85	11	TE
Felix Torres	87	9	WR

James Atkins, Head Coach
Jamie Delverde, Assistant Head Coach
Dennis O'Neil, Assistant Coach
John Hassell, Assistant Coach
James Zouras, Equipment Manager
Nisarg Patel, Associate Coach

CHAPTER ONE

Welcome to Chelsea

Anything can happen any day, but when you're chilling with your boys, something is going to happen, because it's a gang, and you're going to see another gang and you're going to fight with another gang. That's how it works.

—ORLANDO ECHEVARRIA,
CHELSEA HIGH SCHOOL FOOTBALL PLAYER

A silver-haired man in a yellow windbreaker stood among the small bleacher crowd looking out over a high school football field on a cool, September evening. Beyond the field where the lights yielded to the darkness, the leaves were dropping much like the children of Chelsea, Massachusetts, pulled down by forces they couldn't control, drifting aimlessly. But for the first time in a long time, the clean, crisp spring-like air carried a whisper of hope. It was faint, but it was obvious, because in the tiny city of Chelsea, hope didn't linger very often.

"I'll tell you what these boys needed," the silver-haired man said to no one in particular. "They needed a man to teach them how to be men. And they got the right guy."

As he spoke, a large light-skinned black man emerged from the Chelsea High School locker room. He was the pied piper with seventy wide-eyed boys falling in line behind him. They'd follow him off the Tobin Bridge that connected Chelsea to Boston if that's what he told them to do, but on this night, the coach stared into their eyes—eyes of seventy boys stumbling along on their journey into manhood—and closed out his impassioned pregame speech with: "Football is life, fellas."

1

The words were right out of the coaches' handbook, passed down from Knute Rockne to Lou Holtz to Bill Parcells, and so on. The phrase was the mantra of every coach attempting to motivate a team, or to use football as a teaching tool. Sometimes it worked. On the right group of boys or men, perhaps desperate for leadership and direction, the coach's words could be inspiring and profound, but as this coach turned to leave the shadows of the small, foul-smelling team sanctuary, he knew his words were still hanging in the air, hovering, the echo fading before the true meaning of his metaphor was fully appreciated. Seventy boys heard the words. They all listened. A few understood. Most couldn't help but disagree.

The coach had repeated this axiom dozens of times before. The point was simple. Football is about achieving success through hard work. Sure, you get knocked down a lot, but you get right back up and go to work all over again. It's about commitment and pride and teamwork, and it's about knowing your responsibilities and doing your job. It's about leadership and, the coach thought, it was about time these kids started getting the message.

But no, football wasn't like life for these boys. Football, they thought, is fun. And it's fair. It's rewarding and controllable, and it's hopeful. Life, on the other hand, is none of those things. Not in Chelsea. Not in their neighborhoods. Not in their homes.

"Around here, it's like you have to worry about things," Orlando Echevarria said. He was a senior and one of the team's captains. His loyalty to the coach and his Red Devil teammates was only as strong as the ties he still felt to the Bloods, the gang he joined when he was still in grade school. His Blood brothers still tried to pull him back and drag him down into the street life. But they were his friends. That was his life. He loved to play football, but the coach was wrong. Football is not life. It is merely a necessary distraction for the continuation of life, because if Orlando didn't have football, he knew he would be either dead or in jail.

"In some cities, you don't have to worry," Orlando continued. "You always gotta worry what colors you wear. That matters. Around here, people have got jumped because of the colors they wear, just wearing the color red. It's one of those cities where you have to worry, and you have to know how to fight. That's the way I see it. You have to know how to fight or you have to carry something. There's going to come a point when you are going to have to use that, and if you don't have that, then it's going to be tough luck for you."

Orlando was the coach's single greatest challenge. To keep him off the streets, to get him to stay in school and to graduate was not only a more significant task than winning a Massachusetts High School Super Bowl, it was far more difficult. And it was made all the more difficult because Orlando was not the only one.

There was the boy whose brother was wanted by the police for assault and kidnapping, the boy whose father was a heroin addict and died of AIDS, the boy whose mother was a prostitute, the boy whose sister was a prostitute, the boy whose father was a recovering methamphetamine addict, the boy whose mother recently had left him and his sister with Down's syndrome to take up with a drug dealer in New Bedford, the boy who received protective immigration status as he fled from war-torn Bosnia, the boy from Africa whom the coach called "Midnight" because his skin was so black, and all the boys from broken homes where the parent who stayed didn't speak English.

As challenging as Orlando would be, his story only barely stood out above the myriad of unstable home lives faced by his teammates. Each of the Chelsea Red Devils was required to side-step the landmines strewn about his home, his neighborhood, and his city. Not one was immune to the influence of violence, or drugs, or the harsh realities of a fatherless home, but Orlando did stand out because of his size, his talent, and his potential for both good and bad. At 6'4", 230 pounds, blessed with athletic grace and speed and good hands, Orlando had the potential to earn a college scholarship as a tight end. He also had the potential to be just another Chelsea kid who fell through the cracks of the city. He could have risen above or he could have fallen back into the gang life. Orlando's physical gifts were his way out. A better life was there for the taking, but the gang life was always there threatening to take it all away.

"I still chill with my gang friends in school," Orlando explained. "They're my boys. They're always going to be my boys. I stay in contact, because if they need me, they need me. You can't cut all ties, because if you get that phone call and they say, 'This happened or this happened,' it depends who it is. You know the consequences, and I make my own choices, but if someone was messing with my younger brother, I have to do that. If they're fucking with him, I have to fuck one of them up. I don't want them to think they have control of us, or control of me or anybody."

It was a gang mentality Orlando hadn't been able to eradicate from his mind. He'd been associating with the Bloods since he was a tall, gangly twelve-year-old the police nicknamed "Fletch." The Chelsea Police had watched Orlando grow up. They saw him hanging out on the street corners wearing red to signify his gang allegiance. They knew his father, an ex-con, and his mother, currently facing arrest for writing bad checks. The police knew his brother, his uncle, and his cousin—all arrested and jailed for gang-related activities. The police were there when Orlando got into trouble, and they frequently intervened to keep him out of more trouble. And now, one of those policemen, the light-skinned black one with the drill sergeant's voice, was standing on the same sideline with Orlando, the troubled gang kid. Chelsea football coach James Atkins was also Sergeant Jimmy Atkins of the Chelsea Police Department's Gang Unit.

Atkins' first encounter with Orlando took place at a park where members of the Bloods and a rival gang, the MS-13s, were having a meeting. Orlando was there. He was twelve years old, and as Atkins approached, Orlando and a dozen other boys dropped their knives to the ground. Atkins confiscated the weapons and twenty-five bags of weed, and arrested each of the boys for antici-patory breach of the peace.

"If it's a situation that's left to develop," Atkins explained, "you're gonna have a fight. We locked every single one of them up. I look back and I think, 'How did I do that? Why didn't they run? What are they? Retarded?'"

So, Orlando spent an hour handcuffed to a railing and another hour in a cell waiting for his mother to pick him up. Then he was released back into the wild. For the next three years, he was a con-stant on the streets of Chelsea, not getting into a lot of trouble, but when trouble happened, he was around it. He seemed to elude trouble as if it were a defender trying to take him down in the open field. But football is not life. And when Orlando was finally tackled on the streets, it almost killed him.

That day began like many others. Orlando spent the morning sitting on the steps in front of his home on Chestnut Street, just chilling with his boys. Another group of youths, known as the Tiny Rascal Gang (TRG), started gathering down at the other end of Chestnut Street. The peacefulness of a sunlit New England morn-ing was about to be violently interrupted. It was time to have a rumble.

"They came up the street, and we came down the street," Orlando began. "We met up in the middle. They had knives and machetes and all that. We had bats and machetes and all that."

It was a dozen kids in broad daylight swinging to kill. Witnesses stepped inside the nearest doors, lest they become victims. But the violence was reserved for the combatants, the boys wearing oppos-ing colors. When the police sirens could be heard blaring, the boys began to run. Orlando found himself down an alleyway with two TRG kids. One of the roaches, as Orlando referred to them, had a machete. The other had a bat. Orlando had nothing but his fists, his wits, and his desire for survival.

"I was telling the one with the machete to drop the machete and I would fight with him, and then I would fight the one with the bat," Orlando said. "I didn't care about him. He was a nobody. So, me and him got into a fight, and the other kid swung with the bat. That's when I ducked and I hit him, and I hit the other kid, and we were fighting. That's when the cops came. They took all of us in, and we all got locked up."

That was a good day for Orlando. He didn't die. And this time when Sergeant Atkins approached him, it was to invite him to play football. Atkins had been hired in the spring of 2004 to revive the Chelsea High School football program, and he was looking for as many tough Chelsea kids as he could find. He found one in a jail cell. Only a few months into his new job, Atkins swung open the iron bars of Orlando's cell, slammed the door shut behind him, stared into the red, swollen eyes of a frightened kid, and cut him a deal.

"You want to get out of here?" Atkins asked. "I can make it happen."

"I ain't gonna snitch on anybody."

"You won't have to. You just gotta play football."

Confused at first, within a few moments Orlando was shaking hands with his new football coach. Orlando agreed to go to school, keep his grades up, and play for the Red Devils. For that, he walked out of jail a free man. He was fifteen.

The way Atkins looked at it, if he could get Orlando off the streets and on to the football field, he'd be simultaneously accomplishing his goals as a police officer and as a coach. But Orlando, who tried so hard not to show fear on the streets, was afraid of Atkins. After all, it was Atkins who had sent his brother to prison.

"I arrested Orlando's brother," Atkins explained. "His name is Orlando Echevarria, same name as his. They've got the same father, but two different mothers. They both have the same name as their father. The brother was a Latin King, and he stabbed a kid, another kid who was a Blood. The other kid almost died. He stabbed him in his heart. They thought he was dead, but they saved him. The brother's out of prison now. He did five years."

That's why Orlando the Younger had been reluctant to try out for the football team. He was convinced the new coach would treat him the way cops treated a gang kid—either rough him up or lock him up. Atkins did neither. He handled Orlando with kindness and firmness. Atkins' candor and respect disarmed Orlando. The teen wasn't accustomed to civility. But Atkins was never concerned with his players' histories. His concern was for their futures.

"At first I wasn't comfortable with Coach Atkins, because of the whole situation," Orlando said. "But after that he wasn't one of those people who, because of my brother's background, treated me like I was one of those people. Even though he knew about my background and the gang stuff and everything I do, he treated me like I wasn't like that. That's when I started to feel more comfortable, because if other people know that you're in a gang, or you're a Blood, they're going to treat you like one of those people. They're going to treat you like shit. But Coach Atkins was helping me out. That's when I stopped chilling on the streets as much, because I was into football, and I thought I was going to go somewhere. That's when I just started loving the game more, and we got closer."

That night, standing on the sidelines, Orlando was close enough to Atkins to know his coach was more on edge than usual. It was obvious during pregame warm-ups when Atkins barked at his assistant coach, James Delverde.

"Your responsibility tonight is the goddamn balls! Get the balls in the bag. You can go back to JV if you want. Do you want that? Then goddamn do it!"

The last statement was yelled at the top of his lungs, and a few moments later, Atkins let another one of his assistants have it.

"You tell those fucking kids," Atkins began, pointing at several junior varsity kids dressed in khakis, white shirts, and ties, "If I hear them giggling one more time, they're fucking done!"

Atkins' mood was the result of an embarrassing 56–20 season-opening loss to East Boston High School the previous week. The Red Devils were expected to be Super Bowl contenders that year, and even though East Boston played in a higher division and had won thirty straight regular season games, Chelsea's lopsided defeat changed the way they were being perceived, and the coach was in a foul mood. The East Boston game had been a tremendous opportunity to engage his kids with possibilities. If they had beaten East Boston, a perennial powerhouse in an upper division, Atkins would have had no problem persuading his team that a championship season was a realistic goal. With that as an enticement, he was certain he could have gotten the kids to concentrate on football, on school, and on staying out of trouble. Losing games meant losing focus, and ultimately, losing the kids to the streets.

It didn't help Atkins' mood that he blamed himself for what happened against East Boston. He regretted letting his foot off the gas in the week leading up to the season opener. The kids had worked hard during summer camp, so hard that some of them were coming up with assorted injuries. Atkins figured the kids would be pumped with adrenaline to open the season, so he let them rest and recover a little bit before the game by greatly reducing the amount of hitting that went on during practice. But they didn't respond as expected. They didn't hit, and they got pushed around. The first play of the East Boston game was a 42-yard touchdown run by Eastie quarterback Chris Etheridge. That's how the season with Super Bowl dreams started. Atkins stood on the sideline in disbelief. Eastie followed up that score with a 60-yard interception return for a touchdown.

"Just throw it the fuck out of bounds!" Atkins had screamed at his spindly quarterback, Miguel Medina.

"Yes, Coach!" Miguel shouted back forcefully.

"What good is, 'Yes, Coach' doing me now? You're costing us this game!"

Chelsea trailed East Boston 22–0 early in the second quarter, before mounting a bit of a comeback. Frankie Quiles and Alex Caraballo each ran for touchdowns for Chelsea, and the score was 22–14 with just over three minutes to play in the half. Atkins sensed his team was awakening. He called a time-out, brought his kids together along the sidelines, and attempted to rally the troops.

"They cannot stop us. I don't care what defense they're in. They cannot stop us! Guys, listen to me. We need a score in three minutes. Listen to me. You've got to hustle. I don't care if they kick you, or spit at you, they kick you in the goddamn nuts. I don't care. Get up. Get back in the huddle. Get the call. And beat their ass. They cannot stop us. It's impossible for them to stop us. Only you guys can stop you. Get the ball back, and then run it down their throats. We're gonna score here, fellas. We're gonna take the ball and we're gonna run the goddamn ball down their fuckin' throats!"

Seconds later, East Boston's Tyrone Hughes returned the kick-off 87 yards for a touchdown. Eastie added a touchdown before the half and led 34–14 as the teams jogged to the locker rooms.

"Oh, fuck I hate that," Orlando said staring into the distance. "Look at that score!"

"This ain't Chelsea football," another senior, Joshua Rubiera, said. "Let's go! This ain't Chelsea football!"

But it was Chelsea football, at least on that day. It was a disheartening loss for the team, and a humiliating loss for the coach.

Sadly, the kids were used to being overlooked, disrespected. The coach wasn't. He didn't like watching Chelsea plummet in the school rankings. The respect Atkins had restored to the Chelsea football program during his first two years at the helm had disappeared in a flash. The Red Devils had been outplayed, outhustled, and outclassed. But before Atkins could convince people on the outside that Chelsea could still be a force in Division 3A, he had to convince seventy boys whose heads were hanging extremely low. Atkins eschewed the soft approach during the week of practice following the East Boston game. He ran the kids hard and had them flying into each other in a series of long, hard-hitting drills. His voice was booming and implacable. His physical stature, as always, was intimidating. He was tall and muscular, strong-jawed. His eyes switched from kind to maniacal from play to play, moment to moment. The sheer volume of Atkins' voice was startling. Spit flew from the sides of his mouth. His consistent berating of the players was equal parts humbling and motivating. He stepped right up to them and bellowed just inches from their faces, occasionally yanking on their facemasks. Throughout the week, he paced angrily through practice commanding respect and attention.

"You're supposed to be tough fucking kids. You're pussies! You're pussies! Yeah, keep making those fuckin' faces! I'm tired of your fuckin' excuses. Just make a goddamn play!"

Standing beneath a brilliant sky on a barren practice field opposite a busy highway, Atkins paused only long enough to collect his thoughts and catch his breath, and then he continued.

"How many times do I have to tell you to be tough sons of bitches! I don't want to hear anymore goddamn excuses. Coach, he's holding me. Coach, he's tripping me. Coach, he's spitting on me. I don't give a shit! Just make a goddamn play!"

The coach's energy was unrelenting. His outbursts were not calculated. He was genuinely pissed. *Don't let him pick on me,* the players must have thought. *Do it right. Earn his respect.*

The kids worked hard. There was no downtime during practice. Each minute was scheduled meticulously. There were no conversations between drills. If the boys were having fun, it was hard to tell. Sweat poured down their faces. Blood and mud caked onto their uniforms and under their fingernails. This was football, a man's game. But these were boys. Atkins stood several feet behind the tallest boy, and said flatly: "You're gonna be a mediocre player until you start listening."

Orlando didn't turn around to see who Coach was talking to, but he knew. Practice ended shortly thereafter. The boys filed back into the locker room feeling a little freer now to talk and laugh and promise each other they'd beat Madison Park the next night. Only a few of them showered before changing. Almost all of them walked home or rode their low-ride bicycles, the ones that were more suited for an eight-year-old and made their knees go up to their chins as they pedaled. Only a couple of the players were picked up after practice by their parents.

It wasn't yet dark outside, so it was relatively safe as the boys spilled out on to the streets of the city. Chelsea is only 1.8 square miles, so none of the boys had very far to go, and they tended to walk in groups of three or four until they began to split off toward their respective homes. But as they moved along down Ash Street, each of the boys entertained at least a fleeting thought that this was where their classmate, George Chapelle, had dodged two bullets while walking his fourteen-year-old sister home eight months ago. Chapelle, just sixteen years old himself, had either dropped out or had been kicked out of the Bloods. As he and his sister walked down Everett Avenue, sixteen-year-old Chelsea High School student Jesse Camacho came by in a car and exchanged words with George. The car sped away, but Camacho, known as "Baby Jesse," soon got out and waited on Ash Street. He was wearing a gray bandanna on his face, and holding a handgun wrapped in another gray bandanna. When Camacho spotted George, he fired twice, and ran back to the waiting car. George and his sister were not shot, but until police apprehended Camacho, they had to go to school each morning knowing Camacho might be there. They had to walk home each afternoon wondering if Camacho would be there. The football players also had to wonder who might be waiting around the corner for them someday. This was, after all, Chelsea.

"Guys, we have so many things that take our minds off what we're supposed to do," Coach had told them recently. "We walk out in the street and, after school today, how many gang fights did you see? Ten? Ten goddamn gang fights I had to respond to. I know you have to fucking navigate that home, but I don't give a shit! I don't care! When you're here, you're focused. When you're with me, you're goddamn safe!"

Most of the boys had been staring down at the locker room floor while the coach spoke, but as he began to get real with it, when he acknowledged what their lives were really like, they looked up. They looked into their coach's eyes to see if they could detect not just a ray of hope but a glimmer of truth. Were they safe when they were with him? Yes, they believed they were. Their time with the coach might be the only time in their lives they were ever truly safe. As relaxing and comforting as that was, as insulated as they felt from the outside world, inside that locker room, they feared their protector.

"This Madison Park coach was salivating up in the stands last week," Coach began his pregame speech. "He was there watching us get our goddamn asses kicked against East Boston. He watched you get beat on every goddamn play. Miguel, he watched you fumble. He watched you fumble, Frankie. He watched us suck!"

The boys' heads were tipped downward again. They listened as the words bounced against the empty metal lockers. They were used to this. Coach yelled a lot. They knew he was trying desperately to fire them up, but some of them, too many of them, were just waiting for the shouting to stop. That would be their cue to get up and walk out onto the field where the worst thing that could happen was that they would lose. To them, that wasn't so bad. They were used to losing, used to being losers. The ones with that attitude were oblivious to Coach's main message—that this game they were playing was a chance for them to feel good about themselves, to win, and to learn to be winners.

"You know what? We're the underdogs today. In our own goddamn stadium, we're the dog against a goddamn Boston team!"

The coach had pumped up the volume to a full scream now.

"Any goddamn Boston team, we should bury! And we're a goddamn underdog in our own goddamn fucking house! Guys, I want to see you have heart. Frankie, do you have heart?"

"Yes, Coach!"

"Do you have heart, Frankie?"

"Yes, Coach!"

Frankie was a senior and a captain. He was shouting his responses as loudly as the questions.

"I want you guys out there showing some heart. Keeping it focused. If they spit on you, Danny, what are you gonna do?

"Walk away, Coach!"

Danny Cortez was also a senior and a captain. He hoped to be a journalist someday.

"Orlando, somebody calls you a name, what are you gonna do, Orlando?"

Coach left only a split second for a reply. When one didn't come quickly enough, he answered his own question.

"Get your ass back in the huddle and stay focused."

Coach had begun his pregame remarks in a stern, demanding tone and then amped it up to an angry, frothing fury. After bringing it back down momentarily, he finished with another explosive flourish.

"This is the beginning of our run. Only one thing matters, and that's focus as a team. Know your responsibility and kick the living shit out of the guy in front of you! Eleven battles on the field, fellas. Eleven battles going at the same time. And if each one of you wins your battle, we're gonna score a thousand fucking points! A thousand goddamn points and we're not gonna stop scoring! Do your fucking job and take this fucking house back! Make it our home again! Do you understand me?"

"Yes, Coach," seventy boys screamed in unison. Seventy boys who, if they weren't in that locker room at that very moment, would be on the streets either with their gangs, being solicited by gangs, or being threatened by gangs. They were all a team now. A gang of seventy.

"Breakdown!" Coach shouted to begin the team's ritualistic chant. The boys picked it right up.

"Red!"

"Breakdown!"

"Red!"

"Breakdown!"

"Chelsea!"

"Breakdown!"

"Devils!"

The silver-haired man in the bleachers that night said, "Here they come."

The players did not storm from the locker room with enthusiastic or barbaric grunts and yelps. Despite the fact that this was their home opener and their first division game, the players absorbed the coach's fiery speech, and emerged from the locker room with only a modest amount of commotion and conversation. They were excited to get the game under way, but they were not wild. They were reserved, still taking their cues from the coach.

"Guys, one straight line. Let's go, move your butts," Atkins directed. "When they start singing the national anthem, put your helmet over your hearts. I don't want to hear a sound until the national anthem is finished. You hear me? We're gonna wipe the slate clean. We're gonna be beasts. We're gonna go out and kick some goddamn ass!"

The Cardinals of Madison Park marched down the field on their opening drive, needing only six plays and a 2-point conversion to take an 8–0 lead.

"We have the worst fucking defense in the goddamn world!" Atkins moaned. Then he called a time-out and brought his team together for a moment of honest introspection.

"Listen up, get your water, guys. Listen to me, fellas. We're playing a little helter skelter—myself included. Relax. The problem is you're lining up in the wrong places. Guys, Orlando, if there's a wing, you've got to slide out to him. I want the tackles on the outside shoulders. Let's get in there. Let's make a fucking play now. We're getting there. We got it. Let's go."

Things improved for the Red Devils when they scored near the end of the first quarter, and again when junior linebacker Carrington Guillaume blocked a Cardinal punt. Chelsea recovered the ball at their opponents' 28-yard line. Sensing Chelsea was about to take the lead, the small, partisan crowd erupted in its loudest ovation of the evening. It was not a raucous reaction by any means, merely robust relative to the noise level attainable by about three hundred people. Chelsea football did not draw well. It was a beautiful Friday evening. The city seemed alive under the star-filled sky, yet the bleachers were only a quarter full. Fans consisted mostly of students lined up along the running track that circled the field. They gathered in small groups near the concession stand, each new arrival receiving hugs and high fives from friends they hadn't seen in the four hours since dismissal. Some of them were actually interested in the action on the field and the potential outcome of the game. The rest were there to be seen and to socialize. Only a handful of parents attended the game. Some of them had to work two jobs. Others just didn't care enough.

"Guys, we're gonna score," Coach declared before sending his offense back on to the field. "But you've gotta be able to stop them on defense. If you knock them in the mouth on offense, it'll make it easier on defense."

Coach repeated his last thought for additional emphasis.

"Look at me," he said, pausing to make sure each of the boys surrounding him was indeed looking at him. "If you knock them in the mouth on offense, they're gonna crack."

Chelsea was unable to take advantage of the field position. Frankie fumbled. Madison Park recovered, but then Danny Cortez intercepted a pass and brought it all the way back to the Cardinal 15-yard line. Again, Chelsea was in prime position to take the lead before the half. Then, two running plays were stopped for no gain, and Coach brought his offense together. In a rare moment of give and take, Coach resisted the urge to scold his team for mistakes. Instead, he asked them what they thought was happening on the field.

"What's the problem on the sweeps?" Coach asked. "What are we seeing out there that we can't block the sweeps?"

"The linebacker is shooting up," Danny replied.

"Where's he lining up?"

"On the guard."

"Are they on the eagle flat?"

"Yeah."

"Then you just block him backside, that's all. If there's only four, block him backside. How's he getting in? You can't just go out and get him. You have to watch the linebacker blitzing. You understand."

"Yes, Coach," several players responded enthusiastically.

"26-toss lead, guys. Let's get this in."

Number 26, Alex Caraballo, ran for the first down, and Frankie took it in from there. Touchdown Chelsea! Frankie also added the 2-point conversion giving Chelsea its first lead of the season, 14–8.

At halftime, Coach and his assistants met in the hallway outside the locker room to discuss what adjustments needed to be made. From inside the locker room, the kids could be heard doing the same thing. There was much more excitement now than before the game, much more optimism, too.

"C'mon, it's a whole new half," one of them yelled.

Coach entered and began writing on the blackboard. He explained to his defense that the opposing running back shouldn't be able to run the sweep if they spread out wide enough. He told his offense that he wanted the onside guard pulling, but if the Cardinals' middle linebacker started blitzing, they'd have to make a change. Several players felt free to volunteer their thoughts about what had transpired, and the difficulties they'd been having. Coach listened, and then offered advice. It was a constructive and respectful atmosphere. Still, Coach was not satisfied with the first-half efforts.

"When you go at it in practice, fellas, you beat the shit out of each other. Why won't you beat the shit out of them? When we do one-on-ones in practice, you literally beat the shit out of each other. Now, I need you to beat the shit out of Madison Park. The game's too close, fellas. We need to score some points and open it up. You gotta fight. You don't accept being blocked, fellas."

Their second-quarter success seemed to fill the kids with new life. They came out flying around on defense. From his inside linebacker position, Frankie hit everything that moved. He was clogging up the middle putting big licks on any ball carriers or blockers who ventured near him. This was a good sign, because Frankie was undoubtedly a team leader. The other Devils fed off his energy. Unfortunately, that energy could be positive or it could be negative. As hard as he ran, as much as he bull rushed over tacklers, he might just as easily be the first Red Devil to quit.

"Coach tells me all the time, if I fumble, I go into a shell for some reason," Frankie said. "I've been trying to work on that. Sometimes if I fumble, five or six plays later, I'd be like nowhere. If they give me the ball, I don't know, I don't want to run no more. The fumble just kills me. I see things wide open, and it kills me like that, because it could have been a touchdown, and if I score, we can win the game."

There was a part of Frankie that believed he belonged in the NFL. There was another part of him that worried he would let his team down, and that it might happen on the very next play. Sometimes that motivated him. Other times, it immobilized him. He had two distinct personalities, two egos that were polar opposites of one another. Was he the confident kid from a loving, two-parent home in a nice section of Chelsea, growing up not far from a toddler park with a full view of the waterfront and the Boston skyline? Or was he the struggling, conflicted child of two drug addicts? In fact, he was both.

Frankie didn't know too much about his natural father, Francisco Coloazo Senior. He said only that his dad was locked up for a long time because of drugs, and that he was out of jail now, but Frankie didn't know where he was. Frankie's birth mother, Joanne Boone, lived a few towns over in Malden. She was a heavy drug user when Frankie was a baby, but in a moment of clarity, she walked Frankie to the home of Lydia Molina and said, "Here, you take care of him. I can't do it."

Lydia was Frankie's foster mother when he was just eight months old. At that time the Department of Social Services had been alerted to the hazardous environment in which he lived. DSS took Frankie from his mother on what was supposed to be a temporary basis while she went into a rehab and found steady work. Lydia and her husband, Julio Quiles, had met and fallen in love in their native Puerto Rico. Together they had four biological children of their own, Vivian, Antonio, Ernesto, and Julio. They also adopted three more children, Luna from Haiti, Jorge from El Salvador, and Frankie from Chelsea. Lydia and Julio were selected as the 1992 Massachusetts All-Star Foster Family and still beamed with pride fourteen years later when recalling the day they met then-governor William Weld.

"I have a hard time as a foster mom," Lydia admitted. "They tell me my kid's going to go back to his mom. I didn't want to cry, but I have like, I don't want to exaggerate, but I have like a heart attack. Nobody could stop me from crying. But they gave Frankie back to the mom."

Frankie had been living with Lydia and Julio for nearly three years, but in 1993, DSS determined Joanne was ready to resume being a single parent. Lydia knew better. With a mother's natural instinct, Lydia knew in her heart it was a mistake for Frankie to go back to Joanne. She believed Joanne was still using drugs and that Frankie wouldn't be safe with her. Soon after she watched Frankie be taken away, Lydia walked several blocks to the Washington Street apartment where Joanne was living and spied through the window. She could see Frankie in his crib and she watched Joanne leave for work.

"I know she left him alone," Lydia said. "I didn't want to tell nothing to DSS, but I was wrong, because his life was at risk. Thank God, in like two weeks, she bring him up to me herself."

Once again, the drugs and the responsibility of raising a child proved to be too much for Joanne. She had lied to DSS about being clean, but she could no longer lie to herself. She loved Frankie, and she had to do what was best for him. So, she brought him back to Lydia. About a year later, Frankie was officially part of a big family.

"He was five years old when we adopted him," Lydia said. "They think the mother could take the baby back, that she was healthy, but they found out she was lying. The mother love him so much, we did an open adoption. I wanted him to have a relationship with his mom. When we went in front of the judge for the adoption, the judge asked him, 'Do you know what is happening?' And Frankie stood right up and said, 'They are going to be my dad and my mom forever.'"

Little Frankie was right. From that point on, he was part of a stable home, albeit one with an unstable distraction. He never lost touch with Joanne, and though he tended to see her only for holidays and very special occasions, he talked to her often. Many of those conversations included Joanne asking her seventeen-year-old son for money.

"It does bother me sometimes," Frankie said. "Everybody has their problems. But she'll call sometimes with money problems, and it'll kind of mess me up. I'm like 'Damn, now I have to help her and take out money for her.' And I think why can't she work a full-time job instead of a part-time job and then she'd have enough money. I think I handle it pretty well most of the time. I try not to let it bother me as much. I still have to do things for me, not for everybody else. I guess sometimes it does bother me."

Frankie was not bothered, however, by the fact that he was a dark-skinned black kid being raised in the home of two light-skinned Puerto Ricans. He didn't look anything like the rest of his family, but he had been to Puerto Rico dozens of times, and he had learned to speak Spanish fluently. He was comfortable, happy, and accepted in a city where having six siblings who were born in four different countries wasn't especially noteworthy. Perhaps the most unique thing about Frankie was that he was the uncle of his quarterback. His best friend and teammate, Miguel Medina, was the son of Frankie's oldest sister, Vivian. So, even though they had grown up like brothers, Frankie was actually Miguel's uncle, though not by blood.

Frankie and Miguel both were frequent targets of Coach's angry screams from the sidelines. As the second half continued against Madison Park, it was Frankie's turn to get an earful.

"I can't even trust you to give you the goddamn ball! Get over here where I told you to be."

Then to the rest of his offense, Coach said: "Guys, let's put them away. We've got 'em on the ropes. Let's put 'em away. Over right, 24 cross. Left pull."

Then returning his attention to Frankie, Coach warned: "Hold on to the fucking ball. If you fumble, you'll be off the fucking offense. You understand me?"

Frankie nodded, but on the ensuing drive, he appeared to fumble once again. Coach was in an untenable situation. Frankie was his best running back. Alex, only a junior, was quicker, but much smaller. Frankie picked up the tough yards. He could wear down a defense, but if he kept giving the ball away, he'd be useless.

After a pile of players fought to recover the loose ball, the referee ruled that the whistle had blown before Frankie lost possession of it. There was no fumble, but Frankie did not carry the ball again on the game's most important drive. With only a few minutes remaining in the third quarter, Danny Cortez rushed in from his fullback position and added the 2-point conversion as well. That gave Chelsea a 22–8 lead.

Joshua Lewis watched it all unfold from the sidelines. He was one of the biggest players on the team, but he was ineligible to play tonight. Black Josh, as he was known, was over 6 feet tall, and pushing close to 240 pounds of solid muscle. Coach called him a beast. He was also a Blood. Black Josh's mother wouldn't believe her son was a gang member until Coach had shown her a picture of Josh smoking a joint and hanging out with other known gang members.

"They're playing their hearts out," Josh said loud enough for his teammates on the sideline to hear. "We gotta prove it right here. C'mon, guys, this is our first home game. We gotta prove we got heart."

Then, to no one in particular, Josh simply blurted, "I love football. I just do."

But Joshua Lewis was not in uniform against Madison Park on September 15, 2006. He had gotten into trouble at school two days earlier and he was facing the very real possibility of getting kicked off the team for the rest of the season. Josh hadn't been in a fight, or been caught with drugs or a weapon. He had said something to a teacher, a small, demure, attractive, younger Caucasian teacher who was understandably insulted and intimidated when Josh snuck up behind her and whispered:

"Have you ever been with a black man?"

Josh defended his remark by explaining he had just broken up with his girlfriend, and he thought he was engaging in a harmless flirtation with a young female. He couldn't understand what all the fuss was about. He had no idea he had done anything wrong.

Coach tried to make him understand, and he began by sitting Josh for at least one game. In order to get back on the field, Josh would have to apologize to the teacher, and beg the school's principal, Morton Orlov, for a second chance. The begging would be done next week. For now, Josh was a spectator who still wondered why he couldn't be a participant.

The Cardinals scored to cut Chelsea's lead to 22–16, and with less than two minutes to play, the Cardinals were driving for the potential game-winning touchdown. Madison Park decided to go for it all. The ball sailed through the air toward the end zone, a long pass that scraped against the sky. Heads turned to watch. On a play like this, casual football fans see only the ball. Coaches see the field, and Coach Atkins liked what he saw. Danny Cortez was moving toward the ball, timing his arrival perfectly. Moments before it happened, Coach knew it would. Danny hoped it would. And it did. Danny intercepted the ball, effectively ending the game. Chelsea ran out the clock and collected a hard-fought victory, its first of the season.

"Hey guys, listen up," Coach said as his team kneeled around him in the middle of the field. "No long speech tonight. We made it a little harder than it needs to be. Too much fumbling again. We should have beaten them 38 to 8, but a win is a win, fellas."

The team's spontaneous applause was like a giant exhale, more relief than exultation.

"Danny gets the game ball," Coach continued. "Let me tell you something. That's how you step it up when you've fallen to the carpet. You go out there and you lead us on both sides of the ball. That's how you do it. What did you have, about 150 yards of rushing from the fullback spot? Whew! That's a goddamn fullback right there, fellas."

The team's second round of applause began upon Danny's introduction. Danny never quit, not on himself, and not on the team, and he had earned their respect because of it. Coach had singled him out as much for his attitude on this night as for his production.

It was a credit to Danny Cortez that he hadn't quit. His life was not easy. Only eighteen years old, he'd already faced tough decisions and tougher challenges, and they only served to make him more determined, more focused. His uncommon resolve gave him the strength to reject the Bloods when they were recruiting him soon after he turned thirteen. His best friend, a boy he'd known since kindergarten, was sent to do the Bloods' bidding, and when Danny said he wasn't interested in joining the gang, he lost a friend, but said he also got his life together.

His maturity was the product of responsibility. About the same time the Bloods approached him, Danny's parents got divorced. The way Danny told it, his mother, Mira, just didn't want to raise her children anymore. So, she left.

"It hurt," Danny said with some residual sadness. "But I realize she's the one that didn't want me. Not only can I not do anything about it, but I have to move on, I have to be strong."

Danny had no relationship with his mother after she left. He only knew what he heard. First, he heard that his mother had taken up with a drug dealer in Fall River. Then he heard that the drug dealer and his mother had twins. Recently, he heard that the Department of Social Services took the twins away, because they found drugs in the home. If any of this bothered Danny, he didn't let on. He was a football player, a student, and a caretaker.

Danny's day began early. He was the first to rise in the morning, and he went around making sure everyone else was up. He helped his two younger brothers and his older sister, Yvette, get ready for school. Yvette was twenty years old, but she only had the learning ability of a young child. She had Engelmann's syndrome. Danny described it as a form of Down's syndrome, but that seemed to be his way of discouraging any further questions. Engelmann's is a genetic bone disorder that causes a great deal of pain to those who have it. Yvette suffered from increased pressure on her brain, cranial nerve dysfunction, and generalized weakness. She went to special education classes in Chelsea, but still communicated primarily with the use of sign language.

"She's awesome," Danny said with genuine pride, adding, "It doesn't add a layer of stress. It's been this way my whole life. Even when my parents were together, I knew I had to be older than I actually am. I expect to eventually take full responsibility of Yvette. If anything happens to my dad it will fall on me. If I have to help her, that's not a burden. It's just help. If you have to help somebody, you just help."

That was the same attitude Danny adopted when his friend, Fatty, turned to him for help. Fatty Ortez, who earned his nickname and loved his nickname, was looking for some roots. He had spent the past five years living in various parts of Massachusetts, New York, New Jersey, Philadelphia, and Puerto Rico. His father was still in Philadelphia; Fatty hadn't seen or heard from him in several months. Just prior to summer football camp, Fatty and his mother had been evicted from their Chelsea apartment. This happened frequently. Fatty's mother had stomach cancer and couldn't work very much.

So, they were on the move again. But when his mother announced they were headed for Holyoke out in western Massachusetts, Fatty let her know he wanted to finish his high school days in Chelsea. He wanted to play football for the Red Devils. So, his mom moved away, and Fatty moved in with Danny. Danny's father, who delivered auto parts for an East Boston company, was sporadically on welfare, but he never hesitated to welcome Fatty into his home, which now included Fatty and Danny; Danny's brothers, Walter and David; and Danny's sisters, Lucy and Yvette. It was just another typical Chelsea family.

"Fatty and I met each other freshman year," Danny explained. "Now, I'm a captain, and I knew I had to help this player, help this friend. So, if he needed a place to live, I give him a place to live."

Fatty had a home, but he never got a chance to play football his senior year. Just a few plays into summer camp, Fatty was running and stopped suddenly. His weight shifted and his knee buckled. He heard the knee pop three times. His season was over before it began. Fatty had torn his anterior cruciate ligament.

Fatty remained with the Red Devils, though. He would spend the entire season walking the sidelines with a cane, and wearing his varsity jacket, the one he earned as a sophomore, the one that said "Fatty" on it.

"These kids are our banners," said Scott Conley. Conley was a big man with a big voice. He was a barrel-chested, charismatic detective with the Gang Unit who also served as an assistant coach during Atkins' first season. He remembered why it was important to scrape up the funds to buy the football players good-quality varsity jackets.

"Jimmy knew you had to show the other kids that they want to be like the football players. That's why he started having nice lunches delivered to the cafeteria for the team. That's why he wanted to get the kids jackets, and Jimmy's not going to do anything half-assed. He wants nice jackets."

Those jackets were $170 apiece, and sixty players each received one free of charge. There was no money in the Chelsea budget to pay for jackets, just like there was no money for a much-needed blocking sled that Jimmy paid $2,600 for at the start of the season. There was also no money for extra footballs, special quarterback pads, cleats for kids who couldn't afford them, or the pizzas that Jimmy bought the team every Friday before a game. And there was no active Booster Club at the time. No parents stepped up to help. So, in the December following the 2004 season, Atkins opened a Booster Club account at TD Banknorth. For weeks, all that sat in that account was the original $250 deposited by Atkins. Fundraising hadn't begun, but Atkins, who had already spent $3,000 out of his own pocket, needed $10,000 more for the jackets. He bought them by spending $1,400 of his own money, putting $1,300 on his wife Julie's credit card, and then paying off the balance over time as additional funds were raised.

"We raised fifteen grand," Conley boasted.

The money was collected by Jimmy and the other coaches going door-to-door and pleading with local business owners. The donated funds were placed in the Booster Club account with Jimmy as the sole signator. Jimmy named himself president of the Boosters, and he was the only person with access to the account. The money was spent at his discretion.

"We were always in arrears," Atkins recalled. "As I was raising for 2004 after the fact, I was already in the hole for the 2005 season. So, I put a substantial amount of it on my personal expenses."

Basically, his entire $5,500 coaching stipend went toward all the additional things not covered by the high school football budget, and then he randomly reimbursed himself a little at a time.

If there was any school administration oversight of the account at all, it's certain they wouldn't have approved of all the times and places Jimmy reimbursed himself—like when he and some of his cop buddies went out for some fun on a Friday night in February of 2005, and Jimmy used money from the Booster Club account to pay off their $634 bar bill. But Jimmy reasoned it was his money. It didn't matter where or when he accessed it.

All that mattered was that he had started the Booster Club fund for the kids, kids who wanted their nicknames on their jackets, including Fatty. Conley cautioned Fatty that five or six years from now, he might not want the name "Fatty" on his jacket, but Fatty unabashedly told Conley, "But that's my name." It was, in fact, his given name, given to him by Coach Atkins, and if Coach thought enough about him to give him a nickname, that made him special. He wasn't a star on the team, or a starter like Midnight, Pop Warner, and Sunshine, but he stood out as the kid everybody knew as Fatty. He was a lot like the sophomore running back that everybody knew even though he never played, Sabahudin Omeragic, the one coach nicknamed "Alphabet."

And so Fatty had his jacket, and he had one football memory that would last him a lifetime. Atkins' first season was Fatty's sophomore year, and he hadn't played at all until he was pressed into service for the Thanksgiving Day game. Fourteen starters had flunked off the team. Those starters became known as the F-Squad. Atkins made them wear big red Fs on their helmets during practice, and he made it clear that if they didn't show up for practice or the Thanksgiving Day game, they wouldn't be allowed to come out for the team the following year. During the game, the F-Squad stood on the sidelines in dress shirts and ties that were supplied by the coaching staff. They watched as Chelsea lost its final game of the year, and failed to qualify for the playoffs.

During the game, Conley yelled out to Fatty before every snap of the ball, "Stay low, Fatty. Stay low and drive." He was keeping it simple for Fatty, asking him only to submarine the opposing team's offensive line. He repeated it before every play. Finally, Atkins turned to Conley and said, "Would you shut the fuck up!" Fatty jumped offside on the next play.

"Sorry about that," Jimmy said to Conley.

Then, in the final minute of the game, Fatty drove through the line, sacked the quarterback, and recovered the fumble. It was a moment he has carried with him ever since. It was almost certainly the one moment that fueled Fatty's unrealistic dream of one day playing college football at Penn State or the University of Pittsburgh. It would never happen for Fatty, but whether his dream was justified or not, it helped keep him on the right path. He believed in himself, and he believed in his coach, and his friend.

"Coach Atkins is the perfect example of what a Chelsea kid goes through," Danny said. "But he's succeeded. So, he's a perfect example of what we should be. A bunch of us are on welfare just like he needed public help, but he's grown up to be a successful person. Coach knows exactly what we're going through, because he's been through it, and we feel like maybe he does know what he's talking about."

"Guys, be safe tonight," Coach said before dismissing the Red Devils following their first victory of the season. This was how he sent them away after every game, and after nearly every practice.

"Enjoy yourselves, but don't get in any trouble out there tonight. Everybody knows there were a bunch of fights after school today, right?"

"Yes, Coach!"

"Stay away from that. Guys, stay away from that. Stay off the streets tonight."

It was a Friday night. By the time the players showered and changed, it would be after 9:30, and they'd all be released into the streets of Chelsea. Coach hoped they'd all be back on the practice field on Monday, but he couldn't be sure.

"Guys, bring it in," Coach said. "Great job. Congratulations on your first win of the season. Hey, guys, we've got nine more to go. We need nine more wins in a row. Let's run the table."

In the past few hours, Coach had been supportive, frightening, comforting, livid, compassionate, patient, frustrated, and ultimately satisfied with the win. Seeing Coach smiling and shaking hands with some of his police friends and other well-wishers, a boyish teenager rushed up to him and interrupted. The boy began with what was easily recognizable as a whiny explanation of something that had occurred earlier in the game. Coach glared down upon the kid and said dismissively:

"You're a goddamn freshman. You're not allowed to fucking speak. You understand?"

"Yes, Coach."

"Don't even say 'Yes, Coach.' Just shut up!"

CHAPTER TWO

The Black Italian

The kids think I'm Spanish, and they get pissed that I won't speak Spanish. They think I'm trying to lose my culture by not talking Spanish to them, and they get pissed. I'm like, "I'm not fucking Spanish. What's the matter with you? I'm a black Italian. I'm a goddamn black man." They're like, "No, you speak Spanish." And I'm like, "Say it again, I'm gonna smack you in the mouth."

—JAMES ATKINS

Chelsea has always been an immigrant community. Struggling today in the shadows of the Boston skyline just on the other side of Boston Harbor, Chelsea was a favorite destination of Europeans coming to America as early as 1624. The Irish, Poles, Germans, and French made Chelsea their home for more than three hundred years. They were the ones who rebuilt the city after the Great Chelsea Fire of 1908.

Many of Chelsea's residents had just made their way home from church on Sunday, April 12, 1908, when they heard the first fire alarm. The fire department quickly extinguished the fire at the Boston Blacking Company on West 3rd Street, but the winds were blowing hard that day, and the embers were being carried to several nearby houses. Before long, the fire was raging out of control. Buildings made of solid granite crumbled in the heat. The City Hall and Chelsea Savings Bank were among the 1,500 buildings that were destroyed. Eight schools and a dozen churches were also lost, and more than 10,000 people were suddenly homeless.

Chelsea, the little city that could, also had to survive a flood in 1909, a flu epidemic in 1918, a second Great Chelsea Fire in October of 1973 that destroyed eighteen city blocks, and a long series of corrupt mayors. In 1988, Chelsea admitted it couldn't handle the running of its own school system and allowed Boston University to take over total control. And in 1991, Chelsea endured the embarrassment of becoming the first city since the Depression to fall into receivership.

"Chelsea has a self-esteem problem," according to Jay Ash, the city manager. "One of the things I'd like to do is just get that chip off of everybody's shoulder. There is one large collective chip on the shoulder of Chelsea."

Ash was a Chelsea High School graduate, class of 1979. Standing nearly six-and-a-half feet tall, Ash had been captain of the Red Devils basketball team, and returned to work as an assistant coach for six years. He was a smart, hard-working, self-motivated man who could have left Chelsea in his rearview mirror. He knew Chelsea was a joke in the eyes of outsiders. So, soon after high school graduation, Ash drove away. He went over the bridge and down the Mass Pike all the way to Worcester to attend Clark University, but the punch lines kept coming. The tall, lanky kid with a chip on his shoulder was being teased by kids from places like Malden and Revere. Those cities, Chelsea's neighbors, aren't exactly gateways to the Caribbean or cities held in especially high regard either, but as poor as their reputations were, they could still lord it over a place like Chelsea.

"The old days were the old days," Ash said with the knowledge of someone who, as a child, watched the city fall, and as a man, was still trying to pick it back up. "And they were bad old days. There's no kidding about it. We fell into a pit that nobody else had fallen into when we went into receivership, and we deserved every bit of it. This place was chaotic. Politics at its worst was exhibited right out of this office."

Four consecutive mayors contributed to the economic plight of the city that led to it being taken over by the state. Two of Chelsea's mayors were convicted in 1993 of obstructing justice. Another was found guilty of lying to a grand jury investigating corruption in Chelsea, and still another cooperated with the investigation and was granted immunity, but only after admitting he had taken payoffs while in office.

The corruption was woven into the fabric of the city, and it wasn't until a loose thread was observed and somebody pulled on it that it all began to unravel. That loose thread was the city's inability to meet its payroll or open its schools in the fall of 1991. The state legislature swooped in and named James F. Carlin the city's first receiver. By the time Carlin finished cleaning house, only three of the city's department heads were left standing. The rest were thrown out.

"When we went into receivership it wasn't because we owed anything, because we didn't borrow anything," Ash explained. "We didn't borrow anything, because we weren't fixing anything. The mayors of the day took whatever money they had for infrastructure and did whatever they had to do on the surface for people to see to get re-elected. Nobody was doing anything with the water pipes or the sewer pipes. Nobody was doing anything with the utilities. Any infrastructure that wasn't going to get them any votes, they didn't do. So, the neighborhoods were falling apart."

Chelsea remained under the control of the state through 1995 when a new city charter was approved and Guy Santagate, the city's longtime tax assessor, was appointed by a new city council as Chelsea's first city manager. The following year, seven new schools opened in Chelsea, including four elementary schools, two middle schools, and a new high school. Every public school child in the city began the school year in a new, state-of-the-art building courtesy of the state legislature. The state funded 95 percent of the construction costs, or $116 million, and Boston University chipped in a large portion of what was left. Chelsea and its nearly four thousand children were given a fresh start. It was the kind of beginning not afforded to the children of previous generations in Chelsea.

Many people look to a significant vote in 1950 as the day Chelsea began to change, the day its children were abandoned, the day its citizens began looking for a way out. The city's Board of Aldermen commissioned Harvard to do a study on the city's school system. That study, among other things, recommended the city build a new school, which would have been the city's first in over forty years. By a single vote, the board voted not to build the new school. That was the beginning of the end. The people in the city who valued education started to move out.

"What happened was that the people who were left behind probably weren't the best to be able to manage the challenges of the day," Ash explained. "You had less qualified people in all facets of your community and things got tougher and tougher. By the '80s, people we were electing were not the type of people that reasonable people would want serving them. It ultimately collapsed because there wasn't the combination of skill and vision and fortitude in this office to hold things together. Corruption was found here, but I don't think it was corruption that did the city in. I think it was just that there wasn't anyone watching. The community had low expectations, and as a result, the people who got in had low expectations."

Then, with approximately $12 million coming from Boston University, and another $116 million coming from the state, there was an opportunity for Chelsea to redefine itself. By 1996, the Chelsea school facilities were the envy of many affluent suburban communities. But while the buildings were clean, and children were eating lunches in cafeterias instead of classrooms for the first time, educating the children of Chelsea remained a task of significant difficulty.

"For nineteen years now, BU has been managing our school system," Ash said. "The problem is if you don't come to school ready to learn, if you don't have parents at home who are pushing you, then it doesn't matter how good your school system is."

The parents were not pushing. Why they were not pushing is open to debate, but it would seem to include at least two significant factors: language and mobility. Longtime BU president John Silber, who initiated the program to take over the Chelsea school system when his plan to take over the entire Boston school system was met with too much resistance, once defended BU's performance by explaining the continued poor performance of Chelsea's students.

"You can't judge us on those results," Silber said, "because so many of those children have been in the Chelsea schools for only a year, at most. Any child who's transient is going to be deficient. You can't do something with a child you don't have."

Chelsea has had a transient rate of about 35 percent for a while, which means that in any given year more than a third of the students either leave or enter the school district. Only 15 percent of the graduating class of 2007 started their academic careers in Chelsea kindergartens. People just don't stay in Chelsea if they don't have to. Many of the students have entered the school system with little or no formal education from their home countries, but as a public school, Chelsea has accepted whoever walks through the door. That open-arms policy has offered opportunity equally to everyone who lands on the shores of America, but it has created an unstable and difficult educational environment. Chelsea ends up with a student body where minorities are the majority, and most of the minorities are Hispanic. English is a second language for almost half of Chelsea's students.

"We don't see as many parents engaged in their children's educations. That's a fair assumption," Ash asserted. "Language may have something to do with it, but I'll never know that. It's more than that. We grew up with parents who were pushing education, education, education. I don't get the sense here that every parent does that. Part of it is the culture that we live in. It's tougher to do that. It's tough to push a kid towards something that you yourself haven't experienced. So, if you have immigrants who come to this country who weren't educated in their homelands, which is more typical than not, they come to this country and they struggle with language, and there's all this stuff that their kids are getting mixed up in, it may be tough for that mother or father to see that education is the way."

When BU took over Chelsea's schools in 1989, the dropout rate at the high school was an alarmingly high 52 percent, and half of the city's residents lived in households with annual incomes below $10,000. Seven years later when the new schools were opened, the per capita income had only increased to $11,559, and by 2005, the dropout rate for seniors at Chelsea High School had dropped to 11 percent, but that apparent improvement doesn't capture the number of kids who dropped out as freshmen, sophomores, or juniors. Chelsea's dropout rate has remained among the highest in the state, and it increases annually between March and June, because once the kids figure they can't pass their courses anyway, they stop bothering to attend school. That's when some of them get jobs, and the rest start hanging out on the street.

"Because of the failure in school," explained Chelsea school superintendent Thomas Kingston, "the street is more attractive, and that's why there are gang recruiters in Chelsea. We're aware of that and we fight it head-on. The worst thing you can do is to deny there's a gang problem. We have a gang problem."

That problem reared its head in the early '90s. Chelsea police chief Frank Garvin pointed to the day when a young girl walked into the police station on Oak Street and said she had been recruited by gang members at the high school, and that she was afraid for her life. That's when the police and the school became proactive. The Gang Unit Task Force was created, and school resource officers began working security at the middle schools and the high school.

"Over the years it was the 18th Street gang, the MS-13s, the Bloods. It was the Tiny Little Rascals, and the Asian gangs."

Garvin listed the names of the violent thugs who haunted his city as if he were running down a grocery list.

"The gangs, for kids who have no family, they're a family. They're an attraction. They become part of a group. They become people they can hang with, and run with. They may not get that at home or at school, and they get it from them. They don't see the downside. They just see the attractive side. A lot of it was writing graffiti and the attractive stuff, but a lot of it was also selling drugs. And they had beer houses, which are just houses where they'd sell beer at night. When you go to some of these kids' houses, and you try to talk to them about being gang members, you find that their parents were gang members in Nicaragua or Central America, San Salvador. To them, there's nothing wrong with that. It was a way of protecting yourself."

Garvin was a large man with large features, big hands, thick arms and legs, large, round eyes, and a big, bushy mustache. He grew up in nearby Charlestown, and joined the Chelsea police force in 1974. He went to law school, passed the bar, moved up the ranks, and became the chief in 2001.

His office was on the fourth floor of the Chelsea Police Department. It was a building that stood out with its yellow brick facade and the large American flag flying out front. Across the street was a small, triangular park with barely enough room for a half dozen benches. Under the benches were dozens of tiny "nip" bottles of alcohol.

From Garvin's office, he could see the park. He could see up Broadway and down Oak Street where he used to walk the beat from one end of Chelsea to the other.

"We used to walk the square at night," he reminisced. "There were two boxes, one in Bellingham Square, one in Chelsea Square. They don't do this anymore, but you used to walk up the street and pull on all the doors, then ring the box every hour. I did that for years. If you didn't ring the box, they'd come looking for you. They didn't have radios, or even cars for a long time. There was a light down at Bellingham Square, and if it lit up, you had to call the station. They'd tell us to carry enough dimes with us to make sure we could call in when we needed to."

Bellingham Square was an area at the east end of the city's primary business district best known as a meeting place for drug traffickers and prostitutes. It was just around the corner from City Hall. These days, a cop can stand in the middle of the square and wave to his fellow officers back at the police station. That's because there are now thirty high-tech cameras strategically placed around the city. Now, a police officer sits in front of a big plasma television with a joystick. He can zoom in on activity several blocks away. The zoom lens is so powerful the officer can read a newspaper over someone's shoulder. Big Brother is definitely watching in Chelsea, but the residents didn't mind when the cameras were installed in 2004. The city was dangerous enough that its law-abiding residents were willing to sacrifice some of their personal freedoms. Better to be watched than dead.

But the video surveillance was only moderately successful. Only a handful of successful prosecutions resulted. Real police work still needed to be done by real police officers. Jimmy Atkins was a real cop, a throwback. He didn't walk a beat, didn't carry dimes to call in when trouble erupted, but he spent as little time in his cruiser as possible. More often, he would position his imposing frame at the intersection of Broadway and Bellingham, just opposite the bus stop, and across the street from Bellingham Square. He became a friendly and familiar face to the shop owners and customers and various passersby. His gregarious personality wasn't a prerequisite for the job, but it helped him immensely. It helped forge relationships. It helped gain the trust of informants. And on the days it did neither of those things, it at least helped pass the time.

Walking the streets, Atkins could see everything, talk to everybody, learn everything about the people hustling to work or to school, and know everything about the people who were just hustling, the ones with nowhere to go. Atkins was no fool. Not much was going to slip by him out on the streets. He had been a cop too long, nearly twenty years, and before that, he had been a tough city kid himself.

Toughness was mandatory for a kid growing up in the projects of East Boston, especially a kid born in 1965 New England with a black father and a white Italian mother, and especially a kid born into the Mob.

"My dad was as involved in the Mob as you can get as a black man," Atkins said. "I was in those clubs watching all the Italians and my father. My father had more clout than most of the people in the room. He got that because he had a reputation for being fearless. There was this guy who was supposed to be a big-time killer, but they used to say the one guy he was afraid of was Foots, my dad's nickname."

Atkins' father was James Carson, a convicted criminal, a man deep into organized crime. His mother was Jeanette Calley, who also was no stranger to bookmaking establishments and bars.

"They never told me, but I think that's how my parents met," Atkins said. "My uncles and aunts were all bookmakers."

The explanation for why James Carson and Jeanette Calley would have a son named James Atkins is simple. Jeanette was married to Joe Atkins, and while they were separated, but not legally divorced, Calley and Carson got together. The baby was given the legal surname, but Joe Atkins was not his father, and James never had any relationship with him.

"I came along," Atkins explained. "I got named Atkins, but I got no Atkins blood in me—which sucks."

Soon after Atkins was born, Carson was forced to flee from Massachusetts. Atkins' version of the story is that his father owned a nightclub and shot two state troopers one night. Atkins explained they were dirty cops wearing plain clothes and roughing up some of the patrons. His father thought they were robbing the place, so he shot and wounded them. Soon after, Carson took his infant son and the boy's mother to Alabama, Carson's birthplace. As the weary travelers approached the Mason-Dixon Line, Atkins' mother had to get out of the car and go the rest of the way by herself, "because a black guy and a white woman driving down South just doesn't cut it." Atkins finished the story with a smile. He spoke about his father, not with pride, but not with shame either, and even though his father played only a minor role in Atkins' upbringing, he didn't waste time on regret either.

"My father, when he was around, he'd come by on a Friday and he'd empty out the ice cream truck and buy for the whole neighborhood, but then he'd be gone for six months. When he wasn't around, you were always excited when he came around. My mother would yell and scream about it, and I'd get mad at her for yelling about it."

As a young boy, Atkins never lost affection for his father, despite the fact that Carson was constantly in and out of his life, and much more out than in. He wasn't embittered by his father's absence. He relished his presence. And he never resented Carson for seeming to have so much money but still letting his son grow up poor.

When Atkins was with his mother, he spent his Saturday mornings waiting for the National Guard trucks to drive into the projects. The trucks only came by on Saturday mornings, and it was important to get there early before they ran out of condensed milk, and you were stuck with a week's worth of powdered milk.

"Powdered milk sucks," Atkins said with the foul taste still lingering in his memory.

Atkins would return home to his mother with the milk, a big canned ham, a tin of peanut butter with the oil on top that needed to be stirred, and various other grocery items they were too poor to purchase at the store. But when Atkins was with his father, he got to ride around in a big Cadillac. He got to act like a big shot when his father bought the ice cream, or when his father walked into Barney's like he owned the place. Barney's was a well-known bar and grill in East Boston, well known for its Italian sausage and lamb, and well known as a place where the mobsters hung out. It may have been Barney's where Atkins' mother and father met, or it might have been some other after-hours joint.

Bookmaking, racketeering, after-hours card games, and various other illegal activities were an integral part of Jimmy Atkins' formative years. By the time he was nine years old, Jimmy would spend a dime to take a twenty-minute bus ride over to Mattapan, down Blue Hill Avenue into Mattapan Square. That's where they all hung out, the mobsters. And the kids who wanted to be just like them hung out outside.

"I saw it firsthand," Atkins recalled. "I grew up outside those clubs with all the bosses and guys inside. You'd see guys like my father driving a Cadillac and it looked good."

With their fancy cars, wads of cash, instant power, instant respect, and instant gratification, the wise guys had the admiration of the neighborhood kids. They weren't called gangs back then, but the tough kids hung out on street corners, got into fights, and if trouble didn't find them, they went out looking for it.

But Jimmy was different than most of his friends from The Heights in East Boston. He was different, because while he felt the allure and excitement of playing on the wrong side of the law, he resisted it. He was different, because he was always an exceptional athlete and found a sense of belonging away from the neighborhoods. But mostly he was different because he was a black kid with Italian mannerisms. He talked with his hands, and he sounded like his Italian uncles. He was different from the white kids and the black kids, and so he was harassed by both.

"You'd fight all the time," Atkins explained, "not very well in the beginning. You get better as you get older, the more practice you get in. One time when I was eleven, my Italian grandmother gave me these coins. She lived right across the street from Barney's,

and there was a coin shop about three streets over. I'm thinking
I'm the richest man in the world. I'm going to go over to this coin
shop and they're gonna give me a million dollars!"

Atkins told the story as if he were still eleven years old, the
same exuberance. When he told the story minutes after it happened, he is certain to have told it just this way. He relived the
moments in vivid detail. . . . *It is one o'clock in the afternoon. I'm hop-
ping over rain puddles, but the sun is out as I'm walking down the street,
and for the first time in my life, I realize I'm different.*

"Before that you're kind of protected by your family, and I was
good in sports, so I always had a ton of friends. But on this day,
there were these two Italian kids, about sixteen, seventeen years
old with the wife-beater shirts on. I was walking across the street
and one of the kids was emptying out a bottle into the street. It
didn't dawn on me what he was doing. Then I hear him say, 'Nigger, get out of East Boston.' I'm thinking, 'He's pissed at somebody.' Then he says it again, and I realize he's talking to me. I get
pissed. So, I turned around and go back the other way. I was crying
and walking down Brooks Street, and Beneton, and Marion Street.
I was so pissed, I picked up a brick, and even back then I was fast
as wind, and I just ran up behind him, and I smacked him in the
head with the brick. I just kept running to Barney's because I knew
my uncles were in there. I knocked the one kid out, but the other
kid chased me into Barney's. My uncles had a couple of kids take
him out back and beat the shit out of him."

Two years later, at the age of thirteen, Jimmy's uncle, Benny
Calley, got killed. Benny was a bookmaker and a drug dealer. He
had survived one stabbing, but he didn't survive the second.

Two years after that, Jimmy's mother smashed her car into a
telephone pole. Her chest bone, all her ribs, her pelvis, one arm,
and both her legs were broken. She required nearly six months
of rehab. So, Jimmy went to live with his father. Carson had built
a house in Wrentham, a small, rural town thirty minutes south of

Boston. Carson had won the land in a card game and built a house on it. He furnished the place with gaudy chandeliers, velvet furniture, and thick shag carpets.

"He was the only black guy in Wrentham," Jimmy laughed. "I remember the parties clear as day. He'd have a barbecue, and there'd be thirty-five Cadillacs parked along the lawn for two days. Then he'd leave $500 on the dresser and be gone for days."

So, for several days at a time, fifteen-year-old Jimmy was alone, just him and a 1981 Cadillac Fleetwood Brougham, or sometimes his father would leave the El Dorado.

"Whichever car he took, I took the other one. I'm a fifteen-year-old kid driving to school in a brand new Cadillac and nobody questioned me at all. Nobody even thought this was weird for a sophomore in high school."

His unconventional childhood, his battles with poverty and racism, his exposure to violence, and his primarily single-parent upbringing all conspired to shape Jimmy. His difficult past and his rise above it molded him into the adult James Atkins. He was strong willed and goal oriented. He was respectful and respected. He was popular among the law-abiding people he served and protected. He was a tough, courageous, physical cop who was also very squeamish around blood. He was comfortable with the rich as well as the poor, the educated and the uneducated, the drug addict or the king, because no man is better than he. He was affable, and he was angry, but he was not an angry black man. He was an angry football coach.

His anger was layered as he prepared for the Red Devils' third game of the season. Watching the films of the first two games, Atkins noticed an utter lack of toughness on his team. So, he had spent the better part of a week trying to beat toughness into them.

"I just beat their ass all week," Atkins said gleefully. "They're all banged up. They're all bruised up. We had a couple of injuries during camp. So, I pulled the reins back a little bit. That was a coaching mistake. They got soft during that time. I thought we were smart enough and athletic enough that we could teach more and they'd save the banging for game day. But that didn't happen. So, we worked on toughness all week. I kicked their ass."

Atkins laughed, but he was suddenly angry again. Going over his starting lineup, he was reminded that he had to throw Black Josh, his best lineman, off the team. Joshua Lewis had gone to the principal's office to apologize for his sexual remark to the female teacher. He was under strict orders from Atkins to answer every question with either a "Yes, sir" or a "No, sir," and "I'm sorry. It won't happen again." Josh was convincingly penitent, and was allowed to stay on the football team. But two days later, he told another teacher to "go fuck" himself, and threatened to "kick his ass." When he went to explain himself to Atkins, he was met with indifference.

"I really didn't do anything, Coach," he said.

"Josh, you're a lost cause," Atkins replied. "I don't know what to do with you. You're off the team."

Josh stared blankly at the floor for a long moment. The man-child who had just exploded on a teacher was silent before Atkins. The bully who had pushed and shoved his way through the system, never having to face any consequences of significance, was finally out of second chances. There was no outrage. No tears. He was merely stunned. Finally, he turned and walked away. With strides that were long and deliberate, Black Josh pushed open a door and walked outside, back into the streets of Chelsea.

"This is a kid with Division I talent I had to toss off the team," Atkins said with a degree of despair. "Last year, he was ineligible because he didn't do the right thing. This year we got him on the team. He had one F, so we went to the principal who agreed he could play with the F. So, he went to camp, and he's a beast. He's only fifteen, and he's 6'4", 240 pounds, all muscle. Rock-hard stud.

He could stand under the basket, bounce the ball, jump up and grab it and dunk it. He's that much of an athlete. But you can't use up all your energy on one kid. We could have fought for him, but we decided we'd just move on without him. They can be so tough on the streets with guns and machetes and everything else, but they come in and they're just lacking so much. Come in here and let's see how tough you really are. This is a real challenge for me."

A few hours after dismissing Black Josh, Atkins went to a North Shore gang intelligence meeting where officers from several area cities and towns shared information. Atkins took a seat and watched attentively as names and photos of known and suspected gang kids were flashed on a projector screen. Atkins immediately recognized one of the first faces he saw.

"Are you shitting me?"

It was one of his best defensive players, who had been involved in a fight between the Bloods and a rival gang in the city of Lynn. Atkins read the report and talked to the detective on the case. Ultimately, his best read on the situation was that his player was going to a party, and happened to be in the car with another kid who was carrying a Taser. When the skirmish was broken up by police and the Taser was discovered, the officers hauled everyone down to the station. For a Chelsea kid, deeply entrenched in a gang, it was a minor episode. Atkins talked to his player about making bad decisions and being in the wrong place at the wrong time. He threatened to kick him off the team, too, but in the end, he figured this one wasn't a lost cause.

"What do I accomplish if I throw him off the team?" Atkins asked rhetorically. "He's just gonna go back out on the street. What do you do with that one?"

And what does he do with so many of the others? What does he do with a kid who oversleeps and shows up late for school when he knows that kid was sleeping in a friend's attic because his parents haven't been home in days? What does he do with the kid who's obviously distracted during practice when he knows that kid's mother just packed up her things and left town without so much as a good-bye? What about the kid whose father hasn't contacted him in the year since his parents' divorce? Those are the good kids who are staying out of serious trouble, but they're not focused for practice. Sometimes they're late. Sometimes they have detention, because they didn't do their homework. Maybe their grades are slipping and they're in danger of failing off the team. How does a football coach deal with those issues?

Atkins chose to deal with those issues head on, the same way he had been forced to handle kids like Orlando and Black Josh, and Michael Augustine and Brian Roberts. Those were four of the biggest, toughest kids in Chelsea High School, but only Orlando remained on the team.

Augustine was big and strong enough as a freshman to log some minutes on the varsity. He was a potential football stud who could run like the wind, but he also ran with Roberts and the Bloods. After stealing a car, Roberts was arrested prior to the 2005 season with Augustine in the car, but instead of being sent to jail or a juvenile detention center, Atkins intervened and sent Roberts to football camp.

"All right, Brian," Coach said. "We'll get you out, but you have to come to football camp. You're gonna do the right thing. You're not gonna get arrested again. You're not going to get in trouble. This is going to be your probation. You have to come every day, just like going to your probation officer."

Roberts' case was never dismissed. He was put on what's called pre-trial probation, entrusted to Atkins, and given a chance to have the car theft stricken from his record. All he had to do was stay out of trouble for a year. He might have made it, too, except that he separated his shoulder and wasn't able to play football anymore. Once that happened, he started getting into trouble again. No more Brian Roberts on the Chelsea football team.

Meanwhile, Michael wasn't charged with anything when he was simply the passenger in the stolen car, but he was eventually arrested for fighting and for robbery. Still, he could have been eligible to play football in 2006 as a sophomore, but he flunked out. No more Michael Augustine on the Chelsea football team.

Losing three potentially great players could be devastating to a high school football team. Basically, all it takes to win a Division 3 Super Bowl in Massachusetts is three or four studs and two solid running backs. Atkins had the backs in Quiles and Caraballo, but he still didn't know if he had the studs. He was chafed about that, angry that three of his best players were lost for the year, annoyed that so much of his energy was spent on off-the-field problems, and he was still seething about how Minuteman Regional, that night's opponent, had helped screw him out of a playoff berth the previous year.

"We won the league and lost the tiebreaker on a technicality," Atkins bristled. "We should have gone to the playoffs last year, but they sent a team with a 6–4 record instead of us with a 7–3 record. We beat three upper division teams, whereas they lost to three upper division teams. They changed the rule this year—even before they played last year's game, they had changed that rule."

When the 2005 season ended, both Chelsea and Georgetown had one loss in the Commonwealth Small League. Chelsea had a better overall record and a tougher schedule, but its one loss was to Georgetown. So, by rule, Georgetown would go to the playoffs. Chelsea appealed, and Minuteman Regional was among the schools that voted against Chelsea. After the vote, a new tiebreaker rule was instituted that would have sent Chelsea to the playoffs. Atkins saw it as one more example of Chelsea being disrespected. The Commonwealth Small League was made up almost entirely of vocational and technical schools, and Chelsea didn't belong. They were the outsiders, the underclass. At least that's what the people of Chelsea thought, and Atkins made respect, and the lack of it, the theme of his pregame speech before the Red Devils took the field against the Mustangs of Minuteman Regional.

"We had East Boston coaches in the stands last week," he told his team. "You guys know my buddy, Lou, that I hang out with on the gang team. He was up there and he heard them. Lou told me they were shitting all over us. They were saying we suck. They were saying they ran up the score on us. They're talking about who's gonna win the league: Georgetown, North Shore, Northeast. They don't even mention Chelsea. In one game, in one goddamn game, we lost the most important thing that we gained in our first two years, and that was the respect of these goddamn people out there—in that one game we lost it."

The players looked surprised. They knew Chelsea, the city, didn't have much respect from the outside, but they felt their football team had earned respect by beating Madison Park the previous week. The seniors who had gone 15–6 the past two years believed they deserved respect. Could this be true? Was Coach right? One loss and all they had worked for was gone? That's when the doubts began to seep in again. If nobody else respected us, should we respect ourselves? They wondered as the shouting continued.

"Let's get that goddamn respect back right from the kickoff tonight! Let's knock it back right in their fucking mouths, and let them remember who we are. That's what respect is all about. Guys, we need to bring it now. We can't make those simple mistakes. We gotta be ready from the kickoff. And Ato, I need you playing like a beast right from the beginning, son."

"Yes, Coach!"

"Right from the beginning. Luna. I need you to suck up the pain in your knee, Luna, and just come out and take the guy in front of you."

"Yes, Coach!"

Ato Alic and Jonathan Luna were both seniors, and both knew to answer assertively. They couldn't reach their coach's volume or intensity, but they tried. Atkins singled out several other players, each time getting the response he required. Then, just in case his message hadn't gotten through, he gave them one more tweak before sending them out of the locker room.

"By the way, this is one of the fucking coaches here, and one of the goddamn athletic directors who voted us out of the playoffs last year, and then had the balls to change the rule before they even played the fucking game! They took something away from us! Let's take it back and shove it right up this guy's ass!"

"It's up there!" Frankie shouted spontaneously.

"It's up there," Coach said with a smile. "That's right, Frankie. It's up there."

The players jumped up and ran out onto the field whooping and hollering. At that moment, they didn't look like a bunch of troubled teens. They looked like kids who didn't have a care in the world, kids who were playing football and loving life. They looked like happy kids.

And for that moment, Atkins wasn't angry anymore.

CHAPTER THREE

The Gang Unit

These kids aren't afraid of their parents. They're not afraid of teachers, or rival gang members. They're afraid of Jimmy. And really, all he can do is not let them play. And maybe even more than that, it's that Jimmy might not like them. I think that would crush some of these kids. They love him so much, they want him to love them back.

—SCOTT CONLEY, CHELSEA POLICE DETECTIVE

As the Red Devils stormed the field for their third game of the season, there were more than a few spectators standing underneath the autumn sky who thought about what had happened just three years earlier. That was the year the third game of the season was the last game of the season. It was a Friday night. Chelsea lost 43–8, and by Monday morning, the season was over.

"It had to be done. The kids were taking an awful beating," said lifelong Chelsea educator Morry Seigal. "We ended the program strictly to keep our kids from getting killed."

Seigal was born and raised in Chelsea, and he will most assuredly die there, but only after having made a positive impact on the children of the city every day of his adult life. Seigal taught in the Chelsea schools for thirty-seven years, and had been on the school committee for the previous twenty-three years. That's six decades of making changes and watching other changes take place beyond his control.

"The demographics of Chelsea started to change in the middle to late '70s. Folks who could afford it moved to the suburbs and were replaced by a class of people who were poor and immigrant, and had language difficulties. And it's been that way ever since. We have twenty-nine different countries represented in the high school. But when the demographics changed, that's when we started to slide. When our kids go home, there aren't any doctors or lawyers waiting at home to help them with a trigonometry problem. I'm not saying poor kids can't learn. But we're saying poor kids don't have computers in their homes. They've got after-school jobs. It's understandable."

Perhaps, too, it's understandable that with many of the students coming from Latin-American countries, Chelsea does have a strong soccer program, but American football has lagged in popularity. In 2003, under then–head coach Andy O'Brien, the football program hit rock bottom. Only twenty-seven players came out for the team, and only four of them were seniors. A squad of mostly freshmen and sophomores went to battle against bigger and stronger kids from other schools, and they were getting hurt. In their third game of that season against Shawsheen, two kids were unable to walk off the field under their own power. They were carted off. Several other players were also injured, suffering from bruises and sprains significant enough to make their participation doubtful the following week. So, an emergency meeting was called between the school superintendent, Irene Cornish, and the Chelsea High School athletic director, Frank DePatto. The result of that meeting was the cancellation of the football season. O'Brien told his team on Monday after school, but the players already knew.

"I pick up the paper on Monday and find out we don't have a varsity team anymore," Danny Cortez, now a senior, recalled. "I didn't believe it. I figured there had to be a mistake. But we went to practice that day and they told us. We were all down. We understood the A.D. didn't believe we were good enough to play at the varsity level."

Coach O'Brien, described as a nice guy who just wasn't right for Chelsea, had been a football and track star at Stoneham High School, a suburban school about 5 miles north of Boston. He went to Tufts University and switched his major from business to education, and landed a job teaching in the Chelsea middle school. When the high school was searching for a new head football coach to take over for the 2000 season, the young, soft-spoken, and white O'Brien was considered a good fit. He wasn't. The Red Devils had three consecutive 1–9 seasons under O'Brien, and participation dwindled a little more each year. It was tough to get Chelsea kids enthusiastic about joining a team that was beaten so easily and so frequently. They already had a strong familiarity with losing.

"It was my fault," O'Brien conceded. "It was just ignorance, a lack of understanding of the situation. I expected the kids to be student athletes. I didn't support them enough. Instead of getting in front of them, I should have gotten behind them."

O'Brien expected his players to work hard, show up on time, and commit themselves to the team—like he had done, like all his friends had done, like everyone he ever knew had done. *That's just the way you do things,* he thought. But Chelsea was an awakening. The kids there are different. Or maybe it's just kids today.

"I went to a postseason basketball tournament in Revere," lamented Arnie Goodman, a Chelsea educator for more than thirty-seven years and the Chelsea football public address announcer for nearly forty. "And as soon as I entered the gymnasium, the game was already under way, and I heard a group of kids yelling, 'The ref eats shit!' Those kids got away with that. Nobody said anything to them."

Frank DePatto was a Chelsea High School graduate, class of '57, and had been the athletic director for nearly twenty years. He was the best man at the wedding of city manager Jay Ash, another Chelsea native and graduate. Morry Seigal had been around longer than all of them, and his son Jay, class of '76, who also stayed in Chelsea, had been teaching at the high school for the past five years and was now the school's basketball coach. They were some of the caretakers of Chelsea. They had seen Chelsea be better than it was in 2006, or they had heard about a time when it was. They believed in its potential, and they were determined to see Chelsea back on its feet, throwing out its chest, and holding its head up high. It was a sentiment not only understood, but shared by Rich Griffin, a reporter for the *Chelsea Record.*

"I can't leave," he said. "It's an experiment. Nobody's ever done this before. It's democracy being built here. That's how I look at Chelsea. You're talking about a city that was in receivership, and that was corrupt as the day is long. The state came in and had to right the ship. Now you have a lot of people in a lot of different corners of the city really working hard to change that. It's interesting to me, because I don't know what the end game is, I don't know how you declare victory over it, but watching the process, and knowing where it came from and what it's doing right now, to me it's fascinating."

Clearly, there were good people surrounding the kids of Chelsea. These were people with priorities, intelligence, work ethic, people who demonstrated kindness by sacrifice. The kids, therefore, had plenty of opportunities to see another way of life. The streets were not their only option. They had role models who grew up in Chelsea and went to college, and became teachers, and coaches, and cops, and important city officials. If these kids bothered to open their eyes, they would see responsible contributors to the community who were happy with the choices they made—especially the choice to stay in Chelsea.

And these caretakers put their faith in James Atkins. He was the obvious choice when the O'Brien Experiment failed. The football program needed a strong voice and a heavy hand, like Atkins. It needed a no-nonsense disciplinarian, like Atkins. It needed a recruiter, someone who could make playing football cool again, to get the school's best athletes to choose football, to get kids in sixth and seventh grade excited about the possibility of wearing the Red Devils uniform someday. But Chelsea football didn't just need someone *like* Atkins. It needed Atkins.

"It was a rebirth for the football program, and the savior was Jim Atkins," Morry Seigal said. "He's a tough-minded guy. He knows most of the kids, knows the kids who are in gangs, some of them are on the team. He's resurrected this program. He did it through the strength of his personality. He went out and recruited the kids. He's no pansy by the way. When he speaks, the kids listen. There's no nonsense with him. You toe the line or else you're gone. They have great respect for him."

Before Atkins took over, injuries and apathy had depleted Chelsea's forces down to about eighteen kids. Atkins went forth and multiplied that number by more than three. He started by walking into classrooms in the middle schools and the high school and talking passionately about football, about pride, and about winning. Atkins was convincing, in large measure, because he believed in what he was selling. Now, he had more players than uniforms to put them in.

Certainly, Atkins was supremely qualified for the daunting challenge of becoming a head coach for the first time. He'd already served his apprenticeship as an assistant coach, first at Chelsea during their last Super Bowl season of 1995, and more recently at his alma mater, East Boston, under longtime head coach John Sousa. But well beyond approving his X's and O's, the Chelsea school department loved the idea of getting a Gang Unit cop involved with some of its toughest kids.

"I know because I still live in this city," DePatto explained. "The kids in Chelsea, they're gang kids. They shit their pants at him. He has a very, very tough reputation out there. What's the best way to start? You have a coach that's tough, but fair. He knows the game. And he's going to make something from nothing. He has a very high standard. I don't think he'd ever fail at anything he does."

Atkins had tasted the powdered milk delivered to the projects, but he hadn't really tasted the full flavor of failure just yet. After starring on the East Boston High School football and track teams, Atkins attended Suffolk University in Boston, but when the financial aid stopped, he dropped out and joined the Army Reserve. He spoke frequently about becoming a lawyer, but when some of his friends took the police exam, he took it too, and scored well enough to be offered a job with the Boston Police Department.

"I blew it off," Atkins laughed. "I was an East Boston punk having a good time. I didn't want to be a cop. I was doing all right. I was managing a restaurant, drinking and partying."

Atkins still spoke about becoming a lawyer while he was a restaurant manager, but that dream was fading. Instead, the Massachusetts Bay Transportation Authority called next, and since they were the highest-paying department in the state at that time, Atkins decided to go through the motions. He got the job and was hooked. He also discovered racism was alive and well in Boston during the '80s.

"I'd talk on the phone as a detective with the MBTA police," Atkins recalled. "And this one woman got robbed at the JFK train station. Back then you'd bring photo books to people. First, you'd get a general description and then use the book. I said, 'What was his complexion?' And the woman said, 'I don't know, just your regular nigger.' I said, 'All right, I'll be right there.' She comes to the door and it's, 'Holy shit!' They had no idea, because of what I sound like."

Unfazed, Atkins discovered he enjoyed being a cop, and he was good at it. He moved steadily up the ranks while completing his education. Fifteen years after dropping out of college, he went back and received his associate's degree from Bunker Hill Community College in Charlestown, then got his bachelor's degree from Curry College in Milton, and eventually earned his master's degree in criminal justice from Anna Maria College just outside Worcester.

These were the attributes and achievements that made him a suitable role model for the children of Chelsea. But he was not the only one. Detective Scott Conley was one. Sergeant David Batchelor was another. He was a Chelsea High School graduate, class of 1980. An outstanding football and basketball player, Batchelor is a member of Chelsea's Hall of Fame.

"When it was time to hire a new coach," Conley recalled, "Frank DePatto said, 'We need three gang cops down here to make this team work.' You couldn't just have three cops. You needed us."

The three cops ran practice each afternoon, and then drove around in police cruisers at night making sure none of their players was roaming the streets. They were cops and coaches 24-7.

"Who better for us to go to when something went down than our own team?" Conley asked rhetorically. "Before a practice would start, you might hear us say, 'Hey, who was that that stabbed a guy down on Marlboro Street?' It's like we were conducting an investigation on a stabbing before we start practicing."

After putting Conley and Batchelor in their places by reminding them that while they were friends and colleagues on the force, he was the boss on the football field, Atkins began by bringing twenty-five racially mixed, poverty-stricken, troubled kids to Cape Cod for football camp in August of 2004. There could have been more kids, and eventually there would be, but at that point Jimmy had already thrown several players off the team. Right away, the kids knew things were going to be different under this new regime. No hats in the chow hall. No bad language (from the kids). Practice twice a day. It was a military atmosphere. No nonsense.

"When we first went down to camp," Conley explained, "we had Bosnians, Croatians, Muslims, blacks, Hispanics, and a white kid from Alabama. One of the kids, Eddie Rodriguez, super kid, he says, 'Coach, if we don't have a Jihad, we're gonna have a great season!'" Conley also remembered the Bosnian kid tearfully describing the day his parents were murdered back home.

It was an eclectic mix of talent, but the most talented kid didn't show up until the second week of the season. Thomas Cromwell opened eyes and turned heads. He was an amazing physical specimen who transferred from Leominster, a Division 1 high school. Chelsea had managed to win its first two games of the 2004 season without this kid, and with him, an exclamation point could be added to their success story. But Atkins told the strong, talented player he couldn't play right away. He would have to earn his way on to the team by coming to practice. Atkins didn't want a new kid walking on to the team and taking a starting position away from somebody who'd been sweating and working for a month already.

"But in our third game," Conley recounted with vivid recollection and enthusiasm, "we're killing the team, and there's about a minute left. Jimmy sends Cromwell in to play defensive end. They snap the ball, and I've never seen a greater athletic play. In a millisecond, Cromwell comes across the line and murders the quarterback. BOOM! The quarterback's out cold, fumbles the ball. Cromwell picks it up and runs it in. Touchdown! We were like, 'Whoa!' We were so excited. Oh my God! This is great!"

Then it was back to reality. On the following Tuesday, the dean of students, Joe Mullaney, strutted out to practice and asked to speak to Cromwell. The two of them walked inside the school and were gone for several minutes when suddenly, a door was kicked open and Cromwell came running out. He was being chased by Mullaney and two uniformed Chelsea police officers. Conley—watching from the practice field—got on his radio and called in to dispatch that there was a foot pursuit going on at the high school. When asked to describe whom the police were chasing, Conley simply said: "He's wearing number 72."

Still dressed from head to toe in his Red Devils uniform, Cromwell raced across the practice field and easily scaled a 7-foot-high fence. The rest of the team and the coaches stared in disbelief.

Narcotics had been found in Cromwell's locker. He was eventually allowed back into the school, but not on to the football team.

"Jimmy says, 'That's it. You're done,'" Conley said. "This kid would have been All-Scholastic. Jimmy was never blurred by talent."

Cromwell was arrested and found guilty of drug possession. It was Atkins who brought him to court. He didn't speak on his behalf, but he was there for him. It was the beginning of a pattern. Atkins was strict. He suspended kids for games because they were late for practice, or late for school, or a variety of other transgressions ranging from minor to major. But after the consequences were meted out, the kids knew Atkins put the problems behind him and moved forward. He was always moving forward, always looking ahead to the next challenge.

In the third game of Atkins' third season, the coach's challenge was Minuteman Regional. Young Orlando Echevarria's challenge was not allowing the recent arrest of his cousin and uncle to distract him.

Thirty-five-year-old Jose Echevarria and eighteen-year-old Edwin Echevarria were arrested as part of Operation Dethrone II. Following a nine-month investigation by the FBI and state and local police, eighteen members of the Latin Kings were indicted on charges of drug and firearm trafficking. Some of those arrested were Chelsea High School graduates. Investigators also claimed the Latin Kings were involved in a gang war in Chelsea that had resulted in several shootings and stabbings.

So, on September 18, 2006, 125 law enforcement officials rounded up the suspects at four in the morning by either knocking on doors or breaking them down. Edwin and Jose were both in their home on Shurtleff Street. Edwin, also known as "King E," was alleged to be the Carsique, or second in command of the Latin Kings' chapter in Chelsea.

"Edwin was, at thirteen or fourteen, probably as hard-core Latin King as you could be at that age," explained Chelsea detective Dan Delaney. "His family was from Chicago and they were all Latin Kings. Edwin used to carry a newspaper article around in his wallet from a big sweep they did in Chicago locking up the Latin Kings, and he was proud to show you which ones were his relatives. Orlando would follow his cousin Edwin around and some of his buddies. His buddies were all troublemakers."

Also picked up in the sweep was twenty-year-old Sammy Argueta, better known as "Noodles." He was alleged to have been the co-founder of the Chelsea street gang "Kappin on Suckers," which had recently merged with the Latin Kings. Argueta was also friends with Orlando and several other members of the Red Devils.

"Sammy Argueta was on the run," Conley explained. "We missed him at the first two houses, so I grabbed his brother Jonathan and told him this would never end. Chelsea's only 1.8 square miles. I've known the kid since he was eight. I like him, but when I'm not around, he's out stabbing and shooting people. It doesn't mean I don't like him to talk to. So, Jonathan calls Sammy on his cellphone and I get on the line. I says, 'Look, do you want us breaking down the doors of all your loved ones, or are you and I going to meet and have this thing come down now and come down peacefully?'"

Sammy turned himself in. Orlando took the news in stride. Sammy was a friend of his, but he wasn't the first friend to face jail time.

None of this was unexpected, either. Orlando knew what Sammy and his brother, Jonathan, were up to. Still, he considered them good friends, and he reminisced about the days he fought and rumbled with the Argueta boys.

"We go way back," Orlando said. "We met in eighth grade. They were just cool people, him and his brother. When it comes down to problems, you just have to fix those problems. You can't walk away from the problems. You have to handle it. If the problem is there, if somebody is talking shit, you gotta finish the problem right there. That's just the way people are here."

While Orlando was preparing to take the field against Minuteman Regional, his friend, Sammy, was facing twenty years in prison. It had been a tense week in Chelsea.

"When the game's over, and we've won, that's when I'll be happy," Orlando said as he strapped on his helmet and rushed out to start the game.

The Red Devils got off to a good start. Orlando, a wide receiver on offense, caught a couple of passes on Chelsea's first scoring drive. Chelsea was ahead 7–0 in the second quarter when Frankie fumbled again. Though he managed to recover it, he returned to the huddle with his head down. He never looked over to the sideline.

"What the fuck is the matter with you?" Atkins screamed in his direction. "What the fuck is the matter with you? Know what you're doing! And don't drop the goddamn ball!"

A few plays later, Frankie carried the ball through the line. He broke one tackle and looked up toward an open field. *Redemption.* Suddenly, he was hit hard from the side. He never saw the hit coming, and the ball popped out again. This time, Atkins didn't yell from the sideline. Instead, after Chelsea recovered the fumble, Atkins called another running play for Frankie. He responded by bulling his way for 13 yards down to the 3-yard line. Danny Cortez took it in from there and came off the field limping noticeably.

"Stop fucking limping! Stop fucking limping! If you have to fucking come out of this game because of an injury, you're at the back of the line."

And then to Frankie, Atkins said with unexpected sympathy: "You're letting the fumbles affect your play. We scored. We overcame that problem. Understand? We beat that issue. You need to get back there and focus now on defense."

The closing minutes of the first half were a whirlwind of big plays. The Minutemen responded to the Cortez touchdown by returning the ensuing kickoff for a touchdown. Chelsea's kicker, Cesar Camacho, got an earful for that one.

"Don't put the fucking ball in the air. If you put the fucking ball in the air, you'll never see the fucking field again."

Chelsea got the ball back and moved quickly up the field. Orlando made a great diving catch at the 13-yard line, and Alex Caraballo ran it over the goal line on the next play. The Minutemen responded again with an equally swift touchdown drive. Then Chelsea sophomore Melvin Ramirez ran the kickoff back for a touchdown with no time left on the clock. Coach called Melvin "Pop Warner" because he played in his final year of eligibility in the Pop Warner league instead of coming out for the high school team as a freshman. Melvin was immediately swarmed by his teammates in the end zone, and Chelsea raced off the field with a 29–12 lead.

The halftime locker room was a buzz of smiling, happy kids. The Red Devils were laughing and hitting each other on the shoulder pads, shouting out:

"We can't let them score no more!"

"Let's pretend it's zero-zero!"

"Another four fucking touchdowns! We need our fucking respect back! Another four fucking touchdowns."

When Atkins entered, the locker room quieted down. He calmly went over the problems from the first half, first addressing the kicking game, then reminding the kids to be aware of the zone blitz, and to work on the sweeps. He asked for Frankie's perspective on what was happening defensively. Frankie, who also played linebacker, offered his views, and the coach listened. For a moment, there was equal give and take between coach and player. There was a mutual respect.

"Coach, those guys are diving at our knees late on a lot of plays," a player in the back called out.

"Then step on their fucking hands. I don't give a shit. They'll stop diving at you. You've got to walk back to the huddle, don't you? Then step on them. Just don't kick them."

Then, perhaps sensing that the game was well in hand, Atkins turned to Antuan Jagne, one of the only seniors who played sparingly. He was originally from Africa and didn't have any football experience when he moved to Chelsea. Coach named him "Midnight" because of what he considered "excessive blackness."

"Midnight, you're the starting nose tackle in the second half. You're a big strong kid. Just use your speed and your size and tackle the guy with the ball. That's all you'll do."

Then coach added, "You're from Africa. You're used to running down cheetahs and shit, right?"

The locker room erupted in laughter. Midnight broke into a wide grin, his large white teeth standing in stark contrast to his "excessively black" face. Coach waited for the laughter to stop, and concluded with a reminder, and a challenge.

"We let them in the game by not being tough. We stopped being tough, because we thought it would be too easy. Fellas, smack someone in the mouth. They're nowhere near as tough as you. I want four touchdowns this half, four touchdowns and four 2-point conversions. That's 32 points. I want to score 60 goddamn points today. Are we gonna do it?"

They scored 61 points to Minuteman Regional's 12. Running back Alex Caraballo finished the evening with 10 carries for 140 yards and five touchdowns. He got the third quarter started with a 44-yard touchdown run and the Red Devils never looked back. Maybe they thought the rout would put Coach in a good mood. Maybe that's why they snuck up from behind him and doused him with what was left in the Gatorade cooler.

"I'm gonna kick somebody's ass!" Atkins shouted as the cold, sticky fluid ran down his back. The kids wondered if they had gone too far. Coach sure looked angry. But then he smiled and brought them together for the postgame reminder.

"Guys . . . be . . . safe . . . to . . . night," Coach said deliberately. "Okay? Be safe tonight. Don't go out there and get in trouble. Go be with your girlfriend. Go play PlayStation. Do whatever you gotta do. But don't go out there and get in trouble. Stay away from the kids that are causing trouble."

Walking away from the field, Orlando Echevarria felt like a winner. There were a few fans still hanging around to congratulate the players on their decisive victory. The pats on the back felt good. Being a football star had its benefits. Orlando looked across the field. He watched for a few minutes as several grammar school kids tossed a football around, tackling each other and bouncing up to do it again. It was a scene that was undoubtedly taking place simultaneously on high school football fields all across America. That it was happening here in Chelsea gave the city hope, and a sense of normalcy. It gave Orlando reason to pause. While he accepted and appreciated the pats on the back, he couldn't help but notice they were coming from strangers, acquaintances, and just a few friends. He looked around and didn't see his father, or his mother, or his brother, his uncle, or his cousin. Sammy Argueta wasn't there either.

"I'm here with my family," he reflected. "This is my gang. The football team is my gang. This is our gang unit. And Coach Atkins is the leader of our gang."

CHAPTER FOUR

"P" and the Latin Kings

Coach Atkins makes me more of a man. I'm more of a man than I was before. Sometimes in the morning, I hear him in my head. When I don't want to wake up, I hear him saying, 'C'mon, if you don't get up you're not going to succeed in life,' and then I just get up. Even if I'm two minutes late for school, it's better than being absent.

—JONATHAN LUNA, CHELSEA HIGH SCHOOL SENIOR

Jonathan Luna was a baseball player with a football player's body. He was tall and thick, big legs, big arms, thick neck. He could have been a dominating player, but he was playing his first year of organized football, and he was playing in pain. On the eleventh day of football camp, a teammate rolled over on his knee, and Jonathan had to hop off the field. An X-ray indicated he had suffered a bone bruise and a dislocated kneecap. After a few days off and some physical therapy, Luna returned to the Red Devils and played in the first three games of the season. He would also play in the fourth game against Tyngsboro, but it was probably going to be his final game of the season. Because his pain had persisted, Jonathan had an MRI that showed his injury was actually a torn meniscus. Doctors referred to it as a bucket handle tear, and it prevented Jonathan from locking his knee. So, on Friday the thirteenth of October, Jonathan would have surgery. But that was in two weeks. Tonight, he would take the field and play through the pain once again.

Jonathan had another kind of pain. Like Orlando, it involved his older brother. Pascual Luna had once been a promising athlete at Chelsea High School. Now, he was a Latin King who went by the nickname "P."

"He was a great football and baseball player," Jonathan said remorsefully. "He just started slipping away, hanging out with the wrong crowd. After games, he would go out with his friends instead of going home. He got into the thug life. He was smoking weed. That led to problems with my dad. When he was fifteen, sixteen, he used to get into arguments with my dad. I was like eight years old watching my brother and my father get into fistfights. They'd really go at it. It's crazy. I remember crying a lot when I was younger. It's just tough. He was in and out of jail. He's been on probation since he was about fifteen."

Drugs, violence, and carjackings were how P developed his relationship with Coach Atkins and the Chelsea police. Atkins was among the several cops who had put Pascual behind bars. Now, P was on the run for attempted kidnapping and brandishing a firearm. P had a three-year-old daughter named Alizea, and during a dispute with Alizea's mother, P showed he was carrying a gun and tried to take the girl away.

"My dad wouldn't have it," Jonathan explained. "He called the police on my brother. My brother had the baby outside, and was leaving when my dad called. So, my brother let her go to walk back to the house to her mom, and I don't know, they say he shot a gun, and then the cops went to the house. He's on the run right now."

A few days later, Jonathan answered his cellphone just before the start of practice. It was his sister, Jasmine, calling to let him know that the FBI was at the house looking for Pascual.

"I really don't care," Jonathan said. "I have my own life. There's just too much going on."

Contrary to appearances, Jonathan claimed to live in a happy home. His father, Santiago Luna, and his mother, Isabel Valasquez, were not married, but they had been together for twenty-five years. Santiago had been eighteen years old and Isabel was sixteen when they moved to Dorchester from Puerto Rico to start their own life. Jasmine was the oldest of the three children. She was a college graduate and a senior accountant for the city of Brookline. She was twenty-five, pregnant, and planning to be married the following summer. Jonathan looked to her as his role model. Pascual was twenty-one, three years older than Jonathan.

"I try to stay away from him," Jonathan said of his older brother. "Before I would want to speak to him, but I guess he's his own person now, and I'm my own person. I miss him. He's my brother, but I have to stay away from that if I'm going to succeed. I talk to him sometimes, but he doesn't listen. There's only so much I can do for someone before I just quit."

The Lunas had moved to Chelsea ten years ago, about the same time the gang situation was exploding. P fell right into it and he nearly pulled Jonathan down with him. The two brothers looked like twins, and that fact made the streets very unsafe for Jonathan.

"Sometimes I would be scared going out because I look like my brother a lot, and I didn't want a rival gang to come at me, because they thought I was my brother. So, I would carry weapons on me. I'd carry knives. I've never carried a gun. But I'd carry brass knuckles just to protect myself from the gangs. I can go toe-to-toe with anybody, not anybody, but most of the people in Chelsea. But gangs nowadays, they don't want to fight. They bring five or six of their friends, bring bats and stuff. I've seen some of my own friends get beat up. I've seen them beat up other people. It's not the life I want to live."

One of Jonathan's friends was shot in the face and killed. Another friend was shot in the head with a 9-millimeter handgun outside a barbershop in 2005. That incident occurred, according to Officer Scott Conley, when a gang war boiled over at Goodfella's Barbershop in Chelsea. Jonathan Argueta, a Latin King, had been shot in the leg by the Tiny Rascal Gang. When Steven Pisecki, a TRG member, was getting his haircut, a bunch of Kings showed up and called him outside. Pisecki then called some of his TRG friends. A brawl ensued. There were several rounds of gunfire and three arrests were made. Not only did Jonathan's friend get shot, but the incident sparked the subsequent gang investigation that led to the arrests of eighteen Latin Kings.

"I remember going to the hospital to visit him, and he had staples in his head," Jonathan said with a wince. "He couldn't talk. He would move his hands and legs, but they had to keep them strapped because he had staples in his head and he couldn't take them out because he could die. He has a little brain damage. When he speaks to you, you have to remind him of some stuff and finish sentences for him. There might be a pair of sneakers right there, and he can't think of the word *sneaker*."

Despite what they had seen and experienced in their own families, or perhaps because of it, Jonathan and Orlando talked about one day becoming police officers. Jonathan's aspiration was longstanding and he'd been motivated by it. He worked to keep his grades up around a B average. He planned on taking the SATs in November. And he was looking at the criminal justice program at U-Mass Amherst. There was a certain sincerity in his voice when he talked about being a cop. The seed was planted early and it had been nurtured by the dream.

"I struggled when I was younger about my brother," Jonathan said. "By him not doing good and always getting arrested, I decided I wanted to be on the other side. I didn't want to be arrested. I want to do the arresting. Coach Atkins adds on to it, but mainly it's because of my brother."

Orlando, meanwhile, was not as singularly focused as Jonathan. Perhaps he didn't believe in himself, and therefore couldn't believe in the dream. His stated plan was to go to college, but he didn't think he could handle college-level courses. Orlando was part of Chelsea's Alternative Learning Program, the special education classes that Atkins affectionately referred to as the "retard school." Orlando didn't belong in the program. He was not a dumb or slow kid with a learning disability. Orlando spoke with an eloquent narrative. His thoughts were organized. His language was descriptive. He could be a writer, or a cop, or just about anything he wanted to be. But he was still pulled down by the streets. He still wanted to chill with his friends instead of doing his homework. He was lazy. He was afraid of reaching too high and failing. He was a walking, talking contradiction, a leader with low self-esteem. He was a confused kid. And it probably didn't help to have a coach intermittently berating him and then telling him he had so much potential.

There were two paths Orlando could see. They were brightly lit. One was filled with warning signs. It was the path he watched his brother take. It was the path he started down before he reached the crossroad. Now, he saw the other path, the one with the nice house and the white picket fence at the end. It was the path his football coach took out of the projects and into a safe suburban neighborhood.

"I just see Coach has the life that I want," Orlando said admiringly. "He has time for his family, and he has time for us, too. I can't be a coach. I don't know all about that coaching stuff. But if I had a family, I could take care of it. He has a car. I want a nice family and a car someday. He's a cop and he's a coach and he has a nice family. He has time for all that."

Orlando, who walked tall, but who did not walk proud, who walked the walk of a tough Chelsea kid in the streets, but who would often surrender to the will of his opponent on the football field, marched with Jonathan and their teammates into the locker room minutes before the Tyngsboro game. It was the Red Devils third straight home game. They would play seven of their eleven regular-season games at home this year. For as tough and as poor as Chelsea was, the Red Devils had one of the best football fields in the state.

The top-notch gridiron was the brainchild of city manager Jay Ash, with the impetus coming from the Metro Lacrosse League. The lacrosse team from the affluent town of Lexington approached Chelsea with the idea of using their high school field for practices and games, and in return for the time and space, Metro Lacrosse would help pay for the installation of field turf. The project would cost nearly a million dollars, but Chelsea only had to pay about half of that. Metro Lacrosse covered $300,000 of it, and another $100,000 was donated by the National Football League. Suddenly, poor Chelsea had a state-of-the-art football field. They were the envy of the suburbs.

Tyngsboro was an American suburb: 96.8 percent white, less than 1 percent black and Hispanic. It was not an exceptionally affluent community, but as the football team bounced off the bus wearing white uniforms with big orange lettering, the Chelsea kids saw them as just another bunch of rich white kids coming on to their turf. Coach Atkins, who had seen them play, viewed the Tyngsboro Tigers as another upper division team that might very well be the class of the league.

"We'll be lucky if we just stay in the game and don't forfeit," Atkins said honestly.

Atkins was different that night, uncommonly nervous. Tyngsboro was moving up to Division 2 next year, and they probably belonged there now. Their quarterback, Colin Halloran, was college caliber. They were scary big and well coached. Atkins wanted to believe in his team, but he was not sure the Red Devils had the requisite toughness, or the smarts to hang with such a high quality opponent. That was why he intended to change his approach tonight. He said he wouldn't be screaming on the sidelines. He knew how tough this challenge would be for his kids, and he planned on coaching them through it with a kinder, gentler approach.

"Take Frankie, for example," Atkins said. "He's not responding to the challenge. Some of the other coaches want me to stroke him a little bit, and we'll try that tonight. But if that doesn't work, I'll just go back to being myself. I challenge him to be a man. Grab your nuts! Man up! You're going through the combat zone at night and you can't man up on the goddamn football field? Keep your head up and step it up. But I'll work on encouraging him a little bit."

It wouldn't be easy. Atkins didn't just yell because he thought that's what the kids needed. He yelled because that was who he was. He was an emotional, passionate leader of boys, but he wanted to make men out of them, so he treated them like men. That night the boys would see another side of the man they had grown to love and fear.

Atkins spoke to his team before the game in a conversational tone. He singled out several players, including Alex, Jonathan, and Orlando, for their excellence, adding that Tyngsboro "doesn't have players like that." He cautioned his defensive back to be ready to "turn and burn" and to go after interceptions, because the Tigers were certainly going to test them with their passing game. He was calm and optimistic, and then he turned it up a notch before sending them out to the field of battle.

"My linebackers, when you read rush, I want you to lay him out. You're not going to just come out haphazardly and saunter into him. You're going to fly into him like Ray Lewis and knock some balls off!"

This is where the volume peaked.

"You're gonna let them know they're not playing North Shore! You're gonna let them know they're not playing Minuteman! You're gonna let them know they're not playing Manchester or any other goddamn team in our league! You let them know today that they're here to play the Chelsea goddamn Red Devils! And we're gonna show them what Red Devils football is starting today! We are manning up today to that goddamn team! Because when Monday comes and you look at the goddamn *Herald*, there's gonna be a great big sign that says, 'Oh shit. Chelsea kicks Tyngs-boro's fucking ass!' That's what the headline's gonna be. That's what it's gonna be, because I know you can do it, fellas! And you gotta believe you can do it. If you believe you can do it, I swear to God, you're gonna do it. I promise you you're gonna do it. Do you understand me?"

"YES, COACH!"

But Tyngsboro was much bigger, faster, and stronger. They marched down the field on their first possession and took a 7–0 lead. Then Alex fumbled deep in Chelsea territory, and it was 14–0 midway through the first quarter. It was the worst possible start. Then Halloran hit Sam Lovell for a 30-yard touchdown pass, and it was 21–0.

Atkins never yelled. He coached. He encouraged. He cheered. But he never lost his composure. His cheering got louder when Frankie scored on a short touchdown run. He let himself hope when Joey Barbosa forced a fumble and Cody Verge fell on the ball. Cody was an oddity in Chelsea—a white kid who had moved to the city a few years back from California. Coach called him "Sun-shine," naming him after one of the white players in the movie *Remember the Titans*.

"That's what I'm talking about," Atkins shouted. "That's how you be a man. That's how you run the goddamn ball, son! That's how you do it. Guys, this is it. Can you feel it now, fellas? Can you feel it? Guys, are they better than us?"

"NO!"

"Let's get this in. Guys, let's get this in! Where's Danny? Danny, hold on to the fucking ball!"

Atkins then smacked Frankie's helmet several times to fire him up, and watched as Danny held on tight and raced in from the 16-yard line, making the score 21–16 just before the half.

"What did I tell you guys?" Atkins asked excitedly as the Red Devils settled down in the locker room.

"If we listen to you, we'll win," Frankie responded alone.

"What did I promise you? I promised you that if you played up to your potential, we're gonna win this game. Didn't I promise you guys? You know what, we still made too many mistakes and we're only down by 5 points. If we score a touchdown, we win! Let me tell you something. I'll take Chelsea kids over anybody in the goddamn state."

The Red Devils were losing, but they were feeling like winners. They hadn't quit when they fell behind by 21 points. Even Coach was happy. The atmosphere was relaxed, even jovial.

"Melvin, your nervousness should be gone now, pal, because you just hung with a Division 2 team. Forget about Pop Warner, son. You're now a Chelsea High School kid."

Then Coach looked at big Ivan Romero. He was a bright but exceptionally heavy junior who played on the offensive and defensive lines. He usually infuriated Atkins because he liked to debate, and to offer his own opinions.

"Shut the fuck up, and beat the piss out of the kid in front of you. You weigh 350 pounds," Atkins had shouted at Ivan earlier that week in practice. Now, as Ivan sat listening to the new, softer side of Coach, he heard Atkins say:

"Ivan, get into it. Get mean, son, even if you're faking it. Do you need me to call you a name or something, or can you do it on your own?"

"I think I need a hug," Ivan joked. Everyone laughed, including Coach.

"At least you're honest," Atkins said with a big grin. Then he concluded his halftime remarks.

"Guys, you're playing a helluva game. I told you you were gonna do it, and you're playing a helluva game. If you don't feel it now, you're never gonna feel it. We're gonna win this dogfight."

But the game unraveled quickly. Tyngsboro scored on a touchdown pass and a 43-yard fumble recovery to take a 35–16 lead in the third quarter. The good feelings in the locker room were quickly replaced with anger on the sideline.

"You all niggas aren't having any intensity," senior Juan Carrasquillo shouted. "There's no fucking intensity! You all niggas don't have no fucking intensity!"

Juan was the one they called "Kenzi." Nobody knew why, not even Kenzi. He was a hyper kid diagnosed with ADHD, and it was hard for him to stay still on the sidelines. He refused to take his medication before a football game because, he said, "It keeps the anger inside me." And he wanted his anger to be released at game time.

Some of his anger was the result of a typically Chelsea childhood. Both his parents were born in Puerto Rico. They never married and ultimately separated. According to Kenzi, it was "because my mom didn't like my dad drinking." His mother, he added, didn't graduate high school because she had to work. She also spent some time in jail, and came out determined to make sure her kids had more opportunities than she'd had. Kenzi remembers her saying:

"Don't be like me. I want you all to have a good life, have a better life than I did."

Kenzi's father went to jail for a long while, so Kenzi lived in the projects with his mom and his two brothers and three sisters. He thought his mom did an amazing job raising six kids on the money she made working at a deli in Boston, and he laughed when he remembered how she used to punish him.

"It's like a Puerto Rican punishment," Kenzi said. "You put rice in the corner and you have the kid kneel on it and face the wall. And you put gallons of water on his hands, and if he put the gallons down, she would add an extra half an hour to the punishment. After that, we would just chill."

Eventually, after his father was released from jail, Kenzi moved to an apartment with his dad. As a little kid, Kenzi recalled the constant sound of gunshots, and listening to people fighting all the time. From his window, Kenzi also had a good vantage point to witness several gang fights. He'd watch one group come down the street carrying sticks and knives, and he'd wait for the other group he knew would be arriving soon. But Kenzi said the worst thing he'd ever seen was the drive-by shooting he experienced when he was eight years old.

"I was going to the store with my brother and my godfather," Kenzi said. "And I guess there were some Crips inside the store and they came out of the store, and a black car comes up with a bunch of Bloods and they just started shooting them. Then the car just drove off and all I saw was all guys in blue on the floor. That really got to me. For a couple of nights I couldn't sleep. I couldn't get it out of my mind that this happened right in front of me."

The anger inside Kenzi never inspired him to join a gang. He was a big kid, as tall as Orlando, and a little thicker in his legs and chest. So, he'd been approached several times by gangs looking to bring a big, tough kid into the fold. But while Kenzi had avoided being drawn into and pulled down by a gang, he hadn't been able to avoid the violence on the streets.

"Yeah, I've been in plenty of fights," he said. "I fought for my own respect. People disrespected me. I don't fight other people's battles. This guy has a beef with him, so I'm gonna help him jump him? No, I don't do all that stuff. I fight out of respect. I'm gonna talk to you like a grown man. We're men. Me and you are gonna talk. If you don't want to talk we can resolve it in a different way. But I'm not trying to get to that point where we're going to resolve it in a different way. But if you don't want to talk it out then that's what it's gonna get to. That's how we grew up. That's how it was out here all the time."

It was 41–16 with nine minutes left in the game against Tyngsboro.

"Oliveras is out," assistant coach Dennis O'Neil said, referring to Richie Oliveras. Richie was another oddity among the Red Devils. He was Chelsea High School's Student of the Year as a junior.

"Why?" Atkins wondered.

"Because he's blocking like a pussy," O'Neil said angrily.

Atkins turned to Ato Alic and said, "I can't replace one pussy with another, Ato. So, step it up!"

Finally, with the Tigers giving playing time to much of their second string, Chelsea put together a scoring drive capped off by a 3-yard touchdown run by Alex. Frankie was given the ball on the 2-point conversion attempt, but was stuffed behind the line. He came off the field shouting through his face guard.

"All you all motherfuckers quit on me. All y'all motherfuckers quit! Everyone quit!"

The final score was 41–22. Chelsea, the team with the Super Bowl aspirations, was off to a pedestrian 2–2 start. Both losses were against teams from an upper division, so they wouldn't have an impact on the race to the playoffs, but they were demoralizing nonetheless. Coach, who had heard and witnessed his team's spiraling emotions in the fourth quarter, maintained his pledge to bolster instead of bluster. With heads hanging low, the kids heard him say:

"Guys, let me tell you something. You came fucking damn close tonight. I'm proud of you tonight. I'm going out and have a good dinner, because I'm proud of you. We made a couple of mistakes, but I'm not gonna harp on that. We all know we made mistakes. But let me tell you something, as far as hitting, as far as blocking—those guys are hurting. They're hurting, because we put a beating on them. They don't go out of here thinking, we just rocked Chelsea. They go out of here thinking, that's the toughest game we played all year. I told you at the beginning of the game if you played to your potential, we were gonna win. We just came up a little short. But I want you to know that was a great goddamn game, and I'm very, very proud of you. That's the proudest I've been this whole fucking year. If you play like that against our division, I promise you we're not gonna lose another game, and we're going to the Super Bowl, and we're going to go back to East Boston and put a beating on them. You understand me?"

"YES, COACH!"

The dream was still there. The Red Devils didn't have much, but they had that.

CHAPTER FIVE

Senior Night

I told you, nobody gets left behind. You're all going to college.

—JAMES ATKINS

There was chicken parmesan, chicken with broccoli in a light cream sauce, and ziti lined up in aluminum serving trays atop the kitchen counter. Steam rose into a spacious, modern kitchen. Good silverware rested alongside a pile of paper plates. Several bottles of soda waited to be opened. Everything was ready. Soon the seniors on the Red Devils football team would arrive in compact cars and SUVs driven by the ones with driver's licenses or the coaching staff. This was Thursday night, and that meant the seniors were invited to Coach's house for dinner. It was a tradition that had begun three years earlier on Thanksgiving. On the day before the final game of Coach's first year as head coach of the Red Devils, he had casually asked his team if they all had some place to be for the holiday. He was chagrined to learn many of them didn't. It wasn't surprising, really, given that there were several immigrants on the team for whom Thanksgiving didn't have any meaning, and some of the poorer kids were planning on having their Thanksgiving Day meals at McDonald's and Taco Bell. So, Atkins called his wife at home.

"Honey, can you throw another turkey in the oven?"

Julie Atkins discovered on the day before the Thanksgiving holiday that she would need to accommodate a dozen teenagers in addition to her two daughters. It wouldn't be a problem, she said. She'd been married to Jimmy for seventeen years by then, and she had learned a long time ago that he was always willing to extend himself to help the people in his life. These kids were important to him. Of course, she would open her home to them. Never mind that many of her guests were guilty of criminal behavior. Since that 2004 Thanksgiving, she'd been welcoming the Chelsea Red Devils into her home every Thursday night during the football season. She and the Atkins' girls, Courtney and Lauren, were the only women in the house, and commonly, the only white people there.

"I was just never around black girls," Atkins said to explain why the black Italian with a white mother would grow up to marry a white woman. "At Suffolk University, there weren't many black girls, if any at all. It wasn't a preference. It was just a chance meeting."

That meeting took place during Julie and Jimmy's freshman years. Unlike Jimmy, Julie graduated on time and became a vice president for the Internet technologies department for Blue Cross Blue Shield, a job that paid well over $200,000 a year. That night, she was the hostess for thirteen hungry Red Devil seniors. They wore mostly jeans and T-shirts, but they were neat and clean. They had showered after practice, something that was not at all a habit, except on Thursdays.

While Jimmy and assistant coaches Dennis O'Neil and Nisarg Patel sat at the kitchen table, the boys squeezed around the big dining room table. Extra chairs had been brought up from downstairs. Their chatter was loud and gregarious. There was no bad language. The boys all appeared to be close friends. There were no outcasts. Everyone in the Red Devil gang was equal, at least at Coach's house.

Just like at practice, they were on a tight schedule. Coach gave them thirty minutes to eat, and then he hurried them all single file down into the basement.

Coach lived in a very nice, but modest home in Saugus, about fifteen minutes north of Chelsea off Route 1. It was a ranch-style home in a large, established neighborhood. The floor plan was wide open with the den and dining room separated only by a patch of linoleum flooring. The basement was finished with carpeting, brown paneling, and a variety of family photos adorning the walls. It was set up primarily for TV viewing. The couch and loveseats were in a U-shape position facing the flat-screen television. But the boys were not here to watch TV, not even game film. Instead, they crowded into the seats, this time bringing extra chairs in from the garage, and they arranged themselves in a circle. With Julie and the girls escaping to the solitude upstairs, the meeting commenced in the basement. It was a meeting not so much about football, but about the future.

"Are you happy with your performance and your attitude toward football?" Atkins asked no one in particular. "Orlando, start with you."

"What do you want me to say?"

"I want you to tell me what's been going on for four weeks."

"I feel like we should be 4–0. I just feel like we can be a lot better. Me, myself, I just haven't been focused. I gotta start changing that. I gotta start focusing. I can't be like this my last year."

Atkins nodded in agreement, but added that Orlando's focus needs to be on the football field *and* in the classroom. He told Orlando it wasn't a very smart move to be caught with his cellphone out in English class. There was a time Orlando would have been surprised that Coach was aware that that had happened, but Coach always seemed to know everything that was going on.

"That teacher can't stand you and Kenzi, can she?" Atkins said.

This time it was Orlando who nodded in agreement. Kenzi looked up suddenly. He was surprised to hear his name mentioned. He had been thinking about something else, but now he couldn't remember what that was. So, he tried harder to listen to what Coach was saying.

"We gotta focus with the schoolwork," Atkins continued, "because if we make the playoffs, what good are we if we have half the team flunk off. The progress report is coming out next week, and you're not going to be able to lie to me that you've been doing your work. If your priority is football, part of your priority has got to be your schoolwork. Understand. What's the relationship between football and schoolwork, Frankie?"

"If you don't work, you can't play."

But as Coach went around the room asking how the kids were doing in school, he was dismayed to unearth that Danny was missing trigonometry homework. Frankie was not doing well in algebra. Orlando was failing English and art. Ato was struggling in zoology. Only Richie Oliveras expressed confidence that his homework was up to date and his grades were high. He was the only one excluded from Coach's castigation.

"There's no goddamn way you're going to be able to play if you don't get those grades up. Frankie, you're the goddamn captain and a two-way starter. Why won't you get your homework in? You know how to do it. You're just not doing it."

Each child looked guilty and forlorn as Coach continued around the room lecturing each one. They maintained eye contact and nodded gently as Coach made his demands and offered advice. They looked like puppies who knew they'd soiled the rug.

"Guys, this is what pisses me off. Fucking ceramics. Goddamn zoology. Are you kidding me? How do you screw up the basket-weaving courses?"

Mario Hernandez, a hard-nosed, hard-hitting kid who had become a favorite of Atkins for his willingness to play through pain, announced that he'd been doing much better, but that trigonometry was also proving to be difficult for him. David Flores boasted that he was doing great in everything, but he was also failing art.

"Again, give me a fucking break. Art! Come on, draw a picture of fucking Snoopy and turn it in!"

The boys all laughed, and so did Coach.

These Thursday night dinners were more about schoolwork than football, but he really wanted the kids to understand the relationship between school, football, and the rest of their lives. Specifically, they needed to know that working hard and living up to their responsibilities would lead to success and happiness. It was a simple message, but he had already repeated it hundreds of times, and it didn't appear to have sunk in yet. Coach O'Neil, who was sitting outside the circle and had been taking notes on which classes each of the boys was failing, picked up the cause.

"We gotta set our sights higher," O'Neil said raising his left hand to make sure the kids knew where the voice was coming from. "Everett played Peabody the other day, and the kid from Everett had 3 rushes for 127 yards, and they run the same offense we do. You know, we're content with 5 yards every time. We're content to just pass in the classroom, and then it comes time to take the SATs and it's like, 'Oh, fuck. I don't have my 2.0.' Well, if you had excelled in the classroom, if you had set your sights higher in the classroom, you'd have it. And if you set your sights higher in practice, you'll achieve more during the game. In the long run, things will be easier. Effort now, things will be easier for you down the road."

O'Neil was raised as a self-proclaimed "naive sheltered honky from Peabody." He was one of six kids in a traditional two-parent home, but the white Irish guy with the blonde hair related to the Chelsea kids because he understood football, and because the kids understood he chose to come to Chelsea. Nobody chose Chelsea unless they were crazy or they were interested in contributing to the greater good. O'Neil wasn't crazy.

"My thing with these kids is actions speak louder than words," O'Neil said. "Shake their hands. Look them in the eye. Hold them accountable. That's what I know. That's what I know works."

O'Neil grew up on a working farm. His rabbits and ducks and turkeys were not pets. They were dinner. In between school and farming, there was football practice. O'Neil was an all-star in the Greater Boston League as an offensive and defensive end. His title with the team was assistant coach, and his primary emphasis was on the defense, but he admitted "as soon as the other team scores, Jimmy takes over."

O'Neil was an educator who came to that realization later in life than most. After flunking out of college and stocking shelves in a grocery store for a large portion of his adulthood, he returned to school full time while also continuing to work full time, and he graduated with honors from Westfield State in 2003. He was thirty-seven years old. With his teaching certificate in hand, O'Neil landed a job at the Clark Avenue Middle School in Chelsea.

While O'Neil was teaching and becoming friends with Clark's two gym teachers, both moonlighting as football coaches in other towns, Atkins was looking for a new coaching staff. The police chief had allowed three of his Gang Unit cops to coach the Red Devils, but after one season, scheduling and logistics had proven to be too difficult. Batchelor and Conley needed to be replaced. O'Neil, whose prior experience was as an unpaid volunteer coach at Peabody High School, got the job. It was a good match.

"I see myself as a buffer or intermediary, try to be a calming influence on Jim a little bit," O'Neil offered as an assessment. "Head coaches are generally very strong-willed people, and they're head coaches because of that inherent quality. So, on every staff, there's a need for an intermediary. I think it's a natural role for myself, because I do see myself as a teacher. I try to stay calm. I do get fired up, but it's a natural role for me to fill, and I think every team needs one."

And the teacher had to become a student when he crossed over into Chelsea. His days on the farm did not prepare him for his days in Chelsea, except that he knew hard work was the best answer to most problems.

"It's different than Peabody," O'Neil explained. "Like if anybody missed practice in Peabody, they weren't coming back. They quit. Otherwise, everyone just expected to be at practice, and came to practice. But beyond that, some of the things that come up in the Chelsea kids' lives are things I never dealt with in Peabody, like my girlfriend's pregnant. They bullshit you a lot. And they don't fight through things. If a kid starts feeling during sixth period that he'd rather not come to practice, he's got something else to do, then they don't fight through that and come to practice, and then they hit you up with some excuse. You can't always jump to that conclusion that the excuses are legit. You have to look for trends. You have to double-check stories. And it comes down to just holding people accountable. If player X misses a practice or two due to whatever reason, and player Y is there. Well, player X and player Y are the same people. Everyone's got shit going on in their lives. It's kind of a homogenous setting."

Tonight, the setting was Coach's basement, and yes, the kids were very much alike in that they all had shit going on in their lives. Coach Atkins was aware of it; though twenty-five years older, he had gone through similar turmoil himself. He was uniquely qualified to guide and to guard the kids of Chelsea. He tried to be the father or the counselor they needed, but in the end, he wanted them to know that he just didn't give a rat's ass about the shit in their lives. In fact, nobody did.

"I didn't have a father," Atkins reminded his players. "I grew up in the projects. So, I don't want to hear any excuses. I don't want to hear about how somebody got arrested and thrown in jail. I don't want to hear excuses that somebody in my family got arrested. I don't want to hear the excuses that my mother's by herself. My mother raised three little black kids by herself, and she's white. It was tough for me, too. But who gives a shit! Does anybody care?"

They all knew the answer, but it wasn't clear if they really knew the question. Coach wasn't suggesting that nobody cared about them. Clearly, he did. O'Neil did. Dozens of coaches, teachers, city officials, and assorted others who had chosen to live and/or work with the Chelsea kids—all of them cared. They just cared more about the people than the problems. The problems were opportunities for excuses, and Atkins and the rest didn't care to hear how these kids were victims of circumstance. Rise above it. Don't fall into it. That was the message. And Atkins stayed on point.

"And I don't want to hear another fucking kid talk about ADD," Atkins continued. "If I hear another fucking kid tell me that, I'm gonna smack him in the mouth. It's bullshit! If you can come on my field and understand what I'm talking about, then you can understand what everybody's talking about. You let people talk you down. Orlando, you're getting better, but you used to let people talk you down. Kenzi, same with you. You tell me about ADD again, I'll smack you in the mouth."

Kenzi smiled. He did that a lot when Coach talked. He respected Atkins immensely, but didn't fear him. He found him to be as entertaining as he was caring. And at that moment, he was laughing to himself about the first time he saw Atkins refuse to let ADHD be used as an excuse.

"We were at a game and I was really, really hyper," Kenzi began. "You're only supposed to drink like half, but I had a whole thing of an energy drink. And I had another amp drink that I always have at every game."

Kenzi remembered bouncing around and interrupting a lot while Atkins was trying to address the team.

"Would you sit down and shut up?!" Atkins barked.

"I can't. I got ADHD," Kenzi reminded him.

"So take your pills."

"No, I can't do that."

"How about I give you a pill?"

Nobody knew what that meant until Atkins wheeled around and punched Kenzi squarely in the chest and just started laughing when he saw the shock on Kenzi's face.

"It was really funny," Kenzi said with a wide grin, and then referring to Atkins he added respectfully, "He's a man."

But while Atkins considered ADD, attention deficit disorder, to be an excuse rather than a diagnosis, Kenzi found it to be a very real problem.

"I have a difficult time working with the teachers because of my ADHD," Kenzi explained. "I'm always moving around, but that's not my fault. It's not like I wanted to give myself ADHD. That's how I was born. Teachers don't understand that and they blow it to another proportion. They talk down to us like we're dumb, like we don't know what's going on. They act like we're really, really stupid. It gets me mad. It really pisses me off. I don't really like teachers coming up to me and talking down to me. That's how I feel. I'm not dumb. I might be in special needs classes, yeah, but that's not because I'm dumb. It's because I can't control myself in class. I get in trouble for disrupting class. Sometimes it is my fault. I can't say it's the teachers' fault that I'm disrupting class. But sometimes they start capping on us to make us look dumb in front of everybody, but when you start capping back on them, they get mad and kick you out of class."

The meeting flip-flopped from football to schoolwork and back to football. Coach criticized several players for various shortcomings on the field. The quarterback, Miguel Medina, wasn't keeping the ball on his hip on play action. Danny hadn't been taking out the defensive end and sustaining his block. Frankie was too inconsistent, sometimes doing a nice job of reading a play, shooting the gap, and knocking the shit out of a guy, but on the next play, he was out of position. "That's how Tyngsboro scored one of its touchdowns," Coach reminded him.

"I'm gonna tell you why you guys make these mistakes. It's because you don't focus on anything, whether it be schoolwork or football. You guys want everything easy. And that's the problem as I see it. You want to come to school, go to class, go to lunch, talk to your boys, and think you're going to magically pass everything, and magically think you're gonna beat somebody's ass on the football field. It doesn't happen that way, fellas."

Every Thursday night dinner was different, but with unavoidable similarities. The Coach couldn't help but repeat himself, because the goals he wanted the kids to set, and the manner in which those goals could be achieved never changed. Graduate. Go to college. Get a job. Stay off the streets. Coach hammered it home. Each week the kids would write down on a piece of paper what their short-term and long-term goals were. A short-term goal might be to pass an English test. A long-term goal might be to become an architect, or a policeman, or to get out of Chelsea. Each week, three kids would read their goals and everyone would offer suggestions about how to reach them. The smarter kids could help someone study for a test. Someone in the same class could offer to help with homework. Coach could talk to a teacher about providing extra help or a make-up assignment. They were a family looking out for one another. Inevitably the conversation returned to football and the concept of playing the perfect game with total focus.

"Do your job," Kenzi said.

"Don't worry about doing somebody else's job," Mario added.

"We have to come out with the right attitude and stay focused," Frankie offered. "You can't be bringing nobody down. You say one negative thing, like Coach says, 'It's a cancer,' dog. Everybody gets it. I include myself. I get down on myself when I mess up. I see it on film, dog. When I mess up, the next play Orlando messes up.

Then Dave messes up. The whole team messes up. You know what I mean? We all have to do what we have to do."

Kenzi agreed.

"Don't get mad at each other. Everybody gets mad because of one play. Everybody starts getting on top of each other because of one play. Can't be doing that. Know what I'm saying? You gotta make it up on the next play. We can't be climbing on each other and put somebody down, because they might slack off and not do their job."

There was a real give-and-take from the players. They were serious and expressive. They were sullen, but they grew increasingly animated and agitated as the realization hit that the answer was right in front of them, that their goals were within their grasps. They can play better. They can work harder. As they sat on Coach's furniture, they were determined. Coach had seen this before and he wondered if it would carry over on to the field, or if it would die long before the next night's kickoff, or long before the next picture of Snoopy was due in art class.

"Everybody here breaks Cody's balls, shits on Cody. Right?" Coach interjected, referring to Cody Verge, the junior they call "Sunshine." "He's an irritating bastard, isn't he?"

"Yes, Coach." They were all quick to agree.

"He's an annoying little fuck, right? But he was running all over the fucking place at practice today. Do you guys realize how good you would be if you did what the coach says and ran all over the place to hit someone? God forbid if you went like annoying Cody. If you just gave an effort, guys, I just want one game of a complete effort. And then you could see yourselves on the film. And I promise you, you'll never give less than that complete effort again, because once you feel it, it'll be like 'Oh, shit.'"

A few of the seniors were not present for that night's meeting, including the starting middle linebacker, Jonathan Santiago. He had missed three straight practices and Coach suspended him for the Tyngsboro game. It was unclear if Santiago would be allowed back on the team. His absence would be felt. Santiago was a good player.

But football was not his top priority right now.

"How do you guys just let that happen?" Coach asked accusingly. "How do you let him miss three days? Just physically grab him. He was important to us. He's diddling some little ninth grader and you guys let that happen. I would never let that happen. Go to his house! I told you when we won the Super Bowl in '95, Jose Lopez would literally threaten people. He was the toughest kid on the team. If somebody fucked up, he would go to them and tell them, 'You're not fucking up my season. I will fucking kill you.' And people were scared of him. Now, I'm not telling you to go stab anybody. But I am telling you to go to his house and straighten him out."

Coach paused a moment and, perhaps reflecting and regretting to some degree what he had just said about threatening a teammate, he smiled and turned to face Kenzi.

"Don't stab anybody. Okay, Kenzi?"

Everybody laughed, including Kenzi. Kenzi was the perfect foil for Coach's humor and Coach's anger. Kenzi never took either one the wrong way. Coach's words had the potential of bruising weaker kids, or kids who didn't understand where the words came from, but not Kenzi. He knew whether Coach was yelling at him or teasing him. And either way, he knew Coach cared about him.

"It is true. You do feel protected around him," Kenzi said. "You feel like there's a shield there that blocks anything. It's like you're on the Internet and you have the pop-up blockers. You don't get any pop-ups! We just feel more secure around him, because we know he cares about us. He's trying to do good things for us. He's trying to get us into college. And if we don't get into college, he's going to send us into the military. That just shows you that he cares. There aren't a lot of schools that have coaches like that."

Coach's reference to the Red Devils' 1995 Super Bowl season was something the kids had heard before. They knew Coach had been where they were now, poor and on the streets, and they knew he had been where they wanted to be, part of a Super Bowl championship team.

Joe Gaff was the head coach of the '95 Chelsea team. He was a cop from Everett, with a couple of cop buddies, Mike Doherty and Jimmy Atkins, on his staff. The success Chelsea enjoyed when the cops were in charge was one of the primary reasons Atkins was handed the reigns in 2004.

Gaff's relationship with Jimmy went all the way back to high school when they played together at Dom Savio Prep as freshmen and sophomores. Jimmy had gone to Dom Savio for two years before transferring and graduating from East Boston. Years later when Gaff was looking for an assistant, he pegged Jimmy, who served under Gaff for five years, including the 1995 Super Bowl season. Gaff could rattle off the names of his best players and his senior leaders as if he were watching them all walk past. There was Bobby Benson and Jimmy Trovill, a great tailback named Reggie Gresham, and the quarterback Steven Turner.

The Red Devils didn't have a home field during the 1995 season, because the new Chelsea High School was being built. So, they practiced at the Metropolitan District Commission pool in front of a large dirt pit, and they went on the road for all eleven games, including the Super Bowl at Old Colony High School. After beating Old Colony, Jimmy called for a police escort to lead the Red Devils back over the Tobin Bridge and into Chelsea. Several police cruisers were in front of the bus with their sirens blaring and their lights flashing.

"Hey," Gaff yelled. "Isn't it great to be behind the cops for a change instead of them behind us in pursuit?"

Gaff stayed on to coach in Chelsea for a few more years before moving on to Malden Catholic. Jimmy left, too, but eventually returned to Chelsea.

The gang problem was just taking root in Chelsea in 1995, and Gaff had to deal with many of the same problems Atkins was dealing with now, but it wasn't the gangs, the drinking, drugs, or violence that sent Gaff packing. It was the academic requirements. Oddly enough, Chelsea, the city with so many residents for which English was a second language, the city riddled with social issues, at-risk children, and gang violence, had a stricter academic policy for its athletes than any other school in Massachusetts.

"You can't play with an F," Chelsea athletic director Frank DePatto said despondently. "These kids are coming from Czechoslovakia, Africa, from all over. They can't speak English. There's no way they can pass everything. It hurts me when we play against other schools that play under a different academic policy. We're at a disadvantage right away. I don't know if BU understands that, but if they do, they show no compassion about it. The rule is wrong and when something is wrong, it needs to be corrected. But it falls on deaf ears."

The ears belonged to Boston University. The institution that took over the Chelsea School department in 1997 and had since given Chelsea nearly $12 million didn't want any student with an F on their report card to be allowed to play sports. The Massachusetts Interscholastic Athletic Association, meanwhile, had a "2-F" rule which allowed athletes to play unless they were failing two classes, not one. When BU changed the rule for Chelsea, nineteen football players became ineligible. Gaff resigned the following year. Atkins was simply waiting for BU to break its contractual relationship with Chelsea, which was set to happen after the 2007 season.

"Are you shitting me?" Atkins asked rhetorically. "I can play sports at any college in the country, but I can't play here in Chelsea?

I can play at 99 percent of every other high school in Massachusetts, but I can't play at fucking Chelsea? Are you kidding me? Their requirements are retarded. I got one more year of BU. I just can't wait for them to get the hell out of here. They accomplished nothing. In nineteen years, they've accomplished nothing. The grades and academic achievement are the same now as they were when they came in. I think the kids will do better without BU."

Atkins' vocal objections to BU's involvement often made him unpopular with several members of the school board, the city council, and even the superintendent who hired him, Thomas Kingston, but none of the people he alienated could deny that Atkins was improving his players' academic performance. One reason the kids did better was because of all the additional academic support they received as members of the football team, help they wouldn't get once they were no longer eligible to play. Study halls were arranged for players before practice. Coaches divided responsibilities among students and their classes based on the weekly progress reports teachers filled out for the players. Coach O'Neil met with the seniors to go over their essays for college applications. And of course, the Thursday night dinners for the seniors were intended to motivate and to improve academic performance.

"All right, let's talk college," Atkins said seriously and suddenly. "None of you are staying here. I'll make you join the fucking army. You gotta do something. You're not gonna hang out in Chelsea, fellas. I've got some players in Bellingham Square, not from my teams, but from when I was an assistant. You think those hookers in Bellingham Square said when they were young, 'When I grow up I want to suck prick?'"

"Nope," Frankie said aloud. "They had goals, too."

"Right," Atkins continued. "They started somewhere. Things happen quick. Before you know it, you're knee-deep in it. You think Sammy Argueta planned on spending the next twenty years in federal prison? You all know him. A couple of you hung out with him. How quick did he get involved in something that was way over his head? One year. One year he went from just being a knucklehead in the high school thinking he's something. Now, he's in federal prison for the next twenty years."

Orlando, Frankie, Joshua, and others all had raised their hands to indicate they had hung out with Sammy Argueta when he was still in high school. Coach knew the connection to Argueta was strongest for Orlando, so he turned his attention toward him.

"Orlando, we can help you. We can give you ideas. We can get you on the fucking bus, but eventually you're gonna have to try and do something yourself. You're gonna have to try. What are you gonna do, join the Latin Kings and sell dope?"

Orlando shook his head and mumbled the word "No." He was visibly upset that Coach had singled him out. Coach recognized it, offered some comfort, and moved on.

"All right, Orlando, we're gonna come up with a plan for you. Mario, what are you gonna do? You gonna go back to your family in L.A.? What are they doing?"

"Most of them are on the run."

Mario's response was so abrupt, so honest, so unexpected that it caused several of his teammates to laugh out loud, though none of them really knew why. Coach was also surprised. He was taken off guard and, for a moment, didn't know what to say. So, Mario spoke again. He spoke out loud, but he was speaking to himself.

"I don't want to be like them. I want a better life. I'm going to study and make a better life."

Mario's parents brought him and his younger brother, Arnold, to Chelsea when Mario was seven years old. By that time, Mario had already discovered that most of his family members were hard-core gang members. One of his cousins was serving a life sentence for killing a man in cold blood.

"Literally," Mario said. "The guy was on the ground crying for his life with his family right there, and my cousin just pulled the trigger and killed him. For me, it's hard to understand why some people would do that."

It was also hard for a young boy to understand why he had to sleep on the floor and stay away from the windows, but Mario did as he was told. For one week while living in L.A., Mario and his family never left the house. They stayed low to the ground and kept the lights out. It was a matter of survival. There was a hit out on his uncle, who had been caught covering up the graffiti of another gang. Shots were fired at Mario's house, and it didn't seem that unusual.

"We lived in the projects, and just about every house we lived in, we lived on the corner and across the street was a big gang house," Mario recalled. "Literally, all the gangs would go over there. The way it was, each block had beefs. Like this block had a beef with this block. We were right in the middle of it. So every day they would be up on the roof shooting each other, or like, one person can't cross the street, because you get shot at or drive-bys were coming through. And we'd be outside playing."

In an effort to remove Mario and his younger brother, Arnold, from the gang life of L.A., Mario's parents moved the family across the country. They thought they would be 3,000 miles away from trouble, but they moved to Chelsea. Mario grew up being recruited by the Bloods, Latin Kings, and the Tiny Rascal Gang. He never joined a gang, but Arnold did. Mario's little brother, a sophomore, was a Latin King, and he was suspended from Chelsea High for two months for bringing a knife to school.

"Pretty much, you can't escape the gang influence around you, but it's up to you to make the choice," Mario said. "That's the way I look at it. I'm one of the only people in my family that's not affiliated with a gang, and I'm doing just fine."

For the most part, Mario was living up to the promise he had made to himself to create a better life. Despite worrying constantly about Arnold's safety, and recently watching his father move out of the apartment, because according to Mario, "he had a baby with another lady," Mario's grades were up and he had registered for the SATs. While some of his teammates in the room would probably end up in junior or technical colleges, his sights were set on a four-year school, probably Division III, where he could continue to play football. It was the dream that kept pushing him when he didn't want to do his homework, compelling him to do it anyway. It was the dream that kept him home at night when his friends were going out. And it was the dream that had earned his coach's respect.

"After finding out about Mario's family, I mean there's not a tougher family. The Mexican mafia out there in Los Angeles, or the 18th Street, those are hard-core generational gang members. It's in their family. For his mother to take him away from that, and for him to understand why she took him away from that, it just blows me away. This is a kid who doesn't have the talent of half the kids on the team, but he's the toughest kid I've ever seen. He literally played with a broken foot, broken fingers, a sprained elbow, a separated shoulder—all year long! He'd say, 'Coach I gotta get in there.' He'd lay somebody out, crawl off the field, suck up the pain, and then crawl back out there and lay somebody out again. That's a kid that I would do whatever is in my power to help him."

First and always, Mario had to help himself, and Atkins turned to him and reminded him that drugs could send his future up in smoke.

"You'll make it," Coach told Mario, but then cautioned him. "You just can't be out on the street like I see you once in a while with your boys stoned out of your mind. Right?"

Now it was Mario's turn to be surprised.

"You didn't think he knew, did you?" Kenzi said as the rest of the room broke out in laughter. "You have no idea!"

"I'm the goddamn sergeant in the Gang Unit. How many times did I see you and you were wasted out of your goddamn mind? Trying not to look at me, trying not to breathe, holding your breath so I can't smell anything? Kids will be kids, but what happens if you're smoking and a cop comes over. You're up there smoking with Clifton in Lowell Park, a neighbor calls, the cops come up and you get pinched. Why is Luis back here from college right now as a matter of fact? Because he got pinched smoking weed out in the street."

Luis was a gang kid named Luis Verde. He had graduated from Chelsea High School the previous year and was currently playing football at Northland Community and Technical College in East Grand Forks, Minnesota, the heart of the Red River Valley, well known for its catfish and sugar beets. It was nothing like Chelsea, and it was a long way from home, which is exactly what Coach Atkins thought Luis needed when he made the phone calls to help get Luis into the school. His first call was to his former coach in the semi-pro league, Kevin Bradley, who had a contact at Northland Tech. Then came the hard part: telling the Northland Tech coach the truth about Luis, and then hoping the coach would take him anyway.

"Luis Verde had so much anger in him," Coach began. "I could see him killing somebody. He was a gang kid, but he wouldn't be one of the kids who could get talked into doing something he didn't want to do. He was a lot tougher than those kids. They were scared of him. He had a couple of brothers. One was a drug user. The other was a dealer. And his mother was a junkie for so long before she died. She was sick from drug use for a long time."

Luis's mother had died in the middle of the previous season, which was about a year after his father had died. Orphaned, then homeless for a short while, Luis turned to his football coach for help. Jimmy found him housing. Jimmy raised money so Luis's mother wouldn't have to be buried in a cardboard box. Jimmy talked to him when he was spiraling out of control and jeopardizing his college future.

"After last year's football season, he started getting in heavy with the drugs," Atkins recalled. "He lost about 25 pounds. It wasn't heroin. I would say cocaine. So, I grabbed him and said, 'Look, you're gonna kill yourself. Look at your brother. This is it. Your life is going to go one of two ways. Your brother's a scumbag. He's not going to last long. You know that. Is that the way you're gonna go? Look at you. You've lost 25 pounds. If you gain it back, I'll use my connection and get you into college.'"

Luis gained back the weight, but he was still dealing with significant anger issues. During a basketball game his senior season, Luis took particular offense to a hard foul by an opposing player. So, he head-butted the kid. Blood burst out of the boy's nose and cheek, spilling onto the hardwood floor. The boy's father ran down to the court screaming, "I want that kid arrested!" The other coach went ballistic. All Chelsea's basketball coach, Jay Seigal, could do was apologize and try to explain the situation. No charges were ever filed, but Luis was suspended from the basketball team for the rest of the season.

Suspension was nothing new for Luis. Coach Atkins had also suspended him during the previous year's football season. It was a disciplinary action that cost Atkins and the Red Devils dearly. It was the Georgetown game. If Chelsea had won it, they would have gone to the Super Bowl. It was Coach's dream, and he thought it was the Red Devils' dream, too. That's why he was stunned when two of his best players skipped practice on the Monday before the game.

"Are you fucking crazy?" Atkins exclaimed in disbelief. "This is for the championship, and you guys decide not to come to practice? What are you thinking about?"

Luis was the star quarterback and in the previous game, he had scored on a 2-point conversion to lift Chelsea past North Shore, 8–6. It put Chelsea on the verge of something wonderful. In just his second year at the helm, Atkins had his kids on the precipice. But Luis and another senior starter, Larry Gregory, simply didn't show up for practice. No explanation. No notice. And there's no excuse for that, and no forgiveness either. Coach had to suspend them both for the most important game of the year.

It's a tough call when a coach suspends his best players. The boys need to be disciplined, but does the entire team have to be punished? With Luis and Larry on the bench against Georgetown, the Red Devils fell behind 21–0 by halftime. Atkins was going to sit them for the entire game, but he wanted to win, and he wanted the kids to feel like winners, too. So, he reinserted them in the second half. Luis led a spirited comeback, but it was too late, and it was not enough. Chelsea lost and Georgetown went to the Super Bowl. Coach claimed he didn't regret the decision, but he was not sure he'd make the same one again.

Now, Luis and Larry are both at Northland Tech along with two other Chelsea graduates, Clifton Lewis and Eddie Rodriguez. Football and Coach Atkins had given all four of them a chance to move out and to move up. What they did with that chance was entirely up to them. Coach could only "put them on the bus," as he liked to say. Too many of them get back on the bus for the return trip to Chelsea. Too many of them are like Jorge Mercado.

Jorge was the best player on the Red Devils during Atkins' first year as head coach. He hit like a train. He was also a proven winner. As an eighth grader, Jorge was part of a Chelsea Pop Warner team that won the Division II National Midget Championship at Disney's Wide World of Sports Complex in Orlando, Florida. Late in the championship game against a team from San Francisco, Jorge blocked a punt and Orlando Echevarria (the older one) fell on the ball for the go-ahead touchdown. Despite being accused by the opposing coach of playing a dirty game, a claim that nearly set off a postgame brawl, it was a proud moment for Chelsea, and potentially a portent of more great things for those kids. Chelsea's victory was the first time a team from Massachusetts had won a national Pop Warner championship since the tournament began in 1996. With Mercado leading the way in 2004, Chelsea had a chance to win its first high school Super Bowl since 1995.

Unfortunately, Jorge sprained his thumb the first week of the season. It didn't seem like a serious injury at the time, but X-rays revealed he had developed Kienbock's disease. Simply put, it's a post-traumatic condition that causes the wrist bone to die. Jorge had apparently broken his wrist while playing Pop Warner football, but he never had it looked at. An operation was now necessary. The dead bone was scraped out and bones were grafted together. Jorge's season was over before it began. Chelsea went on to post an 8–3 record without him. With him, Atkins was sure there would have been a Cinderella story with a Super Bowl appearance in that very first season, but happily-ever-afters don't often happen to Chelsea kids.

When Jorge learned that his football season was over, he cried. Coach hugged him and cried with him, and tried to console him. Seven months later, he interrogated him.

Jorge was a member of the Bloods, and in May of 2005 he was involved in the killing of an MS-13 gang member outside the Shurtleff Early Childhood Center in Chelsea. Jorge was never charged, but the Gang Unit had a witness who placed him at the scene and identified him as one of the fighters.

"We had a witness who watched the whole thing out his window like he was watching it on television," Atkins said. "The MS guys show up with baseball bats. Jorge Mercado was there with Jamie and Cesar Ramos, and they were all 'Blooded out,' which means they were wearing all red. They ride by on their bikes, and the MS kids jump out and they're gonna give them a beating. Wrong answer. Ramos had a knife on him, not only did he stab them, but he takes the bat and beats the piss out of them, and he smashes the windshield of their car. The victim runs down the street and collapses and dies."

Seventeen-year-old Jamie Ramos accepted a plea bargain in the stabbing death of twenty-year-old Francisco Portillo. Another MS-13 member, Marvin Benitez, was also seriously injured in the altercation. Investigators believe Portillo went to Chelsea looking to avenge the gang-related death of a relative.

At the station the day of the arrests, Jamie Ramos was giving a full confession that would allow Jorge and Cesar to walk. Neither of them would be charged, but that day Jorge still had to face Atkins—as a cop this time, not just a coach.

"Jorge, you've been like a son to me," Atkins said in the interrogation room.

"Coach, I wasn't there."

"Look, I'm not gonna play the tricks on you, but you have to tell me the truth."

Jorge lied again.

"I know you think I'm bullshitting, but if you didn't do it, this isn't about not being a snitch. You don't want to go to jail for life for something you didn't do. Just tell what the fuck happened."

Jorge continued to lie, but as he did, Jamie was spilling his guts in another room. As the truth came out, Atkins asked Jorge:

"Why would you lie to me?"

"Coach, what was I supposed to do?"

"Tell me the fucking truth. Didn't you learn anything from me? Was it all for nothing? When your mother was hit by the drunk out there in the square, who went and got the guy for you? When your sister got beat up by the three girls, who took care of that for you? Wasn't that enough?"

This time Jorge didn't lie. He broke down and cried. He eventually graduated high school, but didn't go to college. His girlfriend got pregnant and had a miscarriage. His mother continues to work at McDonald's, and they all still live in Chelsea.

Coach looked into the eyes of each of the boys sitting in a large circle in his basement. He wondered which of them was the next Jorge Mercado or Luis Verde. Which of these boys would never get on the bus out of Chelsea? Which ones would Atkins put on the bus only to see them return?

Scott Conley called it the "Chelsea Curse," adding that the "city is riddled with guys who can't get out of here" for one reason or another. Atkins was trying to break the curse. He was confident that Danny Cortez and Richie Oliveras would make it out. They were good kids with good grades. He saw Jonathan Luna turning the corner and setting realistic goals. And he liked Mario's chances. But he worried about the rest. Kenzi had so many problems. Jonathan Santiago's efforts were inconsistent. Dave, Joshua, and Frankie didn't believe in themselves. And Orlando always kept one foot in the streets. When Coach encouraged Orlando to fill out his college applications and financial aid forms on time, he detected some reluctance. When he asked for an explanation for the attitude, Orlando spoke sincerely.

"I can't go to college. I could never handle those classes."

"You're not giving yourself a shot," Atkins fired back. "I'm not gonna let you do it, Orlando. Clifton Lewis can do it. Larry Gregory was in the retard school last year. Right? He wasn't even in the regular high school. He was with the kids that were drooling. Right?"

"He was on the mini-bus," Jonathan Luna said above the laughter.

"You know Larry. You know Luis. If it weren't for football, what would they be doing? They'd be getting fucking wasted."

Atkins continued.

"Orlando, you should have been a monster by now," Atkins said. "Your shoulders should have been out to here. Your arms should have been bigger than mine. You should have been just killing people this year. You were too busy with the broad from Atlanta wanting to get your dick sucked."

More laughter erupted. Orlando looked around the room with pride and smiled a knowing grin.

"Am I lying?" Coach asked.

"No, Coach."

"And who remembers Kenzi from two years ago? Was he a fucking mental case?"

"Yes, Coach."

"You were out there," Coach said, leaning forward and looking Kenzi in the eyes. "You made a lot of progress, but still not good enough. You have to control yourself all the time. Coaches in college aren't gonna give a fuck. Kenzi, the coach in college is not going to care that you have all those problems."

But Kenzi's coach in high school did. Atkins played the role of tough cop on the streets, and he relished the role of tough coach on the sidelines, but there in his basement on Thursday nights was a coach who cared. His language was still sprinkled with obscenities and off-color remarks, and his commanding presence still filled the room, but the boys who were there got to see a very different side of the man they sometimes feared and sometimes hated. This was the man they loved. This was the man who had their backs. He helped them in school. He helped them on the streets. He bought them meals and varsity jackets. He got them dress shirts and ties. He told them to stay away from gangs and drugs. He even got them discounts on protein supplements at the American Nutrition Center in Everett.

That had started in 2005 when Larry Gregory became interested in using creatine, the popular and legal sports supplement used by many athletes looking to gain weight and muscle. But Atkins told

Gregory and the other players to stay away from creatine because it was bad for their livers. Instead, he lectured them about their unhealthy diets, the countless meals at Burger King and McDonald's, and said they'd be better off taking protein supplements. Atkins knew a guy who would give them ten- and twenty-dollar discounts. Several players took him up on the offer. They began drinking protein and glutamine drinks. Glutamine, found in soybeans and peanuts, is one of the most versatile amino acids, designed to bring nitrogen to the parts of the body that need it most. The players who added the protein to their diets and committed themselves to the weight room discovered that they did, in fact, get bigger and stronger. Coach was right again. So they listened when he spoke.

"You have to do something, fellas," Coach said as the meeting drew to a close. "I joined the military. I know it wasn't during wartime, so it's a different story. But you can't sit around Chelsea doing nothing. And if you're not going to college, I will push you into the military. It's not bad. They'll train you for something. They might send you off to war, who knows? But it's part of life, fellas. I know when I first mentioned it, a lot of you guys freaked out. But when you walk down the street, you don't have to worry about a fucking bomb blowing up on you, do you? Well, who do you think does that for you? Who protects you?"

The boys stared blankly. None of them was quite sure what the correct answer was.

"God?" Mario answered uncertainly.

"The military!" Coach exclaimed incredulously.

The boys nodded in agreement. *Of course, the military,* they thought. Now, they understood what coach was talking about.

"Guys, I am a patriot. I love my country. I'm going to try to influence you to be good Americans. Help out your communities. It sucks, Orlando, doesn't it, that you have to worry about your little brother on the street? It doesn't have to be that way, does it? So, help out."

Before they all got up to leave, Atkins acknowledged that the game the next day against Lynn Tech would likely be the last for Jonathan Luna. He was scheduled to have his knee surgery on Monday and would miss at least the next four weeks. It was possible his football career was over. His teammates sent him away with a round of applause and good wishes, and then Mario announced that the Lynn Tech game would be a "Luna Special." The Red Devils were determined to send him off in style.

Unfortunately, Orlando didn't play. The next morning, on the day of the game, Orlando arrived for school ten minutes late, so Coach benched him.

"After all the fucking shit we did at my house the night before, do you believe the fucking balls on this kid?"

CHAPTER SIX

Fallen Angel

I think about stuff around New Year's. You start thinking it's another year of living. Damn, I'm still here. I'm a little surprised I got to twenty-one.

—ANGEL ACAVEDO, FORMER RED DEVIL AND EX-CON

Jimmy Atkins was the offspring of a black and white relationship—a black man married to a white woman. He worked with white cops arresting primarily people of color. He worked with a white school administration while coaching a football team that was predominantly black and Hispanic. No wonder he saw the world in black and white. There was very little gray in Jimmy's world. And that was why benching Orlando for being late to school was an easy decision. Orlando wouldn't play that night against Lynn Tech. There would be no negotiation.

Orlando was chronically late for school. He missed most of the season his sophomore year when he simply decided to stop attending the first class of the day. He was late four times, and by rule, that meant he would automatically fail the class. That gave Orlando an easy out.

"I said, 'Fuck it.' I'm not going to school if I'm going to fail anyway."

Orlando was carrying a B average in his other classes, and the principal was going to allow him to play with his one F, but according to Orlando, the assistant principal, Joe Mullaney, intervened. Mullaney made the case that Orlando shouldn't be allowed to play, because he was late for school nearly every day.

"Mullaney is fucking me over all the time," Orlando said. "He's a motherfucker. I hate him so much. I never done nothing. It's my brother who done it. He gave me my brother's background. He swears he knows everything. But he doesn't know nothing. If he hung around in the streets for one day, he'd know what it really is like. He don't live around here, so don't judge nobody if you don't live around here. If you weren't born in a city like this, don't think you know something. He thinks he knows. He was probably born in one of those little white cities. This ain't no white city. He comes from a rich white city and he judges people. He judged my brother and, yeah, my brother was bad and everything like that, but just because he's bad doesn't mean I'm gonna come out bad like him."

For his part, Atkins also called Mullaney a "piece of shit." He claimed Mullaney targeted the football players, in part, because of a strange personal vendetta against Atkins. Some ten years earlier, after the 1995 Super Bowl season, one of Mullaney's best friends was bad-mouthing the Red Devils' head coach, Joe Gaff. Atkins defended Gaff. A heated argument ensued and coarse words were exchanged.

"I basically told him to go fuck himself," Atkins said, and believed Mullaney had been holding a grudge ever since.

It could have been paranoia, or it could have been reality, but Atkins was convinced Mullaney acted tougher on athletes and toughest on football players. Orlando was convinced that Mullaney crossed a line early in the school year.

"There's one thing with gangs—the way they talk," Orlando explained. "If you say 'cuz' to us, it's a bad thing. There was one day, and I heard him nice and clear, just to get me mad, 'All right, fellas, clean up.' And then he looks at me and he says, 'C'mon, cuz, clean up.' He was just trying to get me to react because he knows what I am. All my boys looked at me, and I was like, 'Yeah, he just said that.'"

The Red Devils believed there was an enemy high up in the school administration. When something bad happened, they were convinced Joe Mullaney would look to blame the football team. When Orlando was seen talking to an MS-13 kid in the hallway, Mullaney grabbed him and shouted, "You're out of here. You're done!" Fortunately for Orlando, a teacher witnessed the encounter and told Mullaney that Orlando had been acting as peacemaker. Mullaney sent Orlando on his way without an apology.

When feces was found smeared all over the auditorium stage, Mullaney questioned the football players. Their pleas of innocence were verified later by a videotape that showed the perpetrator, a student who had attended football camp during the summer, but quit the team before the season started.

"This kid would eat a quarter," Atkins recalled. "And I'd tell him not to do it. 'You're gonna fuckin' die. You could get sick. You'll block up your intestines, you fucking retard.' He says, 'I won't eat any more quarters.' So, the next time he ate two dimes and a nickel."

That boy was no longer in Jimmy's charge, but Orlando was. And Orlando was someone who could help the Red Devils win a Super Bowl championship. And that, after all, was the ultimate on-the-field goal each and every season. Atkins didn't know anything less than that, and he didn't think much of a coach who didn't make winning a top priority. Yet, despite Jimmy's desire to win and Chelsea's need to win against Lynn Tech in order to keep their Super Bowl aspirations alive, he never even considered letting Orlando play. He knew exactly why Orlando was late, and why Orlando wasn't focused properly on football. And by his estimation, the excuse was pretty lame.

"Orlando had a girl ruin his whole life," Atkins said. "She moved to Atlanta. So, he takes off and follows her. He misses all the captains' practices, and comes back just in time for camp. Then he finds out she's cheating on him, and he's crying, 'I can't practice today.' I was like, 'Are you kidding me? Quit your crying. What are you, a fucking faggot? Get out there on the fucking field.'"

Orlando had been dating the girl for three years. She was the first girl Orlando ever had sex with and, Orlando said, the only girl. He lost his virginity when he was fourteen, and had remained faithful throughout the courtship. He never wore a condom, but considered it "safe sex," because his girlfriend used birth control pills. When they broke up, Orlando took it very hard.

"Once, I didn't know what love was, but I really can say I love her," Orlando said sincerely. "She was always there since sixth grade. She cares about me. She's my best friend."

As Orlando told the tale of lost love, he peeled off a layer of his self-esteem. He was tall, thin, muscular, and very handsome. But he wasn't always so physically appealing. In grammar school, he was a short, fat kid, and so it always meant a lot to him that one girl liked him long before he became the lean, handsome football star that all the girls fussed over now.

"Now that I've changed, a lot of girls want me because of the way I look," Orlando said without cockiness. "But that's what I like about her. She didn't care what I looked like."

Girl trouble was the primary reason for this year's stress, and Atkins had no sympathy for it. After all, it paled in comparison to the real issues Orlando had dealt with and conquered in the past. The previous year Orlando had found his uncle dead in the house next door. Now that was something Atkins could empathize with, but just barely.

"When the kids start talking trash, I don't want to hear it," Atkins said. "I had brothers and uncles die. My father was in jail when I got married. I don't want to hear a goddamn thing. Just do what you're supposed to do."

Black and white.

And in some cases, life and death.

Orlando's uncle, Javier DeJesus, had a serious drug problem. He was in and out of jail, and on and off crack cocaine and heroin. He was only ten years older than Orlando, and they were friends.

Orlando remembered fondly the many afternoons he sat outside with his uncle just chilling. But the lasting image, the one that haunted Orlando, was seeing Javier's bloody face and lifeless body.

"He was next to a heater, like bleeding from everywhere, like he blew up," Orlando said tearfully. "I just collapsed. It was a crazy day."

It was a day that, in many ways, was inevitable. When he was clean, Javier was a loving husband and father, but he never stayed clean for very long. "He had that one problem," Orlando said. And when that problem put him in jail one too many times, Javier's wife packed up and moved the family to Florida. When Javier was released from jail, he had the option of giving up his drug habit and moving to Florida, or staying in Chelsea. He stayed.

"They were talking again to patch everything," Orlando said. "I guess it was too much. When he came out of jail he was already hooked up a little bit. So he hooked up a little bit more. He was stressing a lot. He was calling the kids every day, because he can't live without them. I think that's one of the things that killed him, his kids not being here. He would get drunk and do drugs and all that, and he would talk about his kids all the time and how he wanted to start a new life."

Javier's end came before his new beginning.

Javier was living alone next door to Orlando. When Orlando's mother, Roseanna DeJesus, denied Orlando's request to have a party at their house one weekend, Javier told Orlando he could throw the party at his place. The party was a tremendous success. Dozens of kids were there drinking and dancing. According to Orlando, Javier left to do drugs with an upstairs neighbor. That's the last time Orlando saw his uncle alive.

"We were knocking on my uncle's door for two days straight," Orlando recalled. "On that Saturday, I woke up and I just felt like checking on my uncle. I was knocking, nothing happened. That's one day straight. This other guy from upstairs kept worrying about him. He would come down the stairs and ask if I checked on my uncle. They weren't like friends, so I kept thinking, why are you worried so much? Every ten minutes he was asking me. He was acting funny. I wasn't catching it at that point. So, the next day I knocked. That whole Saturday he was worrying about it. That whole Sunday he was worrying about it."

Finally, Orlando's father broke in and found Javier. He had died sometime during the weekend, probably early Saturday morning. There were no arrests. The investigation was quick and led to a familiar and obvious conclusion: Javier died of a drug overdose.

"I think about it a lot," Orlando said sadly. "I miss him. We always used to talk. He was like my best friend. And it sucks not having him here."

While Javier wasn't a typical father figure, he was the adult male to whom Orlando felt closest. Orlando lived with his father, but the two had never been close, and their relationship only worsened when Orlando began to bond with Coach Atkins. That's because Atkins was not especially popular with one half of Orlando's family.

Orlando Senior had two daughters and a son named Orlando with one woman. He also had the Red Devils' Orlando and two other children with Roseanna DeJesus. So, when Atkins arrested the older of the two Orlando boys, that side of the family, especially the father, was more upset with Atkins than Orlando, his siblings, and his mother.

"The other side of my family doesn't like him, because he locked up my brother," Orlando explained. "He got caught for murder and all that. They didn't like that I talked to Coach Atkins all the time, and they would see how close we are, and there was a problem about that. First of all, Atkins is a cop and that's his job. And my brother, for murdering somebody, what do you expect? He's a cop! My brother, yeah, it wasn't meant to happen, but it happened. That's my brother's life. I love my brother, and I have his back to the fullest, but it's something that happened with them. It's something that I can't blame Coach Atkins for doing. I am mad. But that was his job to lock him up. If that's what he had to do then that's what he had to do."

And that sums it up nicely. Atkins did what he had to do. For him, life was hard, but the choices weren't.

Atkins was making a difference with the Red Devils, and two key ingredients were hard work and commitment. He saw the difference every day when his team showed up for practice. Kids who routinely skipped school or got in trouble were there when practice started at 3:00. Kids who regularly failed classes were passing those classes to ensure their football eligibility. Kids who never considered going to college, never thought it was possible, were making plans for a better life. The future remained uncertain for kids like Orlando, but the forcefulness of Atkins' message was offering hope and providing new options.

"I have choices to make," Orlando said responsibly. "Either I want a future for myself or I don't. And Coach Atkins, it's because of him pushing me. When I'm outside of school and I want to do something bad, the first thing that hits me is him. I don't want to hear anything from him. I hate it. So I think about what he would say. When you have a person like him pushing you all the time, it makes you think, 'Am I doing the right thing?'"

The answer was often 'No.' Those teenage boys in Atkins' charge didn't do the right thing all the time. They drank and smoked pot. They skipped homework assignments and disrespected authority. They quit too easily on the football field and in the classroom. They made plenty of mistakes. But maybe they made fewer of them now. Maybe now they recognized them as mistakes. Maybe they wouldn't repeat some of them. And maybe, in addition to feeling the brunt of Atkins' rage, they also felt remorse.

For his part, Orlando came up just short of saying Atkins saved him, but readily conceded that Atkins was a father figure who had helped him immensely.

"He helped me from going in a different direction," Orlando said. "Maybe if it weren't for football, I would have gone down my brother's path. Maybe something would have happened in the streets, something crazy. Anything can happen. It still can. But the chances are higher for killing somebody or getting into fights, things that happen with your boys, they're higher when you're in the streets. Now that they're not higher, maybe I can walk down the streets, and I'm not going to get into a fight."

He was also not going to get into the Lynn Tech game. Atkins saw to that. Chelsea was among the smallest cities in the country, but it could be a giant when it came to swallowing up the best and the brightest. Atkins didn't want Chelsea devouring Orlando the way it had chewed up and spit out Orlando's brother, Jonathan Luna's brother, Pascual, Jorge Mercado, Joshua Lewis, Michael Augustine, Brian Roberts, and countless others, including Angel Acavedo.

Angel Acavedo—quite an ironic name. Angel was not a good kid.

Yet, it was through no fault of his own that he didn't know his father, and his mother was a drug dealer and drug user. The way Angel told it, trouble started coming to him when, as an eight-year-old growing up in the South Bronx, he had frequent fistfights with classmates. He was an unsupervised, unloved kid roaming the streets of New York. The violence he witnessed was up close and personal.

"When I was ten," Angel recalled. "They shot my stepfather right in front of me. He was the man who raised me."

The incident had begun when Angel's mother, Laura Fontanez, tried to visit her niece. The child's grandmother was vehemently opposed to the young girl being exposed to a strung out drug dealer. An argument ensued, then some pushing, shoving, and slapping. That's when Angel arrived.

"Outside in front of the building," Angel recounts. "I was running around playing basketball. Some two girls I knew, twins, came and told me my mother was in a fight. I went over and saw it, and my stepfather called me to him, and that's when they shot him. He grabbed me, and he fell on me, because the dude kept shooting at him. He kept asking me if I was all right. I was in shock. That's when the trouble started coming to me."

The only responsible person left to look after Angel was his grandfather, but there wasn't a lot he could do to make sure Angel got off the streets and attended school. Angel was moving in the same direction as his uncles—his dead uncles.

"They got bodied in Puerto Rico," Angel said with more pride than remorse. "They were top dogs in Puerto Rico back in the days."

Angel's grandfather stepped in and forced the family to move, but it was too late—and it was to the wrong place. Chelsea was not a proper destination for a child who found more comfort in the street than at home, or for a mother who wasn't ready or willing to give up using and selling drugs. By the time Angel, his mother, and two sisters moved to Chelsea, it was 1999. Angel was thirteen and already a Blood.

"I got beat into it," Angel said of his gang membership. "It's just a few seconds of guys hitting you. I was in NY when it happened. That's the reason we came up here. I'm still a Blood everywhere I go. You're always part of the nation."

Angel took up with the Bloods in Chelsea and trouble found him again. Soon after his arrival, the Bloods and the 18th Street gang battled at the bus stop on Park Street, not far from the police station. Angel wasn't hurt, but he was caught and sent to the Department of Youth Services on a weapons charge. He spent three months at the Metro Central Community Center in Dorchester, but eventually pled out to probation.

"DYS ain't nothing," Angel said. "You could get out and watch TV, play cards, and go to the gym. It was all right. The worst is when you go to real jail."

Angel experienced that a few years later—after his football career had come to an abrupt ending. He was playing for Coach O'Brien at Chelsea High as a seventeen-year-old sophomore in 2003 when the Red Devils' season was canceled. At 5'9", 190 pounds, Angel was the starting middle linebacker and running back. He was attending classes, staying out of trouble, and having fun playing football for the quiet white man he had learned to respect.

"I judge Coach O'Brien as a great coach," Angel said with a rare smile. "He had a heart. To me he wasn't that bad. As for the school stuff, to my eyes, he used to be involved with it. He used to tell us to be in classes. He was on me the most, because as far as the rest of the team, I was the one that was closest to the streets. Sports was the reason I did all my work. I loved it. I saw O'Brien as a great guy. He was on point with it."

But when apathy and injury conspired to end O'Brien's coaching career, Atkins took over, and Angel's playing days were over.

"I could have played, but I had a little issue," Angel offered as a terrific understatement. "I was more into the streets. When O'Brien left, it hurt me, because I liked him. The streets just came back to me. I had a chance to play. I spoke to Atkins about it, and he told me he didn't mind, as long as I got off the street and went to school. I did that. I tried to do that. But the street life, every time I try to do something good, trouble would come to me. I was just mixed up, so I couldn't handle it no more. Basically, I blacked out."

The "little issue" Angel had with Atkins surfaced when Angel threatened to kill Atkins' wife and children. Atkins had had a series of run-ins with Angel while working with the Gang Unit, and Angel came to believe he was being picked on. He wasn't. He was, however, involved in serious criminal behavior. By 2003, he was selling large quantities of crack cocaine under the street name A-Rock. A street-smart kid, he was tough to catch. He didn't stand on corners and wait for customers. Instead, he stayed in his home and waited for his phone to ring. When the calls came in, Angel would set up a meeting place. He changed the drop point regularly, and the transactions would only take a matter of seconds.

In addition, some might say Angel was a drug dealer with a heart.

"I used to feel bad for them," Angel said, referring to the crack addicts he supplied. "Because crack will make you not want to eat. It'll change your whole body. And it's sad to be looking at somebody that's real hungry. When I see stuff like that, I be bugging like 'Damn.' I tried to do my best. If they hungry, I'd say, 'Do you want some food?' Because I was brought up that way. I was brought up in the street and I didn't have anything. My mother used to sell drugs and all that and she wouldn't buy anything to eat."

So, Angel was dealing, wearing his colors, getting into gang fights, dropping out of school, and occasionally hurting people. These were the reasons Atkins and the rest of the Chelsea Police Department were after him. They asked him questions about selling drugs. They stopped him on the street demanding to know where he was going. They heard about a member of the Tiny Rascal Gang who was badly beaten right in front of Angel's house. And they wanted to know what had happened there.

"I had twenty or thirty kids come to my mother's house, and rang my bell," Angel said with probable exaggeration. "When I looked down I thought it would be two of my friends, but TRG was calling. I gave my mom my phone, and she knew I was going down to take care of business. She knew I didn't want my phone to fall off and break during the fight. They took it to the line.

They came to my mother's house. I went downstairs and started throwing down. Their eyes was so surprised. When they saw me coming down just by myself. I'm being real. Half of them ran. They ran because they don't see that stuff out here like that. I had no weapons. I'm going out there straight with just my hands. Out of thirty only one stood and acted brave, and that's the kid I was fighting with. I was just beating him, beating him to death with my hands."

The Tiny Rascal didn't die, but that fight and many others, along with the earlier weapons charge and the stint at DYS, had placed Angel prominently on the cops' radar screen. He was *known* to them, as they say. And what Angel knew, or at least what he thought he knew, was that the cops were dirty.

"My cousin got jumped in Chelsea," Angel explained. "It was inside work with the police. They didn't jump him, but they gave the green light. Real corrupt. My cousin's sister went to the police and they didn't even have a police report on it."

That, according to Angel, prompted his regrettable threat against Atkins, his wife, and his children.

"Me and Atkins had something between the two of us, real problems. Basically, it started over a comment that I said and he heard. It was serious. I shouldn't have said it. I was angry because of what happened to my cousin. I don't want to speak about it. It was about him, but he took it like his family, too. He took it like I was trying to get at his kids. Since that, me and him went forward with trouble. He was taking it to the streets. Instead of locking me up, he was basically doing the same thing that gangs do. If he would have saw me, he would have beat me up. He didn't want to arrest me. He wanted to take me out, take me off this world. That's when I started worrying about him."

He was right to worry. Plenty of people allegedly overheard Atkins say that if he saw Angel on the street, he'd "kick the crap out of him."

"He is the biggest pussy in the world," Atkins offered as a description of Angel. "He portrays it otherwise. He's a big kid, but I wouldn't want him next to me in a fight. I've known him from the streets since he was like fourteen years old. After football in 2003, I was still involved. He was playing basketball for Frankie DePatto, but he got in trouble. I told him I'd take care of it for him. But he ended up getting in more trouble and got thrown off the basketball team."

Atkins wasn't the only person who wanted to hurt Angel. Atkins' good friend Luis Virella was a tough, once-active Latin King from New York. Atkins and Luis had met when Atkins was walking the beat. He often went into a barbershop during the 1995 O. J. Simpson trial and Luis was almost always in there. Atkins knew Luis was selling drugs, but he took a liking to the kid. The twenty-one-year-old Luis was smarter than the rest of the gang members, and he indicated he might be willing to get out of the gang life. Atkins gave him a reference that helped Luis get a job driving trucks for a meat delivery company. Luis got out just in time.

"Shortly thereafter," Atkins explained, "Marlin Arazzo, who was Luis's partner, got arrested as one of the leaders of the Latin Kings. He had large quantities of cocaine. It was a big story back in '95. Luis had only just gotten out, and some of the Kings thought he was a rat because he was friendly with me."

Luis got married and started living the straight life. But his wife left him for another woman, a fact that gets Atkins howling with laughter. Luis soon found himself a new girlfriend, and during the fall of 2004, long after Atkins and Angel had their falling-out, Luis was walking his attractive young girlfriend down Fourth Street in Chelsea. A bunch of kids, including Angel, started catcalling. Luis kept his composure, but he relayed the story to Atkins.

"So, the next time I see Angel," Atkins said, "I grabbed him and I said, 'Are you fucking crazy? You're barking up the wrong tree. You're in way over your head.' Luis is a real tough guy. He's got a lot of baggage. None of these kids can compare with his history. But the next time Angel sees Luis, he says, 'What are you? A bitch?'"

Luis was with his girlfriend again, so he kept his cool. He dropped her off at home, and met up with his brother. The two of them went to that night's Chelsea High School football game. While Coach Atkins was patrolling the sidelines, Luis noticed Angel and his friends pointing at Atkins' wife in the bleachers. Luis knew the history of Angel's threats against Atkins' family, and he didn't like what he saw. He went after Angel, who was also called "Chippy" due to his chipped front tooth.

"Now Luis is doubly pissed," Atkins said. "He and his brother see seven of them, and they grabbed two of them and beat the shit out of them, sent one of them to the hospital. They beat them bad. Chippy ran away. He left his buddies there to get beaten senseless. That's how tough these kids are. There are like six or seven of them against Luis and his brother, and they run away. Tough gang kids, right? Luis secs Chippy two days later and Luis grabs him from behind, and Chippy falls to his hands and knees and begs for him not to hit him. He was crying so bad, it looked like Luis was disciplining a kid. Luis says to him, 'If you ever open your mouth again, I'll bury you in your basement.'"

Soon thereafter, Angel disappeared from the streets. He would spend twenty-one months in South Bay prison. A-Rock never got caught for dealing drugs, but Chippy eventually got nailed for shooting a rival gang member.

"It's hard to live the good life," Angel reflected. "It's hard like, because you can do it, but I tried it. I tried it a lot. It's just always trouble came to me. That's the problem I got. Whenever I tried to do good, always trouble would come to me. So for me, I was just trying to protect myself when trouble came to me."

Twenty-one jailhouse months of trouble came in April of 2005 on Marlboro Street in Chelsea. That's where and when Angel shot a member of the MS-13 gang. It was the first time Angel had ever fired a gun, and the bullets hit their intended target in the leg and the arm.

"When I got locked up for shooting that guy, I didn't want to do it," Angel explained. "But they tempted me to do it. They the ones what came at me with weapons. They was the ones that were trying to kill me. That day, it was weird. I don't know why I was carrying a gun. But I had it. It was a surprise, and when they came at me, my mind was like 'Please stop.' I didn't want to do what I was gonna have to do. South Bay is not a good place. It's different. The attitude is different. You really feel like you're locked up. Every day something's going on. Somebody's gonna test you. It's not the place to be. You can really feel it. It's like 'Damn.' I walked in there with my chin high, and basically minding my own business. But I walked in there with an attitude. It wasn't like, come pick on me, people. But they knew I ain't no punk. I had one of my cousins in there, and three other guys I knew from Chelsea were in there, and they knew about half the people. My cousin started introducing me to everyone and said, 'This is my family.' So, it was cool."

When Angel got out, he immediately found his way back to a gang hangout. It was a small building with large windows and a cement facade just a few hundred yards away from the Chelsea Police Headquarters. It was a place frequented by hard-core gang members, a place called ROCA.

"We didn't get along very well with ROCA in the beginning," Chelsea police chief Frank Garvin said. "We didn't trust them, because they were working as advocates for the gang members. We would see them in court sometimes with people that we had arrested and people would flip out. 'What are you doing? Blah, blah, blah.' They're trying to save these kids. They're trying to do it that way. We're trying to do it our way. Now, we have a very good working relationship. We rely on each other all the time."

ROCA, which stands for Reaching Out to Chelsea Adolescents, began as a teen pregnancy prevention program in the late 1980s, and over time developed into something much bigger than that. By 2006, ROCA catered to the gang kids, the ex-cons, and the street crowd. Inside the building were recreational rooms, classrooms, a gym, art and dance studios, computers, staff offices, and a day care center. Outside the building, some of the toughest kids in the city congregated. They talked. They smoked. Sometimes they fought. But once they got inside, once that door shut behind them, the dangers of the city were shut out. Unless they were found guilty of domestic violence, no one was turned away.

"Big J," a large, round black man often seen standing under the dim glow of a lone streetlight in front of ROCA, wasn't turned away when he dropped out of high school and started getting into trouble. Eric Santiago wasn't turned away when he finally decided to put his violent youth behind him. Iris Lopez, who gave birth when she was thirteen years old, and Stacey Foreman, who ran away from home when she was fifteen and joined the MS-13 gang, were also welcomed by ROCA.

"I like them," detective Scott Conley said. "Their heart's in the right place. The image is that they're harboring gang kids, and they do bring them into their facility, but that's how they do their thing."

And ROCA's thing was to build relationships. They went out into the field and confronted kids on the street. They knocked on doors. They talked. They listened. They argued and they wouldn't back down from some potentially dangerous situations. ROCA's founder, Molly Baldwin, was a small, thin white woman who spent years in the field without so much as a cellphone. Kids didn't exactly cower when the crazy, white lady showed up, but they tended to do as she said.

"Do we get challenged?" Baldwin asked rhetorically. "Yeah. But we don't feel unsafe. We're out there. We don't have vests. I used to get right out there at night, one o'clock in the morning, pick kids up, pull them right out of stuff, and drive them off. You use your stuff."

And it tended to be the right stuff, but not every ROCA story has a happy ending. In April of 2000, a fifteen-year-old boy named Efrain Calderon shot himself in the head in a room with three other children.

"He was a beloved kid," Baldwin said distantly. "He was in more distress than anybody knew. It was a very complicated day. The police did a big investigation, because there was concern that a rival gang might take these other boys out."

There was some question, at first, about whether the boy had shot himself or had been the victim of an attack. If Calderon's allies thought the kids in the room with him had shot him, revenge would have been foremost on their minds.

Baldwin lost it. Her relationship with the cops already strained, she blamed their ineffectiveness for the tragedy. She barged into the police station screaming at anyone who approached in a uniform. She shouted about guns, and gangs, and violence. She demanded to know what the police were going to do to protect the children. She challenged their willingness to try. She was furious and inconsolable. Members of her staff tried in vain to calm her down. She didn't leave until she had said too many regrettable things to the people she desperately needed as allies. A master at building and maintaining relationships, Baldwin nearly destroyed her relationship with the Chelsea police. Days later she returned to apologize. It took a long time to regain acceptance from the police, and some never accepted her.

"We used to get in arguments with them, because they don't understand that these kids leave ROCA and go out and stab somebody," Atkins said. "So, I lock 'em up on Friday, and they're in court on Monday speaking on their behalf saying they're doing the right thing. There has to be a time when we focus on the kids who can be helped. When somebody robs someone and runs in there, and one of the instructors says they're not here, then they do it another time, that's a problem. There was a stabbing that happened, and they told us he ran out another door. It just happened again last week. There was a woman, an elderly woman who got hit with a baseball bat. All she did was tell someone to stop hitting another kid, so they hit her with a baseball bat, and one of the ROCA guys was standing right there. And one of his kids was the one who hit her, and he won't turn him in because he says, 'I'll lose their trust.' Well, that's a separate issue. Right now, there's an innocent woman who got hit with a bat and you're a witness to it and you're not gonna help. He just hit someone's grandmother with a bat! That's where they lose me."

But Atkins and ROCA weren't so very different. They were both about re-engaging the disengaged. Atkins did it with football. ROCA did it with dance, and art, and alternative education. ROCA did it with a $7 million budget and a large staff. Atkins did it on a policeman's salary—about $100,000 a year—plus the $5,500 more he made as a coach. Both were willing to reach down and pull up the smallest, most troubled kids for no other reason than it was what their heart told them they should do.

During his first year as head coach of the Red Devils, Atkins had a 75-pound freshman, described by Conley as "4-foot nothing with zero athletic talent." The kid was never going to play in a game, but he was willing to work hard in practice. So, when the kid told Atkins he was quitting the team because he had to babysit his brother and sister after school, Atkins wouldn't allow it. He began picking up the siblings at the middle school and bringing them to practice. They would play on the sidelines while their big brother got knocked around by kids twice his size—loving every minute of it.

"And then Jimmy would bring them all home," Conley said with great respect. "And this was a kid who was never gonna play."

ROCA had to employ methods similar to Atkins'. Staff members like Dana Betts, a young country girl with blonde hair and green eyes, were sent into the streets to pick up gang kids who otherwise would blow off appointments and classes at ROCA. Dana worked with the hard-core gang kids. She counted "City Red" among her victories because he regularly attended a charter school. He was still in a gang and recently had been jumped, injuring his foot, but at least he was still in school. On a warm October night in 2006, Dana picked him up in a van that smelled like spilled gasoline while four other troubled youths tagged along, imploring her to crank the rap music up even louder. Dana was a graduate of Holy Cross and she was there to help, not to judge. But most important, she was always there. She earned the respect of the gang kids the hard way—by standing between two boys looking to kill each other and refusing to move until a peace was agreed upon. Then she came back, and she kept coming back. That's why her four passengers, Mercy, Diana, Jennifer, and Kadeem, would listen to her gentle lectures about the need for education. They had heard it a million times, but they listened to Dana.

When they arrived at the Charter School, Dana commanded the others to stay in the van. Members of rival gangs were classmates, and when school let out, students spilled out on to the street. Blood had also been spilled here in the past, and Dana didn't want any more trouble. "City Red" hopped over to the van on crutches and climbed in. Dana asked him about the problems he was having with a certain teacher, and City explained: "Nigga's gonna get punched in the face if he talk to me like that again."

Dana tried to reason with him, but it was to no avail. He was "City Red" at that moment. His gang persona was on display. Maybe when she got him alone, Dana could speak more convincingly to the boy whose given name was actually Mario. Mario has a future. City does not. Dana needed to reach Mario, but it would take years before she knew if Mario had taken over City's mind. Change is incrementally slow. It's hard to know when somebody has truly made it.

When Atkins would drive by ROCA and see Angel Acavedo, he wondered if Angel had made it. Atkins would see him on the corner and think about the Angel who could have been a Red Devil, but chose to stand on street corners and sell drugs instead. Atkins had his doubts that Angel had turned any real corners in his life, but Angel believed he had. Not long out of prison, Angel worked for ROCA's Tacos Unidos catering service for $7 an hour. He was looking for a better job, but it was difficult for an ex-con.

In 2006, Angel sat peacefully inside ROCA. He was physically strong, and though he was uneducated, he was smart. He seldom cursed, and spoke softly and eloquently. He would probably interview for a job well, but it was hard for prospective employers to look beyond the tattoos of his two nephews, Mikey and Mikael, peeking out from under his sleeves. Another large tattoo of his mother's name covered up most of his neck. And there were five ink dots on the fleshy part between his thumb and forefinger on his right hand. Angel wouldn't say what his five-dot tattoo stood for, but it was a common tattoo among ex-convicts letting everyone know about their "bad boy" past. Employers might reasonably question if that past was prologue.

It was the same question Atkins asked. Why should an employer or Atkins invest their time and energy in someone who might be a lost cause when there are so many more that can be helped? Fortunately for Angel, ROCA didn't ask that question. They were trying to help him find some answers. Angel's attitude and demonstrated willingness to show up for work early and stay late gave the appearance that he was not hopeless, but ROCA knew as well as Atkins that appearances can be deceiving. Angel had a bad boy past, and it could reappear at any moment. It's what ROCA faced with Angel and City and Josiah and countless others, and it's what Atkins faced with Orlando and Kenzi and Luis Verde and countless more. The police, ROCA, Atkins, the Boys and Girls Clubs, teen centers, and other individuals and organizations were all working to change lives, and seldom did they know if they had achieved any long-term success. They counted on little victories to push them through the hard times. For Atkins, those victories could come on the football field or the day his players graduated high school. For Baldwin, victory was accepting that significant change could take years, and she'd had nineteen years in Chelsea to see plenty of positive change take place.

Perhaps the biggest development in ROCA's mission came when they introduced peacekeeping circles. It was something Atkins laughed at when recalling the scene: A feather was passed around and whoever was holding the feather got to speak uninterrupted. The first time ROCA invited the Chelsea police to one of its circles, Atkins lasted about ten minutes before leaving. But in truth, the ROCA circles were a lot like senior night at Coach's house. There, the football players sat in a circle and talked about their lives, their futures, and their problems. There was no feather, and Atkins interrupted whenever he wanted, but the structure was very similar to ROCA's, and it worked.

"What the circles taught us is that it didn't matter if they believed in us," Baldwin said. "It didn't matter anymore if they understood what we did. The only thing that mattered is we had to show up in the right way. The big lesson with these circles is that if I show up in a good way things might get better."

Again, Atkins and ROCA were more alike than either was willing to admit. And things were getting better in Chelsea. Help was being given to the helpless, and hope was being given to the hopeless.

As Dana's van pulled up in front of ROCA the night she picked up "City Red," a conversation was wrapping up on the corner.

"That boy shouldn't be carrying no flare gun," a teenager named Josiah said. "That won't do anything."

"It could burn your whole face off if you shoot it from up close," a girl argued.

"Yeah, well a real gun will put a hole in you. Kill you dead."

"Well, I wouldn't want to be going around the rest of my life with a burnt-off face."

Josiah seemed satisfied with the girl's summation. After a brief pause, he noticed a stranger with a notebook and said, "You the guy writing a book?"

"Yup."

"You should write a book about me, nigga!"

"Oh, yeah. How would a book like that end?"

"Rich," Josiah said. "Rich and happy."

CHAPTER SEVEN

Revenge Never Comes

The overall goal is to get to the championship. But once you start working, you can't achieve that without getting involved in their personal lives. It's impossible here in Chelsea.

—JAMES ATKINS

Six games into their season, Chelsea wasn't looking much like a championship team. They barely squeaked out a win over Lynn Tech when Ato Alic, the quiet kid from Bosnia, sacked Tech's quarterback in the end zone in the fourth quarter. The safety secured a hard-fought, but poorly played 8–6 victory. Lynn Tech was an upper division team, but by far, the weakest of those squads. They would only win one game all season.

So, Chelsea had another victory, but it was wholly unsatisfying and somewhat worrisome. The Red Devils were a pedestrian 3-and-2, and one of their star players had left the field in an ambulance.

Alex Caraballo had carried the ball around the left side and was taken down hard. No harder than usual, but this time he didn't get up. He stayed on his back with his knees slightly bent and waited for the trainer to come out and tell him why his neck hurt so badly.

Eve Alvarez was visibly shaken as she watched her son lying on the field. He always got up. No matter how hard he got hit. He always got up. And Eve was always there. She was one of the rare Chelsea parents who went to every game, home or away.

"He doesn't like me at the games," Alvarez said, "Because I scream too much."

She was silent as her son lay on the field and the stretcher was called for. Alex being severely injured had always been her gravest concern. Now, here it was, the stinging reality slapping her in the face. She never liked the physical nature of football, but she had learned to appreciate what being able to play the game did for Alex, and she had grown to love Coach Atkins.

"Football makes a big difference in Alex's life," she admits. "He's a very strong-willed child. So, he does whatever he wants. He has always asked me to play football, but I wouldn't allow him because it's a very dangerous sport. He played soccer for a long time, and once he got to high school, he said, 'Mom, please.' So, finally I gave in. I allow him to play and it has helped a lot in his schoolwork, because for him to be able to stay on the team, he has to have certain grades. He does his work on his own because he wants to play on the team. And whenever he's slacking a little bit, I talk to Coach Atkins and he puts him back in line."

Eve Alvarez was born in El Salvador, but had lived in the United States for over twenty years. She was sweet, smart, and diminutive. She spoke with a heavy accent in a soft voice, at least until Alex carried the ball. She had attended the University of Massachusetts in Boston majoring in human services, but was forced to drop out after two-and-a-half years to support her children. When she spoke about not graduating from college, the sadness in her voice was obvious, but so was the acceptance.

"It's not that I don't have the capacity, or that I don't want to do it," she said. "I would love to do it. But priorities."

She now worked as the community coordinator at the East Boston Neighborhood Health Center, and with the right priorities, she had managed to raise two good boys in Chelsea. Alex's brother was a sophomore at Wentworth Institute of Technology in Boston studying mechanical engineering, and Alex was staying out of trouble, pulling down Bs and Cs and planning to become an auto mechanic.

"I think being involved on the team and in football, he is seeing by himself how important education is," Alvarez said about her son. "He knows if he doesn't make up his grades, he won't be able to play on the team. Now, he's more into education. Before, he was talking about a two-year training school. Now, he's more flexible when I talk about college."

"The only things I'm concerned about are the team doing well and with me doing well in school," Alex told the *Chelsea Record* after his five-touchdown performance against Minuteman.

The message was getting through. In school, after school, and at home, Alex was bombarded with the importance of education. He was listening. Using his older brother as a role model and looking to Atkins as a father figure had made him stronger. In many ways, Atkins was the best father he'd ever had. Alex's real father, Adrian, left when Alex was two years old. He lived in East Boston now and continued to see Alex regularly, but the relationship was friendly, not fatherly. Soon after the divorce, Alvarez married a man named Walter Lemus. They were married for fifteen years, enough time for Lemus to form a strong bond with Alex. But Alex hadn't seen or heard from Lemus since January when Alvarez and Lemus separated.

"Since we separated he hasn't come around," Alvarez explained. "That is a typical man. They divorce the woman, so they divorce the children. The kids say, 'We're okay without him.' We were married fifteen years. That's why I resent a little bit that he hasn't come around. He's the one who taught the boys how to swim and took them camping, and taught them to ride their bikes and ski."

The sudden disappearance of a previously loving stepfather could have been devastating to Alex. But it wasn't. He still had his mom, her large family of ten siblings spread out from El Salvador to New Hampshire to Canada, and he still had his football and his very demanding coach. There was no time to feel sorry for himself. He was too busy, and too tired.

"I worry that if Alex is not busy he will find trouble," Alvarez said. "Practicing every day for football sends him home tired.

For example, I came home last night at nine o'clock, and he was already asleep. That's the responsibility that Coach Atkins teaches them. That's where I can see the father figure in Coach Atkins. He also makes everybody on the team responsible for the rest of the team. Alex says, 'Mom, we have to be very good because if one of us makes a mistake, he makes all of us run.'"

Alex had run earlier in the game against Lynn Tech, all the way into the end zone when he caught a 15-yard pass from Miguel Medina. Alex was still among the league's scoring leaders, and the fact that he was only a junior boded well for Chelsea's future, but right now there was serious doubt as to when Alex would run again.

Lynn Tech's trainer was the first to reach him, and he immediately called for a board to carry Alex off the field. Alex was loaded into the back of an ambulance and taken to the hospital. Eve Alvarez followed closely behind in her own car. Alex had several X-rays taken, and since everything checked out okay, it was determined that he had suffered a "stinger," a temporarily pinched nerve that causes quite a bit of pain, but goes away quickly. By the time Alex was being released, one of the assistant coaches was there to greet him and let him know that Chelsea had squeaked out a victory.

Despite the victory over Lynn Tech, Atkins was in a foul mood. His team had only managed to score 8 points against a bad team, and it was easy to see why. The Red Devils had a strong running attack led by Frankie and Alex, but with Miguel Medina at quarterback, there was absolutely no passing game. Opposing defenses were discovering they could stuff the run by stacking the line because they didn't have to worry about the pass. It was making Chelsea predictable and one-dimensional. Atkins figured it was time to make a change at quarterback. But switching to a new quarterback in the middle of the season could create more problems than it solved. Plus, Miguel was a nice, hard-working kid, and a senior. Although Atkins was prepared to make the switch to the backup, Cody Verge, assistant coach Dennis O'Neil talked him out of it.

O'Neil admitted that Miguel "can't throw the ball to save his ass," and that he was so small "he can't run with the ball without coughing it up." It wasn't exactly a ringing endorsement, but O'Neil believed Miguel was very nifty with his footwork and hid the ball very well, which were two important attributes in Chelsea's misdirection-based offense. Besides, Cody was only a junior, and he had almost no experience as a quarterback.

"Cody is a tough nut," O'Neil said. "He trips over his own two feet quite a bit, but he has the respect of his fellow players as a tough kid. He'll get those tough yards for you. He'll hang in the pocket and take the hit. But he'll also go to throw the toss sweep and just fire it off the running back's face mask. He tends to lack the touch you need sometimes."

It's tough to be a championship team without a quarterback, and Atkins knew that could be his team's downfall. Still, he relented to O'Neil's wishes and left Miguel as his starting quarterback for the Whittier Tech game. What Atkins did instead was change his defense.

"We have a new defense, the 5-2 Oakie," Atkins said, quite pleased on the night of the game against Whittier Tech. "It's a special defense geared to stop the double wing. Everybody has to keep their responsibilities. If you try to be slick or get lazy on a play and they run to where your responsibility is, it's a touchdown. Other defenses, you can make mistakes and somebody else can help you out. In this defense, if the defensive end doesn't crash through the C-Gap, and they run a 26-toss to the C-Gap, it's a touchdown."

The new defense was installed specifically to stop Whittier's all-conference running back, Jason Pina. Atkins had scouted Whittier and identified Pina as the Wildcats' best player. Whether

Atkins truly disliked Pina or not, he made sure his Red Devils didn't like him.

"He's been talking all kinds of crap, all kinds of trash," Atkins said as the team gathered in the Chelsea locker room before the game. "This is a kid, we scouted him last week, and he was so cocky he was turning around talking to the people in the stands. He just figured he was so much better than the other team, he could do whatever he wanted to do. Well, today, we're gonna make sure he doesn't talk to anybody in the stands. Every chance you get to lay a fucking lick on him, I want you laying a goddamn lick on him!"

The anger and volume of Atkins' voice rose steadily. It was one part genuine anger, one part theatrics. He knew Whittier was the better team. They were undefeated, from the upper division, averaging nearly 400 rushing yards per game, and generally much bigger than the Red Devils. This was Chelsea's sixth game in an eleven-game season. They were exactly at the midpoint. It was time to find out if Chelsea could run with the big dogs. Atkins had his doubts about his team. So, he had pounded the kids during the week of practice. He hadn't initially planned on being so tough on them, but when he discovered ten of his starters had Fs on their progress reports, he was livid. They were all permitted to play, but if they didn't get their grades up before the end of the term, they'd be ineligible for the Thanksgiving Day game, and more important, they wouldn't be allowed to play in the postseason. Atkins had no tolerance for laziness, to which he attributed the flunking grades. So, he worked the kids hard. He put them through a hard physical workout while also teaching them the new defense. He hoped it would pay off, but he knew his team needed to be fired up to play its best game of the year.

"Every time you get him," Atkins continued, referring to Pina, "I want the fucking elbow in the face. I want you to go out and stick your helmet right in his goddamn chest. Every time he turns around he should have a Red Devil tattoo right on his goddamn chest! By the end of today's game, I want a big fucking Chelsea Red Devil right on the front of his chest! He is so goddamn cocky, this week we're gonna knock that shit right the fuck out of him. Orlando, every time he looks around, you're going to lay a lick into Number 7. Do you understand me?"

"Yes, Coach!" they all shouted in unison.

"If we shut Number 7 down, we win this goddamn game. It's just that simple."

At this point, Atkins changed his focus, but his energy and his anger never waned. It was easy for him to get up for a Whittier game. The Wildcats were like nearly every other team on Chelsea's schedule, which meant they were unlike Chelsea. The kids were mostly white, and even if they weren't rich, they tended to have homes in the suburbs. Things came easier to them, and Atkins had no patience when he heard Whittier's coaches and school administration complaining about so-called problems with their kids, problems that would be welcomed in Chelsea.

For instance, while the Chelsea kids were dealing with weapons, drugs, violence, language barriers, and crime, Whittier found it necessary to suspend several members of its football team for giving wedgies. For what was deemed inappropriate behavior, six Wildcat players were suspended from school for five days and forced to sit out a game for pulling up the underwear of other football players.

Atkins also had a personal reason for wanting to knock the Wildcats on their ass. Their coach, Kevin Bradley, had been Atkins' coach several years earlier when Atkins was a running back in a local semi-pro football league. Atkins considered Bradley a friend, and he felt betrayed when Bradley cast the deciding vote that kept Chelsea from going to the playoffs the previous year. It still ate at Atkins that Chelsea's appeal was denied, and that even though Chelsea had a better record than Georgetown, Georgetown went to the postseason. He blamed everyone who voted against Chelsea, and that included Bradley. The man he once called "Coach" he now called his enemy.

"Last year, when they voted against us not to go to the playoffs, I was pissed. How could my coach do that to me? So now I know where fucking loyalty lies. There is no goddamn loyalty. The only people who are loyal to us is who?"

"Us!"

"Nobody else. I'm tired of everybody sticking it up Chelsea's ass. Today, we get our goddamn revenge on the SECOND team that took us out of the playoffs from last year. We take this team and we shove it right up their ass. Do you understand me?"

"Yes, Coach!"

"Fellas, they beat the shit out of Manchester. They beat the shit out of Northeast. Those are our rivals. Let's go out there today, and when people wake up and they're reading the newspaper in the morning, they go, 'Holy fucking shit!' Let's go out there today and beat this goddamn team. Send a message to everybody in Division 3A. Let them know who the best goddamn team in this fucking division is! And who is it?"

"CHELSEA!"

"Who is it?"

"CHELSEA!"

"Guys, you gotta believe. You gotta work. We're gonna beat this goddamn team. As long as you play like we practiced this week, I promise you, we're gonna beat this team."

The Red Devils rushed out on to the field whooping and hollering. It was a beautiful New England night. The air was cool. The sky was different shades of pink, purple, and blue. The Red Devils were nervous, but confident. They knew all about the challenge that lay ahead of them.

"We can't make any mistakes," Danny Cortez shouted into the evening, his voice carried by the breeze to each of his teammates. "We have to strive for perfection. We need to be damn near close to it to beat this team. We can do it. We have the ability. We showed all week we have the ability. They are not invincible!"

On the first play from scrimmage, Alex ran for twenty yards. It was good to have him back. Chelsea moved the ball systematically to the Whittier 37-yard line, but the drive stalled there. Atkins called time-out and barked at Miguel. He was already second-guessing his decision to keep Miguel at quarterback.

Defensively, the 5-2 Oakie got off to an impressive start. Whittier couldn't move the ball on its first possession, and when the Wildcats got the ball back to start their second series, Cody Verge rushed through a gap and hammered the quarterback. It was a good, clean hit, and it forced an errant throw. Jonathan Santiago intercepted the ball and ran it back to Whittier's 34. There was still no score in the game with four minutes to play in the first quarter, but Chelsea was knocking on the door. They didn't knock very loudly though. It was three plays and out for the Red Devils.

Whittier's Thane Sanford finally broke the deadlock with a 39-yard touchdown run late in the first quarter. With the 2-point conversion, Whittier led 8–0. Atkins, who began the night nervously pacing the sidelines in his beige khakis, a navy blue windbreaker, and a Chelsea baseball cap, was feeling a surge of optimism that even the Whittier touchdown couldn't deter.

"I'm telling you this is our game," Atkins said as he brought the team together before the ensuing kickoff. "They scored because we didn't do what we practiced to do. I'm telling you, stay on your blocks. Try, try, try, try! We're gonna win this game. Do your jobs. We're gonna win!"

But the Wildcats' Pina was beginning to chew up huge chunks of yardage, 7 and 8 yards at a time. He was as big as his would-be tacklers and quicker than all of them. It required a total team effort and everyone holding their positions to keep Pina from running free in the open. The Red Devils were playing some of their best defense of the season during the first half, but they weren't able to generate any offense. With under three minutes to play in the half, they were still down by eight, and Whittier was threatening. Kenzi was flagged for a 15-yard unnecessary roughness penalty that moved the ball to the Chelsea 20. Atkins called a time-out. He glared at Kenzi, but ignored him.

"Guys, stay in the 5-2 unless Number 7 goes out. If he goes out, switch to the 5-3. I need something from you guys. It's right here, right now. There's three minutes left, let's keep them out of the end zone. It's 1st down, they're on the 20-yard line. We need to stop them. They like the 47 toss pass. My two safeties, if he goes in motion, watch the end. If there's no tight end, you gotta shift down a man."

Chelsea stopped them. Whittier gave the ball back on downs and Chelsea had just under two minutes before halftime to march 80 yards. This was where a passing quarterback would come in handy. Instead, Miguel fumbled the ball at Chelsea's 20-yard line. Sanford scooped it up for Whittier and rushed it in for his second touchdown of the game. Whittier led 14–0. It was a demoralizing turn of events.

"Don't go in a hole!" Coach O'Neil yelled as Miguel came back to the sidelines. "Don't go in a hole. Look at me! Don't go in a hole."

Miguel may not have gone into a hole, but he also didn't go back into the game. After the kickoff, Atkins sent Cody in to play quarterback. On his first play, Cody dropped back to pass, moved well in the pocket to buy a few extra seconds, and then fired a deep pass over the middle. Orlando wasn't anywhere near the pass when it first went up, but he sprinted to the place where the ball was sure to come down. The ball and Orlando arrived at the same place at the same time, and Orlando hauled it in, cradling it in his arms as a Whittier defender dragged him to the ground. First down Chelsea at the Whittier 35. There was still time for the Red Devils to put some points on the board before the half. Cody received several congratulatory pats on the back from his teammates as they huddled again before the next play.

This time, Cody fumbled. Turnover. Atkins looked at O'Neil. O'Neil just shrugged. He had backed Miguel. Atkins had backed Cody. Could they both be wrong?

On the very next play, Frankie intercepted a pass at midfield. Cody had another chance, but he gave the ball right back to Whittier. His pass intended for Orlando floated too long in the air and was intercepted.

"Mistakes," Atkins said to his coaches before they walked into the locker room at halftime. "A fumble for a touchdown. A fumble going in on offense. Penalties. They're not beating us. We're beating ourselves. I preached this all year, and it's just getting old. It's getting goddamn old."

The other coaches nodded in agreement. There wasn't much anyone could say. Everyone was aware of the magnitude of this game. Even though it didn't mean much in the overall standings or the playoff picture, because Whittier plays in an upper division, the game had an enormous emotional significance. This was the game in which the Red Devils could start believing in themselves. A win over Whittier would convince the underdogs and overlooked kids of Chelsea that their dream of a Super Bowl season was possible. If they could beat Whittier, they could beat anyone in their own league. Losing to Whittier would only deepen their self-doubt. And the Red Devils were blowing it. They had committed four turnovers in the first half. Without those mistakes, they could certainly have been leading, instead of trailing 14–0.

"We're a way better team," Orlando said staring at the floor in front of his locker. "Too many mistakes. We keep giving them the ball. Fumbles are killing us. It should be a 0–0 game."

There was surrender in his voice. He wasn't shouting the words in an effort to rally the team. He was merely thinking out loud. Loud enough for others to hear. Loud enough for them to know that he was blaming his teammates. They were the ones who had made the costly mistakes. Not him.

"You're a leader on this team. Let's go. Shake it off."

The words came from the other side of the locker room. Orlando never acknowledged that he heard the words or that he knew who said them. He continued to stare at the floor. His despondence was not shared by most of his teammates. The rest of the room was a buzz of conversation and enthusiasm. Players were gathering in small groups to discuss what had gone right as well as what had gone wrong in the first half. They offered suggestions to one another about what could be done. They spoke the technical jargon of the 5-2 Oakie defense like they had been playing it for years. There was a sophisticated understanding that demonstrated a real intelligence, something they often kept hidden in the classroom.

"Guys, we keep hurting ourselves," Atkins said as he swung open the door. "I don't understand why. I don't know how else to coach it out of you, to yell it out of you, to beg you. I don't know what else to do. You guys have to step up now. Two touchdowns and we win this game. Two touchdowns, Orlando, and we win, because they're not gonna score on us again. We're gonna kick the ball off, shut them down, and then we're gonna score."

He sounded much more positive than he was probably feeling. All season long, he had watched his team beat the teams they should beat, and find a way to lose to the teams that they could have beaten. It was frustrating, but frustration was something Atkins tried hard only to reveal to the other coaches or his cop friends when they asked what was going on with his team this year. He knew his players were also frustrated, and they needed to know their coach still believed in them.

"Guys, we're moving the ball," Atkins said. "We just have to stop two things. Fumbles and penalties. Kenzi, get your head out of your ass. Cut the shit. You're losing your fucking mind. You're not just hurting yourself. You're hurting everybody else, because you can't control yourself. A 15-yard penalty right before the half hurts us."

Kenzi kept his eyes trained on the coach. He made sure Atkins knew that he heard the criticism and that he accepted it. Only when the coach moved on to his next target did Kenzi allow himself to look down and tell himself to do better in the second half. The next target was Orlando who, unlike Kenzi, never met Coach's glare. Orlando was the intended receiver on Cody's interception, and Atkins let him know that he should have adjusted to the ball, and it was because he didn't that the Whittier defender was able to make the easy pick. Orlando didn't look up, because he didn't agree. Coach moved on.

"What happened on that 47 toss pass, Cody?"

No response.

"Why were you on the other side of the field anyway? If you're getting tackled, you're getting tackled. I need someone to run the offense. Somebody has to run the offense. Anybody. I'm waiting for someone to step up, and nobody steps up. Cody, you've got one more shot. It's your offense. Either you pick it up and you run with it or you shit the bed, too. It's just that simple."

As Atkins followed his team out on to the field, he spotted an assistant coach from North Shore, one of Chelsea's league rivals. It was a little surprising to see him, because North Shore was, *at that moment,* playing Shawsheen Tech. Furthermore, Atkins had noticed the coach standing along the Whittier sidelines during the first half. Atkins thought that was suspicious and was convinced the coach was helping Whittier. Using his connections, Atkins had the police remove the coach from the game, and as he was being escorted away, Atkins yelled:

"Worry about your own team, you fat fuck!"

Meanwhile, Atkins had cause to worry about his team. Late in the third quarter, with the score still 14–0, Whittier had the ball 4th and goal at the Chelsea 1-yard line. The Red Devils' defensive line surged forward at the snap of the ball pushing Whittier's blockers backwards. Mario Hernandez, eluding a block and shooting through a hole, was the first to reach Pina. He hit him behind the line of scrimmage and was soon joined by Danny Cortez and Frankie Quiles. The three of them hauled Pina down to the turf. They had stuffed Whittier at the goal line.

It was a momentum-shifting play. Instead of Whittier going up by three touchdowns, Chelsea made the stop it had to make. The Red Devils stood up and pounded their chests. The Chelsea sidelines erupted in wild cheers. It was a proud moment for Atkins. He saw his team rise to a challenge, and he thought, *This is when they know what it's like to do something they didn't think was possible. They can use this moment and take this moment into the rest of their lives.*

But then, on the very next play, Frankie fumbled and Whittier recovered the ball in the end zone for a touchdown. It was stunning. Nobody on the Chelsea sideline moved or spoke for what seemed like a minute. It was unbelievably Chelsea. All the good feelings of the previous moment were vanquished. All the optimism created by the goal line stand was crushed the instant Frankie took the handoff. He never got a good grip on the ball, never was able to safely tuck it under his arm. The Whittier defender was on him too quickly, and the ball squirted free. Maybe it was the fault of whoever missed the block that allowed the defender to invade the backfield so quickly. Maybe it was Cody's fault for handing off the ball too high on Frankie's chest. It didn't matter. Frankie knew it was his fault. He walked to the sidelines, hands on hips, head hung low, and found a place on the bench. Mario was there being treated for a knee injury he had suffered on the goal line stuff. Through the tears welling up in his eyes, Frankie could see the scoreboard change from 20–0 to 22–0. Whittier had just scored on the 2-point conversion.

"Don't worry about it. It's not your fault," Mario said, trying to offer some comfort.

Then Frankie and Mario watched as Melvin Ramirez returned the kickoff 85 yards for a touchdown. Wow! What a roller coaster the last four plays had been! There was still more than a quarter to play, and Chelsea was back in the game. Maybe Chelsea was good enough to beat the best teams on their schedule. They had talent. They had speed and some size—big play potential. But they tended to self-destruct. Turnovers and penalties take good teams by the hand and carry them to defeat. On Whittier's first play from scrimmage after Melvin's touchdown, Kenzi was flagged for unsportsmanlike conduct.

"Please, I'm begging you," Atkins yelled from the sideline. "Control your fucking self. If he pushes you, just get up and get back to the huddle. Can you do that? We just got back in the freaking game."

Whether it was the frustration of watching his team implode once again with a series of costly mistakes, or the acknowledgment that his team didn't have enough leaders, or even a quarterback to go all the way to a Super Bowl this year, or whether it was the adrenaline rush of believing his team really could stage a miracle comeback, Atkins was most definitely on edge in the second half. While he begged his seniors to maintain self-control, he was barely able to maintain his own. His voice cracked as he barked and pleaded.

"Cross sweep, Danny," he said as Whittier marched up the field with the ball late in the third quarter. "Where the fuck are you? He's going in motion, and I'm yelling cross sweep. Why aren't you going out there? I'm begging you. I'm telling you the plays. I'm telling you where they're going. And it's like you just don't give a fuck! Jesus Christ! Guys, we're telling you what they're doing. Make a play! Please!"

It was to no avail. A few plays later, Pina scored on a 15-yard run. With just over a minute to go in the third quarter, Whittier's lead was 30–8. The game was effectively over, but Atkins continued coaching. He coached hard, and he coached angry, but he coached so his kids wouldn't quit. If he didn't quit, they couldn't quit.

"Frankie on this play, slot right, over right, 28-jet. Sprint to the fucking sideline. Move your fucking ass!"

To their credit, the Red Devils never surrendered. They fought to the end, but Whittier's overwhelming size advantage had begun to take its toll. The Red Devils were exhausted. Midway through the fourth quarter, Whittier scored again to make it 36–8. Finally, with very little time left in the game and the Wildcats running out their second string, Alex broke free for a 48-yard touchdown run. When he reached the end zone, Alex simply stopped, turned around, and flipped the ball to the referee trailing the play. There was no celebration. Thanks to a last-minute fumble by Whittier's backup running back, Alex was also able to score on the last play of the game to make the final score a respectable 36–22. It was a demoralizing, but not a devastating, defeat. Again, Chelsea had been soundly beaten by an upper division team. The loss hurt their pride, but not their chances to qualify for the Super Bowl. Chelsea had won its only game so far in the Commonwealth Small division, and that was against Minuteman Regional. However, Chelsea's next four games would be against division rivals. That stretch would make or break the Red Devils' season. Through his anger and frustration, Atkins reminded his team of that fact during his postgame comments.

"Orlando, why did we lose today? Tell us about all our mistakes."

"No blocks outside," Orlando responded. "Penalties. Can't keep our temper down."

"They scored 16 points right from fumbles. Direct fumbles," Atkins interrupted, because he couldn't wait for Orlando to hit the nail on the head. "Cody and Miguel, direct fumbles. I don't know what else to say about that. Fumbles and penalties. I can't coach that. It has to be you. It has to be you. You either are going to step up or it's gonna be tough in our own division. That was an upper division team and we should have won. But we handed them the game.

"Is it a coincidence that someone is always hurt after you make a mistake? Oh, my knee hurts, because I fumbled. That's being a coward, fellas. Frankie, you played well after that fumble. But when you fumble the ball, get the fuck up and make a play on defense. Guys, you don't respond. Our run starts now. The season starts on Monday. Everything else is over. Here's the playoff run. I promise you. If we don't make these mistakes starting Monday, and we prepare for Northeast next Saturday, we'll win. It's that simple."

As the players walked away, some of them believed Atkins when he said they could beat Northeast next week if they prepared well. Others weren't so sure. They had prepared well for Whittier, and look how that turned out. And it was impossible to know which group, the believers or the doubters, would influence the others during the week of practice. Atkins hoped the believers could also be leaders. He needed someone like Frankie, who had played this game with an ear infection, to lead by example. Frankie was as guilty as anyone of getting too despondent too early, for letting one bad play affect the rest of his game. If Frankie could break that habit, he could probably bring a handful of others along with him. For his part, Frankie sounded like he was ready to become a true believer.

"I think we had 'em," Frankie said moments after the Whittier game. "It's just the penalties, too many people not doing their assignments. We worked hard all week, and we come to the games, and people freeze. Coach is right. I go into a shell. I'm just gonna have to work harder. We have to come out strong. No excuses. I'm a senior. I can't make excuses. Go 100 percent, whistle to whistle."

Frankie had said words like that before, but that night he took a step toward actually doing something about it. After his fumble in the end zone, he played reasonably well. He didn't bury his head in the field turf. He continued to try, and that was progress.

Chelsea still had a chance that season. In fact they had as good a chance as anyone in their league of making it to the Super Bowl. There was nobody left on their schedule as good as Whittier. All they had to do was start playing their best football. That, and find a quarterback.

"Miguel's not playing quarterback again for the rest of the year," Atkins said to O'Neil when the last of his players had left. "He fucking sucks. Don't fucking talk me into it again. He's not playing quarterback the rest of the year."

"Well, Cody fucking sucks, too," O'Neil said, defending his position.

"Well, you know what?" Atkins said with resignation. "We're shit out of luck."

CHAPTER EIGHT

Cody's Chance

How many kids walk outside their house and see someone dead on the fucking sidewalk? Chelsea is changing, but it is what it is. The number of crimes and robberies we have would make the news in other communities. It's not even newsworthy in Chelsea. It's not normal. I try to tell these kids. They don't have to live like this. So, get the fuck out. They can live wherever they want. They're getting it, but it's gonna take changing a whole generation.

— JAMES ATKINS

It was another hard week of practice. Atkins had hoped this late in the season he'd be able to let his foot off the pedal, but he just couldn't. He needed his team to be tougher, so the practices had to be physically demanding. He also needed his team to play smarter, so he had to continue teaching techniques and schemes. And he wanted his team to worry, so he had to show them that he was worried. The best way to do that was to push them hard, to let them know that right now, they weren't good enough to reach their goals. It was a fine line for a coach to walk—making a team believe that greatness is a possibility, but mediocrity is the current reality—and Atkins walked it well.

His worry gave way to decision. After two hours of watching Cody stumble and bumble his way through Tuesday's practice, Atkins pulled the plug on that experiment. There was no way Cody could run the offense. He had some of the requisite skills and characteristics of a quarterback, but not enough of them. He was tough, willing to take a hit, he could run and throw, and he was a born leader, but he wasn't familiar enough with the Red Devils' offense, and his feet kept getting in his way.

"We put Cody in there in practice," Atkins recalled. "And he was just God-awful. God-fucking-awful! He couldn't even step. He couldn't even turn his feet. So, we went back to the original plan."

Maybe things would have been different if Cody had grown up in Chelsea, if he had gone through the Pop Warner system where Atkins now had most of the coaches running his offense, so that kids would be well educated in the system by the time they got to high school. Maybe if Cody had played quarterback in Chelsea when he was in junior high school, he might have been ready to take over the reins. But Cody, known as "Sunshine" since his first day at football practice, had spent his early childhood in California.

"He's Sunshine because he was the first white kid we had," Atkins said. "California, blond hair, you know he's gonna be fucking Sunshine."

The fact that Cody was a white kid from the West Coast made him unlike every one of his teammates. That he was from a stable, two-parent family with three well-adjusted brothers who stayed out of trouble, and that both his parents went to all of his games both home and away, well, that made him a bit of a freak in Chelsea. But Cody had more in common with the Red Devils than appearances would suggest. While growing up in California, Cody's father was a drug addict.

"I did drugs real hard," Shane Verge admitted. "It was California. It was methamphetamines. It was about twenty years, from age twelve to thirty-two. When you're in the grips, you're in the grips. I wasn't doing any more crime, but I was still hooked."

Shane's prior life of crime began when he stole a car as a twelve-year-old. A policewoman caught him, drove her knee into his back, and smashed him to the floor, but the theft was written off as a prank. He later stole a moped, got into a series of fights, and spent long periods of time in jail. The longest stretch he ever spent in prison was the nine months he served for stealing a car and driving it under the influence of alcohol and narcotics. He was twenty-three years old then and much closer to the end of his life than the beginning if he didn't jump off the destructive path he was on. He was already a husband and father of two, and while time was running out, his wife and family weren't.

"Betty is my wife," Shane said. "She's a good kid, man. I don't know why she stuck with me. She's got a good spirit. She's never been in trouble in her life. She must have seen some good in me."

His last time in jail was the turning point for Shane. The troubled kid who never graduated high school got his equivalency diploma in jail. The criminal who'd been addicted to drugs half his life attended substance abuse classes and Narcotics Anonymous behind bars. He also went to parenting classes and started to wake up to the idea that he had responsibilities bigger than himself or his addiction.

"I finally woke up from the coma I was in," he said. "My kids were getting older, and I was like, 'What the hell are you doing?' Who was I gonna be to my kids? When they look at me, what did they see?"

For the next twelve years or so, his four boys saw a man waking up, but hitting the snooze alarm frequently enough to continue using methamphetamines. Shane didn't have any more trouble with the police, but ridding himself of the drugs was a long, slow process. Finally, in 2003, he became a welder and moved the family to Chelsea where he took a job at Allied Metals in nearby Revere. Now, when his children looked at him, they saw a man who grew up about the same time they did. The four boys, Michael, Cody, Hunter, and Dylan, all knew the details of their father's travails. His mistakes had shaped who he was now, an honest, tough-minded, self-disciplined, devoted husband and father. And who he was now was shaping who his children would become.

"I have the same mentality the coach has," Shane assessed. "Strict. Discipline. No nonsense. This is a very adrenaline-driven game. Cody's exposure to Coach Atkins is fabulous. His language doesn't bother me one bit. The coach doesn't hide anything, man. He's up-front, honest. He told us when he first took over the program, he sat us down in the parent meeting in the auditorium, and he told us, 'I'm gonna be tough on your kids. I'm gonna yell. I'm gonna scream.' But he said, 'I'm gonna make football players out of them.' And he's done exactly what he said."

And while some of the Red Devils looked to Coach Atkins as a father figure, Cody did not. Atkins wasn't filling up any holes in the Verge household. He was merely reinforcing the foundation.

"My job is to teach my children how to be men," Shane added. "Coach doesn't help me with that. I'll raise my kids. I don't need anybody to do it for me. For me, he's just the football coach. Cody is definitely committed. He's learned to overcome adversity and how to play through controversy and pain, and how to man up."

Now, Cody was learning to live with the disappointment of failure. He had his chance to become the star quarterback, and watched it slip through his fingers. The lesson that came from both his father and his coach was simple: When opportunity knocks, you have to be ready to open the door, or else it'll just go knocking on somebody else's door.

Right now, that somebody else was Miguel. He would continue to be the starting quarterback by default. Other than Cody, there was really only one other choice, and that was Melvin Ramirez, the one Coach called "Pop Warner." Melvin possessed incredible athletic ability. He was the fastest kid on the team, and he threw a nice ball. He was a natural, really. But he was only a sophomore, and more damning, he had missed summer camp. Melvin had no idea how good he was, and his lack of self-confidence caused him to waver on whether to play high school football.

While Melvin wondered if he was ready, Atkins believed he was ready to be a star. But since Melvin had missed camp, he couldn't start the year as the quarterback. Atkins couldn't reward Melvin's lack of dedication to the team, and he wouldn't let Miguel, a senior, lose his job to an underclassman who skipped camp. It just wasn't right, and Atkins wouldn't do it. However, now that Melvin had put in the time, paid his dues, and made himself a full and respected member of the team, Atkins could insert him at quarterback, if he thought it was best for the team. Right now, just as the team was about to enter the most important stretch on the schedule, Atkins decided to play it safe.

Things were anything but safe as Jonathan Luna rode in a car toward his house on Grove Street the Thursday night before the Northeast Tech game. He had met up with his girlfriend after practice, and she was driving him home a little after 9:00. When she got to Grove Street, she couldn't take a left because the police had blocked off the road. Jonathan got out in front of the YMCA and walked up the hill. Several people standing outside their homes were speaking loudly about a man who had just been shot in the head. But they had their facts wrong.

"The guy was beaten with a hammer," Detective Conley explained later. "They opened up his skull. That's why it looked like a gunshot. The victim wasn't a Chelsea native, but he was a Chelsea guy, not in any trouble, not known to the police. It happened around 8:30. He wasn't robbed. Still had his wallet, and he was wearing a pretty nice watch. The guy came up from behind him. The man may recover, but the head injury has really caused him to have unbalanced emotions, and he wasn't able to give a description of any kind."

Jonathan stepped around the crime scene—a body lying bloody and lifeless on the street where he lived—and walked undaunted into his home. He didn't sleep especially well that night, not because of the body, the blood on the sidewalk, or the commotion. Those things weren't about to faze a Chelsea kid, especially one whose brother was still being hunted by the FBI, or especially one who just last year went to the hospital to visit his friend who had been shot in the head. Flashing blue lights, yellow crime scene tape, a throng of cops and a bashed-in skull . . . all this was barely out of the norm. No, the reason Jonathan had trouble sleeping was because of the Northeast Tech game on Saturday. It was the kind of focus that Atkins found both commendable and worrisome.

"Self-preservation. Self-motivation. You have to have it," Atkins said. "I can't articulate it, but I feel it. I try to get my point across when I'm talking to them. They're just bombarded from every angle in Chelsea. You can't get out of it. There's always a gang. There's always a fight. There's always something going on. And the motivation is what do you want to do. Look at your friends. They're arrested. Look at the guy who just got battered. Look at the kid who just got stabbed. Look at the girlfriend who just got all scratched up, because they're fighting. Just because it happens, doesn't mean it's normal. It's not normal to walk out of your house and see some guy beaten to death. It's not normal shit. Just because you're used to it, or you see it and it becomes normal for you, it's not a normal way of life. They have to get out of this area. They can't stay here and hang out on the corner. That's why when you go to college, you see there's something else out there. And then when you come back, you don't fall back into it."

Black Josh wouldn't be going to college, and he had certainly fallen back into it. Just recently, Atkins received a call from Detective Dan Delaney who asked, "What's the deal with Josh Lewis?" Delaney had just stopped Josh on the street late at night and had asked a few innocuous questions like, "Does the coach know you're out?" and "Do you like playing for Coach Atkins?" Delaney didn't know that Josh had been kicked off the team. Being a good liar, Josh said he liked playing for Coach very much, and Delaney slapped him on the back and told him to "get his ass home then."

Once Atkins explained to Delaney that Josh was off the team, he knew not to cut him any more slack the next time he caught him out looking for trouble. And Delaney knew there would be a next time.

There was a lot of chatter on the bus during the thirty-minute ride up to Wakefield for the Northeast Tech game, but Atkins wasn't listening to it. Usually, he spent the time on the road thinking about the game at hand. But on that clear and sunny Saturday morning, Atkins stared out the window and thought about the police officer who had been shot and killed a few days earlier. New Hampshire policeman Michael Briggs had responded to a domestic violence call just before his shift was scheduled to end. Briggs, a 35-year-old husband, father, and ex-Marine, was shot in the head, and died the following day. Atkins was pleased to see flags at the Northeast football stadium were flying at half-mast. Following the national anthem, Atkins spoke quietly to his team about Briggs, adding:

"Give me a moment of silence, please."

The Red Devils respected their coach's wishes and honored the fallen police officer. Then, they went out and played their finest game of the year. It was far from perfect, but it was a glimpse at what could be, and it lifted Chelsea into first place in its division.

It began when Northeast elected not to punt at midfield on 4th and short yardage. Ato Alic sprang through the line and stuffed the ball carrier behind the line of scrimmage and the Red Devils took over on downs. Then, when Chelsea was faced with a 4th down play at the Northeast 25-yard line, Frankie sprinted to the outside, cut behind a blocker, and motored down the left sideline for a touchdown. Frankie also bulled in on the 2-point conversion, giving Chelsea an 8–0 lead. It was still very early in the game, but already there was a sense that Chelsea was prepared to bring a little something special to the field on this day.

The Red Devils had received added motivation when some of the Northeast players had hung posters all over Chelsea High School calling the Red Devils a Pop Warner team and inviting everyone to come watch Northeast give Chelsea a good beating.

"They were trying to get into our heads," Danny Cortez said. Danny wasn't playing in this game because of a deep thigh bruise, but he paced the sideline and cheered incessantly. "It's a rivalry. They put up signs that said they were gonna beat us, but it didn't work. They psyched us up."

Northeast and Chelsea had a friendly rivalry generated by the fact that Northeast was the technical school of choice for a lot of Chelsea kids. That meant a lot of the players on the opposing teams knew each other or had played with and against each other in junior high school.

"Everybody, let's go," Atkins cheered during a time-out, then he calmly added, "Hey guys, listen to me. Quiet now. We've got them on the ropes. We cannot let them off. They're already starting to get aggravated. They're taking penalties. Don't worry about it. We're gonna beat them on the field. We're gonna stay composed, but we're gonna take it to 'em. All I want you to do is stay alert."

Some of the optimism was quelled when Melvin was called for a personal foul. Northeast was getting a little chippy, and Melvin reacted impatiently and violently. He shoved an opponent after a play was dead, and it cost Chelsea 15 yards.

"What did we just talk about?" Atkins yelled to no one in particular. Then, to Melvin he shouted, "Get over here! Answer me. What did we just talk about?"

Melvin sheepishly defended his actions by claiming the other kid hit him after the whistle. It was not an acceptable defense.

"That means nothing to me. So what! I don't care if he spit in your face. He got the first down because of your stupidity. What means something to us is the win. You see the difference? Your ego, because somebody pushed you, versus the win for the team.

You sacrifice it, get back in the huddle and smile. And if you're a real man, the next time you get a chance to lay him out, you lay him out legally. That's what you do."

Melvin's lapse in judgment was one of only two mistakes Chelsea would make in the first half. Miguel's interception near the goal line with under two minutes to play in the half was the other. It appeared to be a costly turnover, because Chelsea was going in for a score that would have given them a 14–0 lead. Instead, Northeast had a chance to ride out the clock, and despite being thoroughly outplayed, they could go to the locker room and regroup knowing they were only down by one touchdown.

Inexplicably, Northeast didn't sit on the ball. It was a poor decision. Chelsea's defense had been dominating the entire first half. Ivan Romero, the Romanian who tipped the scales at over 300 pounds, was finally the huge defensive-line presence his size dictated he should be. He filled up the middle, stuffed the run, and occasionally got to the Northeast quarterback, Brian Rose. Kenzi, Orlando, and Ato were also beating their blocks, applying pressure, and flying to the ball.

When Northeast faced a 4th and 11 from their own 12-yard line and less than a minute to play in the half, everyone knew that a punt was the safe call. Northeast chose to pass. Ivan jumped in the quarterback's face forcing a bad throw, and Frankie stepped up from his safety position, grabbed the ball, and ran it back 15 yards for the touchdown. Again Frankie rushed in with the 2-point conversion. Chelsea raced to the locker room with a 16–0 lead. Frankie had scored all the points.

The halftime locker room had a different feel to it today. It was professional. Collaborative. Atkins drew on a white erase board and meticulously went over the changes he wanted to see on the offensive and defensive sides of the ball. He offered specific advice to individual players about how to beat a block, or make a run more successful. And he listened to the players when they offered their insights about what was happening on the field. Coach was clearly happy with a 16-point lead, but he didn't want his team to be satisfied.

"This is a defining moment, fellas," Atkins stated soberly after getting his team to quiet down. "What happened against Whittier and Tyngsboro? They finished us off. Both of those teams are better than us. We're not gonna lie to ourselves. They played better than us, so they beat us. They came out in the second half and they went right down the field. Let's do that to somebody else. Get the ball and march right down the field and put 'em away."

Coach was trying to teach his players the difference between a good team and a great team, and perhaps, the difference between a great team and a championship team. Based on their performances against the upper division teams, and their dominance in the first half against Northeastern, the Chelsea kids could justifiably begin thinking they were pretty good. But Coach knew something they didn't: Great teams may believe they're good, but they never believe they're good enough.

"Manchester, North Shore, and Georgetown are all here," Atkins continued. "Are they gonna say we put these guys to bed? Manchester had all kinds of problems with Northeastern. So, let's knock them out and let them worry all week about us. Let's take it to them and finish them off. Guys we have to put them to sleep."

The kids raced out of the locker room jumping all over each other. They were ready to bury Northeastern and bury their own self-doubt along with it. They felt good. They felt powerful. On this cloudless day a few miles away from home, they were happy. That all changed in a hurry.

Chelsea received the ball to open the second half. They ran three completely ineffective plays and punted. Alex came back to the sidelines with his head down.

"First drive, I don't know what's wrong with us," he said. "We thought we were going to do good, but we didn't make our blocks. We have to play tougher. I have to run harder."

Northeast took over at midfield and, a half dozen plays later, finally moved the ball across the goal line. The Knights failed on their 2-point conversion attempt, and the score was 16–6. Atkins could see all the progress from the first half unraveling before him. He'd seen this from Chelsea kids before. They were so unaccustomed to feeling hopeful and proud that when they got a little taste of it, it could actually throw them off their game. Optimism was a foreign concept and it confused them.

"You have to get your head out of your ass," Atkins screamed at Frankie after the Knights' touchdown. "It started with the punt. What did you do? You jogged down there. You've got to fight! You've got to want to goddamn win! Let's go!"

Frankie stood on the sideline with his hands on his hips as Northeast kicked off. Tears were welling up in his eyes. He was angry at himself and angrier at the coach. He may have jogged down the field in punt coverage, but what harm did that do? Northeast didn't score on a punt return. *What's Coach mad at me for?*

Determined, but still distracted and upset, Frankie joined the huddle as Chelsea took over on offense. The first play was a hand-off to Frankie. He took the ball from Miguel and gripped it tightly with both hands, head up and eyes up the field for daylight. As soon as he saw it, he burst through the hole and picked up a 1st down. A Northeast defender grabbed Frankie by the arm and spun him around. Just then another defender came flying in from the side and delivered a jarring hit. The ball popped free and Frankie knew immediately he had screwed up again. Northeast recovered the fumble, and as Frankie got up from the ground, he could hear Atkins screaming his name.

Fortunately for Frankie, he also played defense, so he didn't have to face Atkins on the sideline. He stayed on the field with his head down until the next snap of the ball. Northeast's running back rushed for 40 yards down the sideline before he was finally hauled down at the 9-yard line. Atkins called time-out.

"Frankie, I see you walking around with your head down. You're doing it now. You're goddamn doing it now! Orlando, it's coming outside. Why do you keep getting hooked outside? You have to extend. You have to be tougher than him. It's simple. Is he tougher than you?"

"No," Orlando said sheepishly.

"Then fight off the goddamn block! Frankie, you need to step up and stop feeling sorry for yourself, because nobody in those goddamn stands feels sorry for you. As a matter of fact, they're laughing at you. They're saying, Frankie quit. Are you gonna quit?"

"No," Frankie barely managed to verbalize.

"Well, then let's go!"

Northeast scored a few plays later, but Orlando stuffed the 2-point conversion. With less than a minute to play in the third quarter, Chelsea's lead was down to 16–12.

Suddenly, the momentum swung in Chelsea's favor. Frankie had back-to-back big runs, and as time expired in the third quarter, Chelsea was at the Northeast 9-yard line, looking to extend its lead. Atkins called time-out and waited for the entire team to circle around him.

"We've got them on the ropes," he bellowed. "You gotta finish it! You gotta feel it from inside your gut! We're here. We're knocking on the door. We gotta take it to them. Let's go, guys! Let's get this touchdown, guys. Forty-seven toss sweep!"

The call was for Frankie and he responded with an 8-yard run. On the next play, Frankie pushed through the line and scored his third touchdown of the day. Frankie also added his third 2-point conversion. Frankie carried his head low for part of the afternoon, but he had scored all of Chelsea's 24 points, and the Red Devils' lead was 24–12.

The final minutes of the game moved rapidly. A late hit call against Kenzi helped Northeast pick up a 1st and goal, and the Knights scored to make it 24–18. The Red Devils responded with more big running plays from Frankie and Alex. Frankie would finish the day with 24 points and 170 yards rushing.

Meanwhile, Atkins still had his frustrating moments with his quarterback. At one point, he called a play, and then noticed the offense wasn't in the right formation, so before the snap Atkins signaled for a time-out and waved for Miguel to come over to him.

"Miguel, get over here! What did I call?"

"Over right," Miguel answered incorrectly.

"No, I didn't. Regular formation, you asshole. You fucking asshole. Twenty-six toss pass, asshole."

That play didn't work, but Alex rushed in on the next play and Chelsea won, 30–18. It was a convincing victory over a good team in their own division. For all the worrying, the hanging of heads, the distractions, and the lack of a big-time quarterback, Chelsea was in first place. The Super Bowl dream was alive and well. There was no final trip to the locker room. The Red Devils had arrived in their uniforms. No one brought a travel bag or a change of clothes. No showers after the game. The team simply gathered on the sideline and knelt down as Atkins gave his summation. They had no idea if he'd be blisteringly angry, or benevolently complimentary. He paused before he spoke. Perhaps, he wasn't sure which mood to put on display.

"Guys, way to have a good goddamn game!" he shouted, and almost as a collective sigh of relief, the Red Devils erupted in applause. Coach was happy, and that was always a good thing.

"That's how you do it," he continued. "The only negative thing I'm going to say is we have to work on putting a team away, fellas. A good team will come back and make you pay for it. Other than that, great goddamn job, fellas."

As he walked to the bus, Atkins was already thinking about Manchester, Chelsea's opponent the following week. Manchester was a passing team, so it would be important to put pressure on the quarterback and try to force quick decisions, which at the high school level, were usually bad decisions. Atkins was also concerned about his own quarterback. He thought about the interception Miguel had thrown about an hour ago, and he visualized the time Orlando was wide open for a touchdown but Miguel missed him by 5 yards. They had to be able to pass.

But as Atkins stepped aboard the bus and grabbed the seat directly behind the driver, he turned around and looked at the kids behind him. They were troubled kids who seemed trouble free at the moment. He thought about the senior dinner two nights earlier at Coach O'Neil's house. O'Neil had made his famous pasta salad with chicken and cheese. There was tortellini salad, too. And there had been a lot of smiling that night as well. When the progress reports had come out, there were twelve seniors with at least one F. So, Atkins ordered the kids to complete the work that was missing, and then asked for a second progress report. They all brought their grades up. Even David Flores raised his 3 Fs to poor, but passing grades. Things were looking up in Chelsea.

"We got a win," Atkins said through a boisterous laugh. "We need three more league wins. Two down, three to go. I couldn't be happier."

CHAPTER NINE

They Accomplished Nothing

I told Jimmy, "You need to know right up front that this is a one-year contract. If you do things in your manner that aren't acceptable by the athletic department, we may have to post the job again."
We have to kind of keep him on the reins.
—FRANK DePATTO, CHELSEA HIGH SCHOOL ATHLETIC DIRECTOR

At arrival time and at dismissal, Chelsea High School looked like any other public school. Kids dressed similarly in baggy clothes and T-shirts. They carried large backpacks presumably filled with books to do their homework. They entered and exited the school laughing, talking, and shouting. Loud, indistinguishable noise emanated from and mixed with the hustle and bustle of the orderly chaos. Some boys walked with their arms draped over a girlfriend's shoulder. Some girls generously offered demonstrative hugs to friends they hadn't seen in nearly twelve hours. Surveillance cameras monitored their every movement. A security guard and a school resource officer supplied by the Chelsea Police Department were always prominently positioned.

"We keep the schools as secure as we can by keeping a single, common entrance," superintendent Thomas Kingston said. "It's protected. We have lockdown procedures. We do not use metal detectors. We think they give a false sense of security. We do random searches, both in the middle grades and in the high school. I tell the parents there is no such thing as 100 percent safety. You always have to be vigilant. Parents are very concerned, especially in the middle schools. There's even a myth on the streets that the middle schools aren't safe because people see things happening on the streets. There's lots of stuff you see on the streets, but you're not going to see it in our schools."

Many of the kids entering the school on a cold and windy morning in late October would never exit as high school graduates. Chelsea's dropout rate was routinely around 10 percent, and that number only represented the senior class. It didn't take into account the number of underclassmen who dropped out every year due to pregnancies, financial problems at home, or pathetic academic performance. The number of students dropping out increased dramatically in the early spring when they began to realize there was no way they were going to pass their classes anyway.

Coach Atkins thought about this as he watched students filter past his office located between the cafeteria and the football locker room. It was more of a workspace than an office. Atkins had a desk. It was littered with paper and photographs, along with a clipboard, a whistle, and other tools of the trade. The desk was positioned just a few feet from Frank DePatto's small office. If he leaned back in his chair, Atkins could see into Frank's office and shout about whatever happened to be bothering him at that moment, and he frequently did.

"B.U.," Coach announced spontaneously. "They accomplished nothing! In nineteen years, they've accomplished nothing!"

DePatto rolled his eyes. Whether he agreed or not, he wouldn't reveal. He knew that at his best, Atkins was a straight shooter. At his worst, he was a loudmouth. Conversely, DePatto was a quiet man looking to keep the peace. As an employee of Chelsea High School, he was an employee of Boston University, which had been running the Chelsea school system since 1987. DePatto was sixty-eight years old, still with a full head of blond hair and a youthful gait. He was either unwilling or unable to retire, so he chose to ignore Atkins when the coach was looking to stir things up.

"Everybody gives them credit for the schools," Atkins repeated many times. "We got the new schools because we went into receivership. Those things happened at about the same time. The receiver said to B.U., 'Okay, come in and you can change the school around.' Well, the grades and the academic achievement are the same now as they were when they came in. They accomplished nothing!"

DePatto knew that Atkins was not wrong. He'd seen the numbers. In statewide testing, Chelsea students consistently scored well below the average of suburban and other city schools. There were plenty of reasons for that. First and foremost among them were the language barriers and the transient population. Only 25 percent of students that started out in the Chelsea kindergartens graduated from Chelsea High School. The rest were constantly moving in and out. There's nothing B.U. could have done about that, but the fact is, the university takeover didn't fix the problem. The fact that Atkins gleefully liked to point that out had not endeared him to the administration he worked for.

"We have policies that he's not happy with," DePatto explained accurately. "But those policies were in place before he took over."

His constant complaining about the "1-F" rule and his vocal criticism of B.U. were sufficiently ignored by his bosses, but Atkins frequently found himself on thin ice when he failed to follow proper procedure.

"Coach Atkins is very aggressive," DePatto said. "It's either his way or the highway. But I told him that's not the way it would work here. He can't just make decisions without clearing them with me first."

Atkins did his best to oblige. He did ask permission from time to time, but when he didn't get the answers he was looking for from DePatto, he went out and did what he wanted. He asked Frank for money to buy the varsity jackets, heard the word *no,* and bought them anyway. The same scenario occurred prior to the team banquet held at The French Club following the 2004 season.

Julie Atkins wrote a check for $2,400 from her Discover Card account. That paid for the food catered by Spinelli's. Jimmy covered the $600 cost of the rental hall, plus the trophies and other items presented at the banquet. Holding the event without proper authorization and never bothering to put in an invoice or provide receipts for his expenses landed Coach in hot water with B.U. administrators. They believed Atkins' autonomous behavior indicated he didn't respect their authority. And they were right.

Jimmy acted alone. He ran the team and team's finances as he saw fit. Control freak that he was, it wasn't until early in his third season that Jimmy accepted any help running the Booster Club. Shane Verge, the recovering drug addict, who had taken it upon himself to hold raffles and fund-raising events, was added to the Booster Club account. Verge would try to organize Atkins' haphazard recording of money going in and out of the account, but Atkins retained control of it.

It was Atkins' no-nonsense, get-things-done, independent style that helped get him hired in the first place. City manager Jay Ash advocated behind the scenes for Atkins, citing his "tremendous dedication to the kids."

"I see in Jimmy a guy who is an incredible leader that I could see kids falling in love with and falling behind," Ash said. "I felt this was important. Jimmy the person and Jimmy the gang police officer were so important to inject into these kids' lives. I felt it was the place for me to speak up."

Superintendent Kingston was ultimately responsible for hiring Atkins for the start of the 2004 season, and during an extensive interview, he didn't ask any questions pertaining to wins and losses. He only wanted to know what kind of man Atkins was.

"What I'm interested in is how many kids did we get out for the football team this year?" Kingston explained. "How are they doing academically once we get them out there? What kind of habits and discipline are you engaged in? One of the virtues of Jim is that he's a streetwise and tough kid, not just because he's a cop, but because he grew up in this environment. He is a commanding presence, a disciplinarian, and committed to academic support, making sure the kids have a taste of success, but also maintain their academics."

Certainly, Jimmy's strengths overpowered his weaknesses, but those weaknesses, especially his autonomy, were affecting his popularity among his bosses. The principal at Chelsea High, Morton Orlov, offered nothing complimentary about Atkins, saying only that he "inherited" him. Jay Ash, who championed Atkins' hiring, now cautioned that Atkins was not what he appeared to be, and shouldn't be "painted as some kind of hero." Clearly, Atkins' support was waning mid-season in 2006. His aggressive use of language among his players was another area of discontent from above.

"I think if you get to know Coach Atkins and his motivating style, sometimes he gets carried away," DePatto said. "He's not personally insulting any individuals. But I did have to talk to him a few times. I have some concerns about that, because I think it would be unacceptable to some members of the school board. I wouldn't want him to be using every third word as a swear word. If that were the case I would have to step in and have him clean it up a little bit. I think he has a job to do, though. He just has to follow guidelines. He's done enough good things here now, and he has the potential to build a dynasty. It would be a sad, sad day if Coach Atkins decided to pull up his shingle and go somewhere else."

Leaving Chelsea was the furthest thing from Atkins' mind. Even though he worked tirelessly to convince and enable his players to get out of Chelsea, he had no plans to go anywhere. He was committed to both the school and the community. He was invested now. From the time these Chelsea kids were still in middle school and playing Pop Warner football, Atkins was intricately involved with their lives. The futures of Orlando, and Jonathan, and Mario, and Kenzi, and many others were significantly more hopeful, because of Atkins' influence. In his heart, he knew he was doing more to help them than B.U. ever could. B.U.'s control of the Chelsea schools would only last one more year, and Atkins couldn't wait to see them leave.

Also on the way out of Chelsea was Richie Oliveras, the quiet, olive-skinned Puerto Rican kid. Richie was a senior, born and raised in Chelsea, but he was not a typical Chelsea kid. He had two parents at home who stressed education. He had been Student of the Year as a junior pulling down a 3.69 GPA. He was a member of the Honor Society. He had never been in trouble, and he had a dream to become an architect.

"Richie wants to go to Virginia Tech," Richie Oliveras Sr. said at his home in October 2006. He was looking for the photo albums that chronicled Richie's academic career. He found them and opened them up proudly. The albums were filled with every report card from first grade to the present. There were certificates of achievement, ribbons, photographs, and a letter from the city manager recognizing Richie as the Student of the Year. When Richie Senior finally looked up from the albums, he stared at his son, whom he respectfully called "Papi."

"Papi's got a good head," the father said softly. Richie Senior appeared incapable of shouting, or even speaking in a loud voice. Everything about him suggested an inner peace.

"I don't know how he does it," Richie Senior continued. "Since he was a baby, I've been talking to him about college. It's imbedded in him. He knows what his ultimate goal is, which is college, having a great job, so that eventually he can have a good life. I tell him, you don't measure life by the size of the house. You don't measure a good life by the amount of money you have. You measure life by the amount of happiness you can give yourself and the people around you that you love. As you can see, I don't have the biggest house, but I'm the happiest man in the world."

It wasn't always like that, however. Richie Senior grew up in the Bronx. He was thirteen years old when his parents moved back to Puerto Rico, leaving Richie and his older sister behind with relatives.

"My parents just wanted to go back home," he said. "They weren't happy in New York. They figured I would finish school there and live with my sister, who was well grounded. It all worked out great."

True, except for the fact that Richie dropped out of school in order to sell drugs on street corners. His sister couldn't control him, and by his own admission, he got heavily involved in drug activity, never doing them, just selling them. He never got caught, never spent time in jail, but right through his teen years, he was a tough kid going nowhere.

"My sister said, 'You want to be a man, you have to behave like one.' So, I started working odd jobs, a little construction here and there. It was tough. I got into a lot of trouble at a young age—until I met my wife."

Richie met Shelley during a visit to Puerto Rico. She was sitting on a rock reading a book, and she wasn't perturbed at all when the small, round-faced twenty-year-old man-child came up and introduced himself. Shelley was a year younger than Richie, and she fell in love almost immediately. So did Richie, and nothing had changed in the past twenty years.

They lived in a small two-story house on the edge of the city. The Oliveras home was not at all spacious, but there was plenty of space. It was filled with family photographs and tasteful decorations, but it was not cluttered. The backyard was a triangular slab of cement big enough for a barbecue grill and nothing else. The children, Richie and thirteen-year-old Natalie, each had their own room upstairs. Shelley worked at the Early Learning Center in Chelsea, and Richie Senior was a caseworker for the Department of Mental Retardation. He hadn't received his GED until he was twenty-seven years old, but then he went to Mass Bay Community College and earned a degree in human services.

He was one of only a handful of involved parents at Chelsea High School. He attended every football game and even many practices. And he helped Shane Verge organize and run Booster Club events.

Back in 2003, Richie Senior noticed an increase in graffiti in his neighborhood. More and more he saw kids wearing gang colors. He was worried for the safety of his own children and his own home. So, he got involved. He went out and solicited donations from local businesses and started a Gang Prevention Basketball League. When he spotted kids out on the streets with nothing to do, he invited them to play ball. Soon he had enough kids to make up six teams. More parents got involved as coaches and refs. Others rolled out their grills and cooked hamburgers and hot dogs. The community came together a couple times a week and kids were taught to respect one another. They all had to sign a contract that said they wouldn't fight and they wouldn't swear, and their parents had to sign it, too.

"I think everything happens for a reason," Richie said. "You go through the struggles, but it builds character. I think as a parent you can use it as a tool to lead your children in a positive way. The problem here is education. A lot of folks migrate here and their first thing is not how they can get their kids educated. It's how can they get food on the table. So, academics is secondary, or maybe not even thought of. That's a big problem. You have to make time for your kid's education. You have to make sacrifices."

Richie Junior sat quietly as his father spoke. It was hard to tell if he was listening, or if his mind was somewhere else. He was definitely a thinker. He responded to questions slowly and thoughtfully, but with a strong, deep voice and a certainty more suited to someone much older. Clearly, he had spent time away from the football field and out of his schoolbooks long enough to reflect on his life in Chelsea. He had seen friends swallowed up by gangs. He'd heard the stories, and he'd walked through dangerous streets at the wrong time of day. Still, he had risen above it. And soon he'd be out of it, out of Chelsea for good.

"We're moving to Virginia right after Richie graduates," the father announced. "We want to start a new life. We think Chelsea's been great to us and great to our children academically. I just feel like it's time for us to settle down. We're young enough to assimilate into a community very well. Natalie is psyched. She wants a little dog and a tree house, and we'll do that for her."

The plans were already in the works. Richie would try to get into Virginia Tech and the family would move to a town nearby. If it was not Virginia Tech, Richie could certainly get into Roanoke College or one of several other colleges in the area. No matter. Come next June, the Oliverases would be packing up and putting Chelsea in their rearview mirror. Before they left, however, Richie would try to help the Red Devils win a Super Bowl. He was not just an excellent student. He was also a tough kid.

When Richie was a freshman, he broke three bones in his right foot while playing Pop Warner football. Richie heard the snap and felt the pain, but he didn't know how badly he was injured. He sat out the rest of the game, but it wasn't until the family had already ordered their food at a nearby Burger King that Richie finally spoke up and told his dad how much his foot hurt. The Oliverases got their food to go and went to the hospital where the X-rays revealed the breaks in Richie's foot.

Richie was a running back then, and he played some fullback now for Coach Atkins. He was a big, strong kid with powerful legs, but he wasn't as fast as Frankie or Alex, so he only got to carry the ball in short-yardage situations. The rest of the time he played center. But in the biggest game of the year, the one against Manchester that would likely decide which team from Chelsea's division would go to the playoffs, Richie was likely to carry the ball a little more often. That's because Frankie was being benched for the start of the game.

"It's the never-ending saga of Chelsea High football," Atkins said as he began to tell the story of why Frankie wasn't starting. "It's about one o'clock on Tuesday. I'm working my shift and I'm driving up Essex Street, and who do I see walking down the street? It's one o'clock in the afternoon! It's fucking Frankie Quiles. I say, 'Frankie, what are you doing?' He gives me the 'Oh shit' look. He says, 'I'm going to the hospital.'"

Frankie had hurt his foot at the end of the Northeast game. It didn't appear serious at the time, but Frankie had been bothered by it ever since. Still, instead of going to the doctor over the weekend, Frankie took Tuesday off from school and walked to the hospital on his supposedly injured foot.

"Frankie, that's just bullshit," Atkins said and drove away in his cruiser. He made the decision at that moment that Frankie wouldn't start against Manchester. Later, Atkins spoke to his assistant coaches, and they debated not allowing Frankie to play at all. Each of them remembered the Georgetown game last year when Luis Verde and Larry Gregory were benched because they skipped practice. The coaches agreed it was the right disciplinary decision, but it cost Chelsea the game and a shot at the championship. Punishing two players had actually punished the entire team. Would they do it again?

"It's a little bit different scenario than last year," Atkins explained. "Because it was our quarterback. But we've got ample backups at two-back and linebacker, and Frankie's not even playing very well at linebacker. So, it's not going to hurt us on defense. It'll hurt us on offense for the tough yards."

After seeing Frankie walking the streets on Tuesday, Atkins arrived at practice Wednesday still in a foul mood. He was met by Frankie's blank stare and complete lack of acknowledgment that he had done anything wrong, and that set Atkins off. When the rest of the team didn't show enough effort in practice, Atkins stormed off the field.

"Guys, I don't know what else to say to you. I've done everything for you. And you guys give me absolutely nothing back. Why am I even here? I've got a hundred job offers. Why am I putting myself through this, sacrificing time, family, money for you guys, and you guys don't want to even give anything back. That's just bullshit."

With that as his exit line, Atkins walked away. The players stared for several moments until Atkins reached the double doors leading to the locker room and disappeared. Everyone was quiet, wondering if the doors would swing back open and their coach would return to them. Even the assistant coaches didn't know what to do. The doors never reopened. So, whistles blew and the assistants got the boys running and hitting again. Their lethargy was replaced by confusion, and practice never reached the intensity one would expect with the Manchester game just two days away.

Thursday was better. Frankie went to Atkins and said he honestly didn't think he had done anything wrong. He defended his decision to have his foot checked out by a doctor, but he listened when Atkins explained that he should have gone at a time that didn't conflict with school. Frankie ultimately admitted that he didn't need to miss an entire day of school.

"I wanted to freak out, but I'm staying calm and letting him talk," Atkins said. "It's the same old shit. I've heard it all before. But by the end of the discussion, Frankie says, 'I understand it now. I let my teammates down.' Then we had a great team dinner."

Back in Atkins' basement the Thursday before Manchester, the Red Devil seniors had an emotional and beneficial meeting. Instead of being the one giving the advice, Coach began by asking the kids for their help. With an uncharacteristic vulnerability in his voice, Coach told the kids he felt like he had failed to reach them this year, and he wanted to know how he could do a better job next season of getting the team to understand the importance of setting goals and working hard to achieve them. Orlando piped up with the suggestion that Coach should have walked out of practice a lot sooner. That, they all agreed, had been very effective.

"Why?"

"Because it made us believe that if we didn't start doing good, you might quit on us, too."

"But what I'm trying to do is talk to you guys as adults and get you self-motivated in reaching goals and responsibilities," Atkins said with some exasperation. He had always thought it was important to treat them with respect, because so many adults didn't. He tried not to talk down to them. Instead, he talked them up. He told them they could do anything. More than anyone else in their lives, he believed in them. That was more respect than they got at home, or at school, or at the stores when security kept an ever vigilant and distrustful eye on them. Yes, Atkins cursed at them and called them names, and it hurt them. During his frequent diatribes the pain and sadness were evident on their faces. But the outbursts always subsided, and then Coach was there the next day, and the day after that, believing in them again. His words were gone, but he wasn't. His anger was temporary, but he had become a permanent fixture in their lives. His actions spoke loudest. Besides, they had heard Coach say the same types of things to his assistant coaches, and to his cop buddies. That's the way he spoke to his friends and co-workers, and that's the way he treated his football team. No better. No worse. Like men. And for Chelsea kids, that was respect.

Yet it was when he disrespected them, when he turned his back on them and walked away, that was when he finally got their attention. In essence, he had done what they believed so many of their teachers had done. He gave up on them.

"Do you really like it when your teachers talk down to you and they think you can't do something?" Atkins asked.

"I hate it!" Jonathan Luna said with a sudden burst of anger. "It's not right."

Jonathan was nearly in tears thinking about the times he had been made to feel stupid in front of his classmates. Everyone in the room, except for Richie, had experienced the same feeling.

"Well you give them motivation by the things you guys do," Atkins said. "How can you not know what we're trying to accomplish here at this late stage in the game?"

Atkins pressed Jonathan, demanding to know what he was going to do about it. If he hated being belittled in class, how was he going to make it stop? What was he going to do to improve things for himself? Jonathan didn't respond right away. He rose from the couch and walked over to where his jacket was. He pulled a piece of paper out of one of the pockets and returned to his seat.

"My mid-term goal is to graduate high school and get into a good college," Jonathan read. "And my long-term goal is to become a police officer."

His assertion came as a surprise to Atkins, who immediately wondered if he had had something to do with Jonathan's desire to be a cop. More than feeling proud of his possible influence, Atkins was just glad Jonathan had a goal. He explained that Jonathan would need to look at colleges that offer degrees in criminal justice, and if he wanted to continue playing football and baseball, he'd have to start lifting weights.

"I think you'll make a great cop," Atkins told Jonathan. "It helps that you've seen a lot of things firsthand. So, you might understand what people need and how to help them."

That brought the conversation around to Jonathan's brother, Pascual, who was still on the run from the police. Atkins told the kids how Pascual had approached him when he first got out of prison and asked if he could play football for him.

"'Sure,' I told him. 'If you get enrolled in school, then sure.' Then I started thinking. I've been chasing him around for five or six years, so I says to him, 'How old are you?' He says, 'Twenty-one.'"

Then with a big grin and a wave of his hand Atkins finished the tale.

"No. You can't play. Get the fuck out of here."

It was a funny story that caused the boys to break out in laughter, but they also breathed a sigh of relief. Coach was back. He was talking to them as adults, sharing his life with them. They were in his home, laughing, almost crying, feeling like they were part of something, and once again secure in the knowledge that Coach cared about them.

"Atkins has seen what I've gone through, because he's a police officer," Jonathan said later. "And my brother, he's not that much of a good kid. So, Atkins has gone through and he's seen it from both perspectives. I don't think the teachers have gone through that. They're more of an outsider. Eighty percent of this team can relate to Coach, because he lived in the projects. He knows what it's like to be poor. And he knows that just because you're poor doesn't mean that you have to stay down. You can go to college, even if it's not a big Harvard college, you can still succeed and become mediocre, and have a little bit more money and take care of your family. This is what he's showing us."

It was interesting to hear Jonathan make success analogous with mediocrity. Did he truly understand that the word means common or insignificant? Would he really describe success that way? His body language and tone suggested he did use the word appropriately. His dream was to be ordinary. And considering where he's coming from, perhaps that would be extraordinary.

The meeting closed with Julie Atkins being summoned when Miguel Medina announced his long-term goal was to become a computer systems analyst. Julie, a vice-president in the information technology department for Blue Cross Blue Shield, offered Miguel a summer internship. Miguel seemed genuinely interested.

"You can't remember the plays from the time Coach tells you on the sideline to the time you get to the huddle," Jonathan teased Miguel. "How are you going to be a systems analyst?"

So, a tense week of practice ended with a lot of smiles and a return to family. The long-term goals were in place, and the short-term goal was at hand. The Red Devils were about to play the most important game of the year.

"Whoever wins this game is going to the playoffs," Atkins said flatly. "If we don't make mistakes, Manchester's in some trouble."

CHAPTER TEN

Orlando Quits

Manchester's a nice, rich town. Remember going up there last year? Next to the high school, all the nice houses out there. They've got no goddamn worries. Let's show them what it's like to play a real city team, fellas. When they look across and they see Midnight, and they say, 'Oh shit, what the fuck is that?' Then they look across and see Ivan, and they say, 'Holy fuck.' Let's give them some 'holy fucks' to say all game, fellas. This is our goddamn house.

—JAMES ATKINS

It was the biggest game of the year, and Coach had them laughing in his pregame speech. It was funny to think of another rich, white suburban team coming into Chelsea and staring across the line of scrimmage at a kid as black as Midnight or as large as Ivan. But it was a nervous laughter that filled the Red Devils' locker room on the coldest night of the fall season so far. They all knew what was at stake. Any divisional loss could be a devastating blow to their Super Bowl chances. This was the kind of moment when championship teams respond. As for Chelsea teams, well, sometimes they quit. Coach didn't know if he had champions or quitters, but he feared the worst. That's why he was as nervous as they were.

"Guys, this is it," Atkins began when the players had quieted down. "This is for first place. Whoever wins this game has the fast track to the playoffs. It's that simple. You win this game, and you're 3–0 in the league and everyone's chasing us. You saw what happened last year when we lost to Georgetown. We had to hope somebody lost, and all that tiebreaking crap. Do you want to get into all that again?"

"No!" Several players shouted.

"You control your own destiny, Orlando," Coach said. Although Atkins was speaking about the game, Orlando had heard him make the same comment about life many times before. Coach paused a moment, taking the emotional temperature of the room. Were the kids afraid, or just appropriately nervous? Could they sense his own anxiety, and if so, should he give a calming speech, or would a change in his personality confuse and worry them? Did they need a kick in the ass or a hug? They were all staring at him. No heads were tipped to the floor. No eyes were wandering around the room. They were waiting for their leader to tell them how to feel. So, he told them to be angry.

"That shit-bum team is ranked above you. So, all the things you've done, they just dismiss us, like they always do. I try to get you motivated, and I try to say things to you to get you fired up to go out on the football field. That alone should be enough, fellas. On top of that right here, fellas, this is for the goddamn league championship. That's what it is. This is it. We've got to show them. I don't know who the fuck Manchester thinks they are, but we're the best team in our league, not goddamn Manchester. Every week we prove it. No team has beaten us yet. We've beaten ourselves in our losses. And we're not gonna let Chelsea beat Chelsea playing goddamn Manchester today. Nobody ever again is gonna come down to Chelsea and take our championship away. We let it happen last year, and we're not gonna let it happen this year. We've got to do it from the first goddamn hit. You've got to get out there right now. We're gonna take that ball and shove it down their goddamn throats!"

When he was finished, Coach waited for the roar that generally follows an impassioned plea like that, but it never came. Perhaps the players were looking for something different, something more. Perhaps they didn't know he was finished, and once a few seconds had passed, the moment was gone. But more likely, the players were distracted by their uncommon nervousness, and frozen by fear and apprehension. That would help to explain the bad week of practice, and why Frankie had skipped out to see a doctor and would be benched for the first quarter of tonight's game, and why Austin Hightower had missed two practices and would be benched for the entire game, and why there was no focus and little effort leading up to Coach storming out of Wednesday's practice. The kids were setting themselves up for failure. Whether it was intentional or not didn't matter. They were not approaching the game the way champions do. They were behaving like Chelsea kids.

They walked out of the locker room finally quickening their pace as they got outside. Awakened by the sudden chill in the air, the Red Devils sprinted across the running track and on to the field. Once they reached their sideline, several players began pounding each other's shoulder pads and violently butting each other's helmets. Kenzi took a few steps in the direction of the stands and raised his hands in an effort to get the crowd to rise and respond, but the crowd did not reflect the magnitude of the game. The few hundred people who got there before kickoff were more interested in keeping warm than welcoming the Red Devils on to the field.

Manchester was a good team, but it was hard to gauge just how good. They had beaten up on a couple of bad teams from Mystic Valley and Hyde Park by a combined score of 95–0, but they had been crushed by Whittier, 44–8. Chelsea had given Whittier a much tougher game. And the Red Devils had beaten Northeast more easily than Manchester did. So, there was reason to believe Chelsea was the better team, but only by a slight margin.

Manchester got the ball first and began at their 24-yard line. On the first play from scrimmage, Manchester's quarterback, Pat Orlando, slipped and fell in the backfield for a 7-yard loss. The Chelsea defense celebrated even though nobody had made the play. Atkins clapped his hands on the sideline. He was looking for a good start. He knew his team would play much better with the lead.

On the very next play, Pat Orlando faded back to pass. There was no pressure being applied, so he waited for a receiver to get open. Finally, he spotted Sam Cohen, who grabbed the pass well short of a 1st down. Cohen turned, faked as though he were headed for the middle of the field, and then took off down the sideline. He outran every one of the Red Devils who bothered to give chase. Barely a minute had run off the game clock and Manchester had just scored on an 83-yard pass play. Atkins looked on in disbelief. The defense trudged off the field with their heads down.

This is where Atkins would find out if his gamble would pay off. With Frankie on the bench, a large burden would be placed on sophomore Melvin Ramirez, who was making his first start of the year at running back. The kid they called "Pop Warner" would be getting his hands on the ball for the first time with Chelsea already down by a touchdown.

Melvin, who usually wore number 14, was wearing number 5 tonight. He began by picking up 5 yards on his first carry. A nice run by Alex was negated by a holding call. Then Melvin rushed through the middle of the defense, darted to his left and right, and was finally hauled down around midfield. The drive stalled three plays later, but it was a nice start for Melvin, who appeared comfortable, and was clearly the quickest player on the field.

Meanwhile, Chelsea's defense looked slow and confused. The defensive line wasn't getting into the backfield, and therefore couldn't put any effective pressure on the quarterback. Three times on their second drive, Manchester was able to convert 3rd downs into 1st downs, once because Ato had jumped offside. When Manchester completed a 30-yard pass when Mario was caught out of position, Atkins called his first time-out.

"You've got to want it, and you don't want it right now," he began. "You gotta fight for it. Danny, you got tripped. You're supposed to slide out. You're fucking in la-la land. In goddamn la-la land! You need to make some plays, fellas. It's goddamn sad that we have the opportunity to do it, and we're not gonna fucking do it. Are you gonna quit, Ato?"

"No, Coach!"

"Well, then let's make a play. Jesus goddamn Christ."

Manchester moved the ball inside the Chelsea 20-yard line. After two good defensive plays, Manchester faced a 3rd and 4 from the 13.

"You need to stop them right here!" Several Red Devils yelled from the bench.

"Stay focused!"

The Red Devils needed a big stop. If Manchester got a 1st down, they'd have 1st and goal, and it would be hard for Chelsea to keep from falling two touchdowns behind. The Red Devils broke from their huddle and rushed up to the line of scrimmage. They got into their three-point stances, pawed the ground with their feet, and prepared to explode into their nearest opponent. As the ball was snapped, the whistle blew. Ato had jumped offside again.

"Oh, you've got to be shitting me," Atkins said out loud to himself.

The Chelsea defense stood stout, actually pushing Manchester back to the 13-yard line. But again, on 3rd down, Manchester made the play, and Chelsea didn't. Heads hung low again as Manchester's Jared Clamenzi ran the ball in for a 14–0 lead.

"QUIET!" Atkins screamed as loud as he had ever screamed before. "Just stay onside! Watch the ball. What's the goddamn problem, fellas? We're jumping around like we don't know what we're doing and we can't make a goddamn tackle. It's 3rd and 13 and we give them a goddamn touchdown. You got to suck it up!"

Now that the game had moved into the second quarter, Atkins decided Frankie had served enough of a punishment. After Melvin returned the ensuing kickoff to the Chelsea 37-yard line, and then ran for a 1st down to the 46, Frankie was sent into the game.

Miguel Medina took the snap and shoved the ball into Frankie's arms. Frankie hugged the ball with two hands and rushed behind fullback Danny Cortez who stood his man up long enough for Frankie to get by. Then he was gone. Fifty-four yards! On his first play of the game, Frankie raced to the end zone and put Chelsea back in the game. Atkins pumped his fist, but immediately looked over at Coach O'Neil. In that moment, they both wondered if they had made the right decision to bench Frankie at all. If they hadn't, maybe the scoreboard would look a little different right now.

Frankie was stuffed on the 2-point conversion attempt, and the score was 14–6. Manchester went right back to work with its aerial attack, needing only two plays to move the ball down to the Chelsea 25-yard line. The Chelsea sideline began chanting "Defense! Defense!" and Mario responded with the hardest hit of the game, but it came after an 8-yard run.

"They're just coming through the holes," Jonathan Luna observed. "I don't know why. I guess we're getting lazy."

Ivan came to the sidelines breathing heavily. Manchester's up-tempo passing attack was especially tough on someone as large as Ivan. He was sometimes a huge presence, both literally and figuratively in the middle of the field, but today he was watching the ball sail over his head, and trying unsuccessfully to chase down much quicker receivers. Manchester had scored on its first two possessions, and it looked like they were going in again.

"We're playing the biggest game of our lives," Atkins said. "And what the hell is going on out there? Orlando, on that last play you just didn't rush. Nobody's making a play. Nobody's flying to the ball. We need a play made out there, fellas. They're going to try to draw you offsides right here. Don't move! It's that simple. Dont'e, don't go offsides on this play, or you won't see the field again. I want everybody, I want 5-3 regular, but I want everybody up tight."

The Red Devils did as they were told, but they couldn't stop what they never expected. Manchester's quarterback, Pat

Orlando, rolled to his right and looked like he was either going to throw to the corner of the end zone, or keep the ball and take it outside. Then, just as Ivan was about to wrap him up, Orlando quickly released the ball with his nonthrowing hand, under Ivan's outstretched arms. It was a shovel pass to his fullback, Paul Martyn, who had completed a block and then turned to catch the ball. Before the Red Devils could react, Martyn went into the end zone untouched. It was 21–6 with four minutes to play in the first half.

"We've got to stay focused!" Cody yelled as he fired his water bottle to the ground. Atkins liked Cody's fire and wished he saw something like that from Orlando, who so far, hadn't made a block on offense or a tackle on defense.

"Orlando, I need you playing harder," Atkins said quietly, a hand on Orlando's helmet. "You've been sauntering. I don't know what's wrong with you today, but you gotta play hard. Let's go!"

With Frankie taking his regular turn at running back, the Chelsea offense started to run more efficiently. Melvin and Alex were there to provide quick bursts of speed to the outside, while Frankie handled most of the plays between the tackles. On 1st and goal from the 5, Frankie plowed through the line and scored his second touchdown of the game. The Red Devils had committed twelve penalties in the first half, and looked outclassed on defense, but they were only trailing 21–14 at the half. There was still plenty of time, and plenty of hope.

"First of all, Orlando, you're sucking the most."

That's how Atkins began his halftime speech.

"Even on that last play when I said I needed you, you grabbed a teammate and you watched. You made no effort. All those swing moves we worked on this week, and I told you what I needed you to do, and you're totally disregarding it. You're literally saying, 'Fuck Coach. He must not know what he's doing, because I'm not gonna do it.'

"You gotta fight to get to the quarterback."

Atkins wasn't shouting. He knew his words would be enough. If he yelled, he ran the risk of losing Orlando for the rest of the game. If he was too hard on him, Orlando could sulk his way through the second half. So, as angry as he was, Atkins kept his temper in check.

"If you want it, fellas, if you want something, you've got to fight for it," he continued. "You have to fight for everything you get. And you're not fighting right now! And you know what? We're only down by a touchdown. After all that bullshit, you're only down by a touchdown. So now what I need you guys to do is what you're supposed to do."

At this point, he turned his attention back to Orlando, who had the cool, distant look of a teenager who was trying to detach himself from a situation. Coach had embarrassed him, but Orlando didn't want his teammates to know it bothered him, so he took a relaxed position on the bench and leaned far back against the lockers. Atkins noticed the posture and realized apathy was setting in. So, he singled Orlando out again, but this time he gave Orlando the chance to stand up for himself.

"Orlando, I need you to rush the fucking quarterback. Do it, or I'll find somebody who can do it, and who wants to do it. Can you do it?"

"Yes, Coach." Orlando spoke softly.

"Do you want to do it? Will you do it? Will you give fucking a hundred and five percent effort?"

"Yes, Coach."

"All right."

But it wasn't all right at all. Orlando's second response was a bit louder, but no more convincing. He was mentally and emotionally gone, and Atkins knew it. But he didn't have time to focus on Orlando anymore. He needed the rest of his team to recognize the urgency they were facing.

"Now, my defensive line, you've got to stay on side. You guys are just bull rushing and not making any moves. Ivan, throw him the fuck out of the way! He weighs 160 pounds. Just grab him and throw him the fuck out of the way! Our line is just engaging and then you're stopping. Guys, make some goddamn moves! You got a swing move and a club move. We worked on this hard this week."

Atkins swung his arms wildly and aggressively as he demonstrated the moves they had practiced. He glanced around the room, and everywhere he looked, he found reasons to be upset.

"Hightower, you're hurting us too, because if you didn't take two goddamn days off, I could have used you today."

Atkins was growing more and more agitated.

"My linebackers are running around like chickens with your fucking heads cut off."

His speech rambled. Whatever popped into his head, he simply blurted out. He hoped something would connect, but he wasn't having any success.

"Guys, they have five blockers and we have five rushers. Are you telling me they can block us? Not one of our guys can beat one of their guys? That's what it's coming down to. That means one-on-one they're beating us, and that's a dirty, crying shame, fellas. Are you shitting me? Those fucking puppets up in goddamn Manchester are tougher than us. Orlando, are you just going to say okay if the guy's beating you?"

Orlando didn't respond. In fact, there wasn't any kind of response from any of the players. They simply sat there like stones. Nobody nodded in agreement. Nobody defended themselves. Nobody cried. Nobody so much as shuffled their feet, sniffled, coughed, or scratched. The only noise in the room was Atkins' voice, and it was growing louder.

"You have to fight, fellas! They're gonna fight you! We're in a goddamn fight now, fellas! You've got to want it! You have to fight through the goddamn blocks!"

Even with Atkins screaming at the top of his lungs, there was no reaction. And that seemed to set Atkins off. He began screaming louder and longer than anybody had ever heard him before.

"You have to hit somebody!!" He screamed and pounded Danny Cortez on his shoulder pads.

"Hit somebody like you want to win the fucking championship!"

This time it was Ivan who felt the force of Atkins fist coming down on his shoulders. As he spoke, Atkins punctuated each sentence by hitting a different kid's pads. His powerful arm swung down violently, but none of the kids were hurt or afraid. Unfortunately, they weren't jolted awake either. Instead of being inspired, the Red Devils were caught up in the surreal vision of their coach totally losing his cool.

"I don't want to wait and hope somebody else loses so we make the playoffs!" Atkins yelled so loudly the word *playoffs* took several seconds to complete.

"I want to win it today! Right now!"

Atkins gave Frankie a forceful two-handed shove sending him clanging into the lockers.

"And I can't keep preaching! You have to do it your fucking self, fellas! You have to wake the fuck up and do it your fucking self! You can't sit there and goddamn accept it! You have to fucking fight for it! You have to want it! You have to go out there and fight tooth and nail. You can't sit at the end, Orlando, and play so soft. You have to fight through that man and make a goddamn play."

By this point, Atkins was breathing heavily and his voice had grown hoarse. His raving appeared to have little or no impact, so he changed his tone, and reverted to a normal speaking voice.

"This is a fight now. We know what they're going to do. Enough of the scheming. We know what they're going to do. Now, it just comes down to toughness. They're doing exactly what we practiced, but right now they're tougher than us, and they're outfighting us."

Then, in one last-ditch effort to shock his team and fire them up for the second half, Atkins screamed.

"Make some goddamn plays! Make some fucking plaaaaays! I need some help today, fellas. I can't do it. You have to do it! I can't get on the field. You're on the field. You have to do it! This is it!"

As in the pregame speech, Atkins was met with a moment of silence, but this time, when the Red Devils realized he was finished, they leaped from their seats and began cheering wildly.

"We want it!"

"Let's go!"

"C'mon! We can do this!"

The players began hitting each other on the shoulder pads, slapping each other's helmets, and chanting, "Let's go Chelsea!"

It was a positive show of adrenaline that left Atkins wondering if it was genuine. Where had this energy been before the game or during the first half? And where was all this emotion when he was screaming in their faces and hitting them on their shoulders? And would this enthusiasm last as they took the field for the second half? Atkins wasn't so sure.

Chelsea got the ball first in the second half, but only managed to move backwards. First, they lined up offside. Then Frankie lost yardage on two consecutive carries, and Miguel threw an incomplete pass. On 4th and 19, the Red Devils punted the ball away.

"Defense, let's bring it in," Mario said on the sideline as the punt sailed through the air. "We got to fucking put pressure on the quarterback. You have to do your job. Cover your guys. That's it. One-Two-Three defense!"

Manchester drove the ball quickly down the field. Orlando looked to be making a better effort, but he couldn't get to the quarterback in time. Manchester systematically chewed up yardage, finally scoring on a quarterback sneak to make it 27–14. A two touchdown lead wasn't insurmountable, but Chelsea needed to score in a hurry, hope they could finally stop Manchester's offense, and then score again.

"Waggle left. Screen right!" Atkins told Miguel. It was a relatively safe pass, but the play broke down and Miguel threw an interception. Three plays later, Manchester's running back Paul Martyn threw an option pass to Don Kennerson. It was a trick play that took Chelsea completely off guard, and the result was a 54-yard touchdown pass that gave Manchester a 33–14 lead with less than five minutes to go in the third quarter.

The crowd was motionless. The Red Devils were silent. For a moment the only sound that could be heard was the faint din of cars driving by on the road behind the stadium and the distant celebration being held on the other side of the field. The quiet was finally disrupted by the referee's whistle.

"Slot right. Over right. Forty-seven counter," Atkins called out. He was coaching with more urgency than ever.

The play looked like it would be stopped for no gain, but Frankie kept pumping his legs and refused to fall. He escaped the grasp of two Manchester defenders and took off down the field for a 35-yard gain. He scored on the next play, and when Richie bulled his way in on the 2-point conversion, Chelsea was back in the game trailing 33–22 with ninety seconds left in the third quarter. There was still time.

"We have to get pressure on that goddamn quarterback now," Atkins implored. "We're in the game. We need the ball to get points. We're gonna score. Just give me the ball back, defense."

Manchester didn't score again, but they went into a ball control offense that chewed up a lot of time on the clock. When Atkins recognized the change in the Manchester offensive approach, he called a time-out.

"Guys, they're not going to pass it. Play the fucking run. Our d-backs will play the pass. Everybody else play the run."

But Manchester was still able to run the ball. To Atkins, the reason was simple. He stood on the sidelines with his eyes trained on Orlando. Play after play, he saw Orlando getting pushed around by players he should have been able to manhandle. Finally, Atkins had seen enough. He called out Orlando's name and waved him over to the sideline. He then signaled for Ato to get in the game and take Orlando's place on the defensive line. Orlando was furious. Everyone could see he was being benched. He tried to avoid Atkins, but Coach's words followed him to the bench.

"You're blowing the game for us, Orlando. Why would you stop? Why wouldn't you try your hardest to get back? You're quitting. You're fucking quitting, Orlando."

On his first play back in the game, Ato was called for jumping offside. It was Chelsea's nineteenth penalty of the game, and the Red Devils went on to lose, 33–22.

Orlando walked slowly back to the locker room several yards behind the last of his teammates. It was hard to tell if he was despondent because of the loss, or because of how poorly he had played. He certainly wasn't in a hurry to hear what Atkins had to say, so he stopped for a moment to talk to a couple of friends.

"Guys, look within yourselves," Atkins began, but he stopped suddenly to look around the room.

"Where's Orlando? This is exactly what I'm talking about. Get him the fuck in here! Right now."

Orlando stepped just inside the locker room and leaned against the doorframe. He looked up just long enough to notice that none of his teammates bothered to turn around to see him. Then he looked down at the floor.

"We're gonna see the character of this team," Atkins continued. "We're gonna see what you're made of. The stuff I saw today, Orlando, you quit. I saw you kick a kid in the back. Two plays later Coach Jamie saw you do something else. Then you got a holding call. And on that last interception, that was your fault. You watched him intercept it."

Atkins paused again. He looked to see if Orlando's body language gave anything away. Did Orlando accept responsibility for the interception, or was he thinking, *Coach is just picking on me for no reason again?* Ultimately, it didn't matter. So, Atkins turned his attention to the rest of the team.

"We're gonna see what you're made of now. We're gonna see who starts missing practice. I'll tell you right now. I have nothing to lose by throwing you off the team. Hightower, if you miss one more practice, you're gone! Because we could have used you today. So you have to decide if you want to play football the rest of this year. If you miss one more practice, you're gone. Is that clearly understood? Any starters that miss a practice, I don't need you, because you're quitting. Orlando, do you understand me?"

"Yes, Coach."

"Ato?"

"Yes, Coach."

"Mario?"

"Yes, Coach."

"Juan?"

"Yes, Coach."

"Barbosa? Ivan? Frankie?"

"Yes, Coach."

"So don't be the test case and start missing practice. You understand me?"

"Yes, Coach." This time every player responded loudly and in unison.

"That's number one. Number two is we had nineteen penalties. We gave them that game on nineteen penalties. We scored 22 points. We should have scored another two touchdowns, but you kept getting penalties. Offsides. Offsides. Holding. Facemask. False start. Personal foul. Guys, I'm beside myself. I don't know what to say. Some of you played well. Pop Warner, you played well. Frankie, you played well. Linebackers, Jonathan, you played horrible in the middle today. You made one tackle, I think, in the fourth quarter."

This was as hard a postgame speech as Atkins had ever had to give. He was bitterly disappointed, not only in the outcome, but in the effort of several key players. He also felt he might have painted himself into a corner by convincing the kids this game was critical for the team's playoff chances. Now that they had lost, how could he motivate them? How could he tell them to keep chasing their dream, if the dream was dead?

"Now, we have to hope that Manchester loses a game. Now, we have to hope North Shore or Georgetown can beat Manchester. And then we're in the same position we were in last year. We put ourselves there. You're a better football team than that, but they wanted it more than you. They fought harder. I can't wait to watch the film and show you. I'm not gonna talk about it tonight. But I want to see what your character is. We have three games left. We have to win those three games, and hopefully Georgetown or North Shore can help us out. And that's a possibility. Georgetown and North Shore are good teams. So, it's not like last year hoping Minuteman beat somebody. We're on the outside looking in, instead of holding our own destiny. It's all about character now. I want each of you to look at me."

Only a few players in the back were looking at him.

"Look at me," Atkins repeated. He waited until all eyes were trained on his. Then he said: "It's all about character now. Learn your lesson. Let's finish the season strong and sneak in the back door."

Atkins clapped his hands together and walked briskly out of the locker room. Orlando, still standing in the doorway, shuffled his feet to the side to let Atkins pass.

CHAPTER ELEVEN

Halloween in Chelsea

You've seen it all in your first year as a Chelsea cop, dead bodies, murder scenes, everything. The "sudden death" call is the worst. You don't know how long the body's been laying there. The smell is sickening. It makes you wonder if you want to be a cop anymore.
—Detective Scott Conley, Chelsea Gang Unit

Hundreds of ghosts, ninjas, Spider-men, and princesses scurried up and down Broadway in Chelsea. They had converged on the city's restaurants, liquor stores, and other small businesses, darting in and out, and squealing with delight as they were weighted down with candy. Although darkness had fallen, the streets were brightly lit. The decrepitude that frequently anesthetized residents and visitors had been replaced by a new energy. The sky was clear, the air was merely cool, and there was a genuine festive feeling. That alone made Halloween a special night in Chelsea.

"But Halloween is a potentially dangerous evening," Chelsea detective Dan Delaney cautioned, "Because everybody's wearing masks."

As the weather cooled, everybody was also wearing winter jackets and bulky clothing. That was a concern for the police, because it made it easier to carry and conceal weapons. Delaney recalled the Halloween two years ago when he, Jimmy Atkins, and Scott Conley arrested a thirteen-year-old kid with a gun.

"He was in the park with a .357 Magnum looking to shoot somebody."

As a large group of trick-or-treaters made its way into the Chelsea Police Department at the west end of Broadway, the dispatcher came out from behind the bulletproof glass with a large basket of chocolates and lollipops. There was only enough time for a few pleasantries, "pleases" and "thank-yous" before the children rushed off to discover treasures somewhere else. As the children left, the dispatcher heard another call come in. It was a domestic situation and police were quick to respond.

Three police units arrived simultaneously. They sprang from their cars with radios in hand and guns holstered. Uniformed cops as well as members of the Gang Unit gathered momentarily before responding to a noise coming from an apartment building to the left. They were only inside for a moment when a few of the officers, but not all, rushed back out and into another building across the street. They had been told by a woman in the first building that her ex-boyfriend had violated a restraining order and was hiding across the street. The officers quickly discovered the man they were after. There was a struggle. A beer bottle was smashed, and the suspect was brought out in handcuffs, smelling of beer, and with a small cut on his forehead.

Coach Atkins, working as Sergeant Atkins tonight, was the ranking officer on the scene. He was among the first responders, but not part of the scuffle. As the suspect was put in a cruiser and taken away, Atkins stood in the middle of the street with the remaining officers. They agreed it had been a slow night so far, and then they discovered a possible reason why. One of the cops just heard on the scanner that fifteen Chelsea Bloods had been stopped by the police in nearby Salem.

Apparently, the Chelsea Gang Unit had been doing surveillance when they spotted a large group of Bloods getting on a train headed for Salem, which was a popular destination every Halloween. The Gang Unit alerted the Salem police that the Bloods were coming, and when they arrived, the police stopped them and found drugs, knives, and a flare gun. Four of the Bloods were arrested, including Michael Augustine.

"That's another one of mine," Atkins said as he told his fellow officers about Augustine failing off the team. "I never had a problem with him. He's a big, strong kid. Tough kid. He could be a good football player, and he's not stupid. It's another waste. Another fucking waste."

He repeated the phrase the second time to himself as he walked back to his cruiser. His drive through the city appeared to be random, but he was cutting down side streets and into neighborhoods where disturbances were known to occur. He stopped once to tell a group of adults sitting on a stoop to bring their beers and tequila inside. He stopped again when he spotted two other officers defusing a minor incident with an elderly drunk. And he stopped several times to call kids over to his car.

"Hey, Kielbasa!" he yelled to a hefty twelve-year-old who played on his Pop Warner team. "You staying out of trouble?"

"Yes, Coach," the boy said. He had a broad, natural smile, and he was obviously comfortable with Atkins and excited to see him. He approached the car quickly and put both his hands on Atkins' door where the window rolled down.

"All right then. Make sure you get home soon. And I better not find out you're taking candy from other kids."

"I won't, Coach."

Atkins had similar conversations with several other kids. He was cruising a dangerous city and loving every minute of it. He was well known among all the locals, and well liked by many of them. During his regular shift, he routinely stood outside his cruiser at the bus stop on Broadway, or he walked up and down the street speaking to and socializing with passersby. He was charming right up until the time he needed to be tough. He loved being part of the Gang Unit because, as he said simply, he "loves putting bad guys away."

Atkins and the other officers were in constant motion. Each police car continued going round and round the city. Chelsea was less than 2 square miles, so even with a series of detours down side streets and slowing down near known trouble spots, it didn't take long to go from one end of the city to the other. Atkins made a U-turn off Broadway at the police station and headed past ROCA. Standing outside on the corner was Angel Acavedo. Atkins ignored him, and answered his cellphone.

"I'm not surprised," he said into the phone. The caller was another officer letting Atkins know that Joshua Lewis was with the Bloods in Salem. He wasn't arrested, but he was there.

"So, you tell me," Atkins said while remembering the day he kicked Black Josh off the football team, "Is that a lost cause, or is that a lost cause?"

Then he answered his own question.

"That's a fucking lost cause."

Atkins rolled up to a stop sign and waved a couple of pedestrians across. One of the walkers was a tall, gangly black man in his early twenties. He looked at the police car, saw that Atkins had his window rolled down, and said very clearly:

"I'm gonna fuck somebody up tonight if they hit me with an egg. I'm too old for this shit. Somebody's gonna get fucked up, if I find out who it is."

While Atkins was asking him what he was talking about, an egg crashed on the street about 50 feet away. Several people were ducking for cover and looking up at the roof of the apartment building. Two shadows ran across the roof, and another egg smashed into the stop sign to Atkins' right. He got out of the car, but stayed behind the door. Another police unit drove up, and for the next few minutes, everyone just stared at the top of the building. No more eggs were thrown and the small crowd of people that had gathered to see the commotion started to disperse. This was not considered a dangerous situation, and the police were not going to spend valuable time chasing after a couple of egg tossers.

The police were out in full force tonight to make sure something big didn't go down, like the time Scott Conley chased a suspect up Hawthorne Street and caught up with a suspected terrorist. Conley had been sitting in his police car when he saw a man run by wielding a machete. He immediately ran after him and just as he was within arm's length, the man spun around and took a violent swing with the machete.

"I'm wearing a sweatshirt, so he mostly got clothes," Conley recalled. "But he cut me a little on my side. Just a scratch. But there's no doubt if he had swung for my head, I'd be dead right now."

And the man who took the swing was Elmer "Tiger" Tejada, a twenty-two-year-old member of the MS-13 gang. Tejada had been deported to El Salvador as a criminal by the Department of Homeland Security's Immigration and Customs Enforcement agency, but was still able to sneak back into the United States. That was especially unnerving to intelligence officials who had reported seeing MS-13 members in El Salvador meeting with known al-Qaeda terrorists. The possible link between MS-13 and al-Qaeda was of extreme concern, because many law enforcement officials believed MS-13 controlled alien smuggling routes along the Mexican border, and the gang could become involved in bringing terrorists into the United States. Finding Tejada a mile and a half from Logan Airport was alarming, but Conley had no idea what he was getting into at the time.

"Anyway, after he swings at me, he goes, 'I'm sorry. I didn't know it was you.'"

Conley and Atkins and the other Gang Unit cops enjoyed telling their war stories. It was a big part of their brotherhood, the bonds that form in combat, at football practice, and at weekly poker games. They got together and laughed about the time a suspect turned on Jimmy and Jimmy punched him and broke his cheekbone in two places. The suspect's eyelid was split in such a way that when he closed it, you could still see his eye.

That reminded them of the accident victim they found with his right eye literally lying on his cheek.

"It was on a Friday night once in Bellingham Square," Dan Delaney began. "Me and Jimmy are having a cup of coffee. An off- duty cop was following a van that was all smashed in on the passenger side. It had a flat tire, and it was going down Central Ave, and left on Highland. So, this officer wanted us to stop the van. So, we started flying up Bellingham Street toward the hospital, and we go up and over the hill, and I see the van pulling into the hospital. So, we get up there and Jimmy pulls in, and it's his call. Now, the driver gets out and runs into the hospital. So, as I walk past the van I see the passenger lying out in the front seat with his eyeball sitting on his cheek. 'Whoa!' I says, 'Jimmy, you gotta go see this.' And he's like, 'I'm not going in there.' I says, 'Jimmy, it's your call. You gotta go in there.' Jimmy went in there and turned white as a ghost."

"He drove into a pole, and the pole just took his eye right out of his fucking head," Jimmy said, picking up the story. "It's round like a ball just laying there on his cheek. I went, 'Oh shit!' and ran away from him."

There was another time Jimmy ran away, and this time, he just kept running. Delaney liked to tell the story.

"Two years ago we're out checking on MS-13 graffiti, and we're in an alleyway that runs parallel to the expressway on Third Street, and there's this gigantic pit bull. I mean it looks like a ravaged, maniac pit bull standing on a back porch. So, as we get closer, I notice the dog's not leashed, and Jimmy's like, 'If that dog comes after me, I'll bust a cap in his ass.' We keep walking, and then I notice there's no chain-link fence where there's supposed to be. Then the dog lets out a couple of loud barks. Next thing I see, it's

Jimmy running past me. What an asshole! Luis Rodriguez, another cop with us, is a tall, thin Spanish guy, and he's gonna run by me too. So, the dog's gonna maul me. We run up the street past a parking lot where the church is emptying out into. There goes old Jimmy running, and there's a fence, a Jersey barrier, and then our cruiser. And Jimmy, like a gazelle goes over the fence and the Jersey barrier, lands on the ground, and in one jump, lands on the roof of the cruiser, and he's standing there yelling, 'Shoot it. Shoot it!' I'm running for my life, and I knew I couldn't jump like Jimmy, so I just dove over the Jersey barrier hoping the dog was gonna get Luis. Luis turns around and pulls his gun and yells 'Freeze!' at the dog. And it worked. The dog just stopped and walked away. Jimmy was still on top of the car with about two hundred people watching us. I was cut to shreds."

Good times. There would be no such drama or danger on this Halloween night, however. The only other significant call the officers responded to was a crack deal going down off Broadway. Conley and his partner watched a white man and a white woman drive up to a light-skinned Puerto Rican with a large Afro who pulled a brown paper bag out of his jacket. They knew immediately the Puerto Rican was slinging—selling drugs.

Conley pulled up in the cruiser and jumped from the car. The crack dealer threw what he was selling into his mouth, but before he could swallow it, Conley hit him with a forearm shiver, knocking him to the ground. Conley forced the man to spit up the crack, and the evidence was bagged. The dealer remained sprawled out on the street for several minutes. Conley noticed he was lying in a puddle of spilled beer, so he grabbed the suspect by his belt buckle, picked him up like a suitcase, and moved him several feet away. While he was being carried, the man repeated several times that he hadn't done anything wrong.

"Well, I guess he didn't do it," Conley boomed. "He says he didn't do it. Maybe we got the wrong guy with crack in his mouth!"

The relatively quiet night would end soon. As Atkins drove back to the police station, he began the transition from cop back to coach. He thought about his team and Ivan, who always needed to debate everything.

"Shut the fuck up," Atkins thought aloud. "Beat the piss out of the kid in front of you. You weigh 350 pounds."

He considered Danny, a kid who would do anything to please you, but who somehow had gotten worse as a football player.

"He was better as a sophomore. I don't know what happened his junior and senior years, but he's gotten worse. School is going good though."

Atkins smiled when he thought about Mario, Kenzi, Jonathan, and Richie all scheduled to take the SATs on Saturday. They'd miss the first half of their big game against Georgetown, but that would have to be okay. Taking the SATs meant they were serious about going to college. Richie was a given, and he'd do well, but the others still needed to be pushed. Certainly, Atkins needed to remain vigilant with Orlando.

It was 11:00 p.m. as Atkins parked the cruiser in the small parking lot opposite the police station. He hadn't seen Orlando walking down the street by himself, but perhaps he sensed he was there, because he spent the next several minutes worrying about him.

"He's had issues," Atkins admitted to himself. "His mother is screwed up. She's always partying, sniffing coke on the weekends."

He recalled a conversation he had with Orlando's mother after she had been arrested and charged with committing larcenies by check. She was put on probation and ordered to pay restitution, but she never did. So, there were warrants out for her arrest.

"Why haven't you been paying it?" Atkins had asked her.

"I don't have the money," she replied.

"You go out every Friday night. Don't go out every Friday night, and bring that $60 you're spending to the court."

Sometimes the parents could be as bad as the kids, Atkins thought. But the time for quiet reflection was over. After a solid week of practice, it was time for the Georgetown game, and the Red Devils simply had to win. Atkins needed to instill a sense of urgency in his team. He had to make sure they understood what was at stake.

The forty-minute bus ride from Chelsea to Georgetown High School had bothered Atkins. The problem: There was nothing different about the team's demeanor. An hour before the game, while the team was going through drills, there was still no discernible difference. And there should have been. Atkins stood in the middle of the field and watched his players behaving exactly the same way they did before every game. He didn't like what he was seeing. The Red Devils should have been more nervous, more hyper, or more quiet—more of something, or less of something, but there definitely should have been something different. The seniors especially had to know that if they didn't beat the Georgetown Royals today, they would probably never play another meaningful game. Where was the screaming, the rage, the fierce determination, the leadership, or even the search for solitude where a player could escape from the norm and concentrate on rising to the challenge of this day? Atkins wasn't seeing it. So, when the pregame calisthenics were complete, Atkins and the Red Devils walked off the field into the locker room. It was time for a little heart-to-heart.

"If we want to save our season, we have to win this game," Atkins began calmly. "We cannot lose another league game. You understand that?"

"Yes, Coach!"

"If we lose this game we have no shot at making the playoffs. Zero. We need to win this game. And you guys can easily win this game, and I hate to even say that because you might take it too literally and think that you can just walk out on the field and do it. That's not what I mean. I mean, Orlando, if you play like you practiced this week, you're gonna have a monster game. Danny, if you double-team down and you hit that linebacker like you practiced this week, you're gonna have a monster game. Ato, you had a great week of practice. We worked hard this week. Now, we need you to put it on the field."

At this point, Atkins' intensity level began rising.

"Guys, let's not be nervous today. Let's just play football. If you guys just play football, fellas, you're gonna blow this team up. Just be hard-nosed. Beat them up. Let's leave here today with blue jerseys littered all over the field, getting carried off the field because we beat the shit out of them. Let's let North Shore know that we're coming for them next week. They're up in the stands, and they're the ones who were breaking my balls when we were playing Whittier. Show them that they have a lot to scout today. If you play every single play like it's the last play of the game and you need to win that play to win the game, if you play like that, I guarantee, not just a victory, but a goddamn ass-whooping!"

Atkins was shouting now.

"If you play with that fire, PLEASE! I want to see it one time this year. I want to see it one time, the fire for a complete game, so that people go 'Holy shit! Where was that team all year?' So that they know we're not full of shit! So they know we know what we're doing here at Chelsea High School. So they know you guys are tough Chelsea kids."

The players, who began leaning back against their lockers, or sitting with their heads down, were sitting forward now with their heads up. Atkins had their attention, and he had their respect. Plus, he was so loud and demonstrative now he was putting on quite a show.

"Let's show them that you are tough goddamn Chelsea kids," he bellowed. "Beat the living shit out of Georgetown today!!

When you get on the field, look at the guy across from you, and knock his dick off! Knock his goddamn dick in the dirt and let him pick it up, but before he does step on it and squoosh it in, and when he comes back for the next play, do it goddamn again. Make them quit on the field. And watch the feeling you get when you beat a team into submission. Let's beat that team into submission!"

Chelsea went three and out on its first possession. Then the long snapper lost his grip on the ball, so the snap only made it halfway to the punter. The ball splattered in a puddle and Georgetown recovered at the Chelsea 28-yard line. Three plays later, George-town quarterback Joe Esposito threw a bomb to the corner of the end zone, and Georgetown had a 6–0 lead just a few minutes into the game. Chelsea junior Hamza Abdul was beaten on the touch-down pass, and as he came to the sideline, he announced apolo-getically: "I turned and got burned."

Coach O'Neil got in his face and yelled, "Are you pissed now?"

"Yes," Hamza said angrily.

"Good. Use it."

But the next time Georgetown got the ball, Hamza was beaten again by the same wide receiver. Georgetown's Tim Lynch had scored twice, and Chelsea trailed 12–0 at the end of the first quarter.

"Hamza, will you cover him?" Atkins shouted from the side-line. "Do you think you might want to cover him?"

While Alex's mother came down out of the stands to clean mud out of the players' spikes with a stick, Ivan just missed sacking Esposito. Instead, the Georgetown quarterback eluded the rush and found a receiver standing all alone about 30 yards down the field. The catch was made, but the ball was fumbled. Georgetown's Mike Rue recovered the ball and ran straight for the end zone.

The game and the season were slipping away. Chelsea was down 18–0 and showing no signs of life.

Chelsea was still struggling to move the ball on its next possession. In need of some inspired play, Coach looked to Cody, perhaps his most consistently passionate player, and screamed, "Cody, make a goddamn block! C'mon, Cody!"

But on the next play, Cody missed a block that looked like it might spring Alex for a long run. Alex was stuffed and Chelsea had to punt the ball away again. Cody was playing injured. He'd had an MRI earlier in the week to find out why his knee kept swelling up like a balloon. He was advised to take a week off from playing, but a full night of ice and very little sleep had gotten the swelling to go down, and he wasn't about to miss such an important game. Several other players were also playing hurt, including Mario, Frankie, and Joey Barbosa.

"I'll play, Coach," Joey said as Atkins looked for someone who could cover Georgetown's receivers.

"You can't even move."

"I can play. I want to play."

"All right, get in there!"

Down 18–0, Chelsea began blitzing on every play. Each time it was someone different rushing into the backfield. First, it was Frankie coming up the middle. Then it was Richie or Ivan or Mario looking for a hole in the line. But even though Atkins was correctly calling out Georgetown's plays before they snapped the ball, the Red Devils couldn't stop them. The Royals continued to chew up huge chunks of yardage. With less than a minute to go in the first half, Georgetown was threatening to score once again. Atkins called time-out.

"Everything they've done, we've practiced," he said. "Every single thing. It's on you now. You have to perform, fellas. You cannot continue to let them catch the ball. You have to come up and make a play. It's called being a football player."

"Yes, Coach," they said in unison. Then Atkins put his face within inches of Hamza's and demanded: "Get out there and make a goddamn play."

But with three seconds to go in the half, Esposito threw the ball toward the sideline to his receiver, Brandon Wade. Wade made the catch and ran back toward the inside, managing to elude Miguel and then breaking Orlando's arm tackle. Touchdown.

"Now, I'm just questioning your manhood," Atkins said as Orlando passed him on his way to the bench. "I've got you exactly where you're supposed to be. I can't tackle. You've got to tackle."

Orlando took a seat in the middle of the bench. Nobody else sat down. The Royals squibbed the kickoff and the first half mercilessly came to a close. When the whistle blew, the Red Devils trudged to the locker room. No one spoke. Shoulders slumped. Heads hung low. And they all braced for the worst.

Atkins met quickly with his coaching staff outside the locker room. He was unexpectedly calm. The coaches, speaking in low, steady voices that belied the score of the game, volunteered suggestions and alternate strategies. They spoke very little about what needed to be done offensively, but they all agreed they should switch to a man-to-man defense in the second half. Then Atkins threw open the door and looked at his team. He stood in front of them for only a moment before summing up what had gone so terribly wrong.

"Guys, we have to be tougher. I implored you at the beginning of the game to go out there and beat them into submission. Those two interior linemen are kicking our ass. Orlando, what's the difference in this game?"

"They want it more," Orlando said barely loud enough for anyone to hear.

"They're making plays, and we're not," Atkins continued. "We each know what the other team is doing. So coaches on both sides did their jobs. There's nothing to tell you. You know exactly what they're doing on offense. You just have to make a play. You have to make a block. Jonathan, Frankie you have to make your blocks. Miguel, you have to hit wide-open receivers. I can't throw the ball for you. Hamza, you've got to make a play. Don't just shake your head and say 'Yes.' Just do it."

Atkins was not shouting. He was not berating, or belittling. He was aware that their fragile egos were on the verge of breaking. This was not the time to beat them down. It was time to build them up. He began asking them questions about what they thought was happening on the field, and he listened to their responses. Instead of criticizing them for making excuses, he considered their opinions as if he valued and respected them. And he did. And the players respected each other. When players explained why something had been unsuccessful, other players offered helpful suggestions, and talked about what they could do better in the second half. Suddenly, the energy in the room started to rise. Kids were becoming engaged. Several conversations were going on at once, each one designed to fix a problem. Maybe they forgot what the score was, but they spoke with enthusiasm and hope. Did they really think they still had a chance to win? Georgetown had the ball four times in the first half, and scored on every possession, but the Red Devils were acting like a team that could still save their season. Atkins saw the transformation, and knew they were ready.

"Guys, I have nothing else to say to you except that your season is in this half. If you want to have two meaningless games, it's on you. Let's go out there and fight, fellas."

Finally, early in the second half, a big play for Chelsea. The man-to-man defense worked, and Georgetown was stopped for the first time. Then Alex ripped off a 50-yard run to the Georgetown 17-yard line. Three plays later, Frankie, who consistently limped back to the huddle, bulled his way over the goal line. Alex scored on the 2-point conversion, and Chelsea trailed 25–8.

Georgetown's offense, so effective in the first half, was struggling to adapt to the change in Chelsea's defense. On 3rd and long, Esposito spotted an open receiver, but Hamza delivered a crushing blow just as the ball arrived. The receiver and the ball fell to the ground. On the next play, Ato burst through the line and blocked the punt. The Chelsea sidelines erupted with shouts of joy. Meanwhile, they actually looked worried on the Georgetown sideline.

"Would you get around the corner?" Atkins implored Alex. "Sprint to the outside and get in the goddamn end zone. Get in the end zone. C'mon, Alex. C'mon, we need this!"

Alex obliged with a 20-yard touchdown run, but the play was called back because of a holding penalty. Atkins merely placed his hands on his hips and rolled his eyes. Chelsea scored a few plays later, and with another 2-point conversion, it was 25–16.

The Red Devils had momentum on their side, but not time. Down by 9 points, they would need to score twice in the final ten minutes. Time was running out in the game, and in the season. Then Joey Barbosa intercepted a pass! Chelsea still had a chance.

Back on offense, the Red Devils kept the ball on the ground with Alex and Frankie sharing the load. Together they moved the ball deep into Georgetown territory. Then, on 4th and 2 from the 22, Miguel kept the ball on a quarterback sneak. His legs churned while his feet slipped in the mud. He fell forward and reached as far as he could in an effort to get the 1st down. Where the ball was spotted would make all the difference.

The referee took the ball from Miguel and placed it on the ground. Atkins immediately sprang several yards on to the field and barked at the referee.

"That's a bad spot! Ask for help! That's not where the ball should be spotted!"

The referee did as he was told and asked another official for help. After a short conference, the ref picked the ball back up, and moved it a good half-yard forward. The chains were brought out for a measurement, and by the nose of the football, Chelsea had gotten the 1st down. If Atkins hadn't intimidated the ref into re-spotting the ball, Chelsea would have lost possession, and the game would have effectively been over.

The Red Devils still had the ball, but they couldn't do anything more with it. After three straight runs netted little more than a yard, Chelsea ran a reverse. Cody went in motion from the slot position, took the handoff, and gave the ball to Frankie who was coming over from the other side of the line. Frankie pushed until he was hauled down by four Georgetown tacklers, but he was stopped well short of a 1st down. Georgetown ball.

The Royals attempted to run out the clock, but with exactly one minute to go in the game, they were forced to punt. This is where Atkins may have had his greatest victory of the season. Orlando, who had hustled and fought the entire second half, vaulted from his down position, adroitly sidestepped the man in front of him, and sprinted unimpeded toward the Georgetown punter. The kick went right between the "3" and the "2" on Orlando's chest. With near certain defeat staring him in the face, Orlando hadn't given up. He was fighting to the very end. He wasn't alone. Every Red Devil player had made a conscious decision to not quit.

Quitting was the easy choice. It was a choice they'd made many times in their lives. It was a choice they routinely made when they didn't do their homework, or study for a test. It was a choice they frequently considered when looking at their futures. But on this day, they chose to fight. That they lost 25–16 and their playoff dreams would once again be unfulfilled was tremendously disappointing, but their coach was smiling.

"Fellas, that is exactly how you play football in that second half. You should be proud of yourselves that you didn't quit. You came out and played a helluva second half of football. That was the best half of football I've seen all year. Be proud of yourself the way you played that game. You understand, Orlando? You played like a goddamn beast the second half. That's what you're supposed to do."

Orlando was down on one knee with tears in his eyes. Several other players were visibly weeping.

"Guys," Atkins continued. "I want to watch the films and show you, I can't wait to show you how good you are. In that second half, you came out and you fought. We got off to a slow start. We made some adjustments at halftime. Remember that I said you have to play a whole game, Orlando? If you play a whole game of football, we kill that team. If we play a whole game of football, it's 32–nothing instead of 25–16. They didn't move the ball on us. You guys came out and decided we're gonna stop them, and we're gonna play some defense. You played a helluva game. I don't want anybody here to be upset at all, Orlando. You should be disappointed because you lost the game. But I'm telling you guys, the coaches are as proud of you as we've ever been since I've been coaching. This is the first team that was down so big that said, 'No we're not gonna quit on you, Coach. We're not gonna quit on ourselves.'"

Sitting in the front seat on the bus ride home, Atkins looked out the window. It was another beautiful day. The sun hit his face and he felt warm. Yes, it was killing him that they had lost that game. He hated the idea of being eliminated from playoff contention. It would be at least another year before he could raise a Super Bowl trophy and share it with his kids. The seniors would never know that feeling. He had wanted desperately to give them that, to give all of the kids something they could carry with them for the rest of their lives. Atkins wasn't able to give the Red Devils that sense of accomplishment, but he had given them something else that day. In the midst of another discouraging defeat, the Red

Devils found self-respect. Maybe they could carry that with them for the rest of their lives. And maybe, just maybe, that was better than winning a championship.

As the bus rolled on to the highway and headed back to Chelsea, Atkins closed his eyes and thought about the wins and losses, the missed opportunities, and the day's disappointment. He looked back on the season thus far and saw fumbles, interceptions, and penalties. He remembered how blatantly Orlando had quit against Manchester. He heard the people who criticized his coaching abilities, especially in the aftermath of the Manchester defeat. He knew he'd hear more of it this week from people wondering why he didn't switch to a man defense earlier.

And then, with his eyes still closed, Atkins saw Orlando rushing toward the Georgetown punter with a minute to play. That's when he relaxed and wondered if this had been his most successful season after all.

CHAPTER TWELVE

Pop Warner Gets His Shot

If I can get Kenzi out of Chelsea and into college, the last three years will have been a success. Just using one kid, because he's had it the worst, even worse than Orlando. Kenzi, I know the mother a lot better, I know the family, and I know what shot he has. He has no shot. This kid has no shot. If he can make it, yeah, it was a success.

—JAMES ATKINS

The goals were different now. From the moment the Red Devils were eliminated from playoff contention in 2005, the goal had been to make the playoffs in 2006. Atkins and the Red Devils didn't achieve that goal, so they created three new ones for the last two games of the season. It was time to focus on having fun, gaining experience for the underclassmen, and looking for a new quarterback. The two options at quarterback were Cody and Melvin. Coach went with Melvin.

"What's gonna suck here tonight is if he goes out and has a stellar game," Atkins said. "I put it right back on Pop Warner. I says, 'If you come out and play great tonight, I'm happy for us, because next year we have something to look forward to, but also you fucked us. If you had gone to camp like you were supposed to, you would have been the starting quarterback from the beginning, and we wouldn't have had to go through any of this crap.' What do we have to lose now? We can't make it to the playoffs."

Melvin hadn't gone to camp because he wasn't convinced he was ready to play on Chelsea's varsity team. Just a sophomore, Melvin debated whether he should play high school football at all, or just stay in Pop Warner, thus the nickname. But Melvin shouldn't have had any doubts. He was a tremendously gifted athlete. In most games, he was the fastest player on the field. He could throw the ball far and accurately, and he was a leader. His teammates trusted him, perhaps because he was so much like so many of them.

"My father's in jail right now," Melvin said. "I don't really talk to him that much. I have met my father. He's been locked up a couple of times, drugs and stuff. He hasn't really been there for me, but that's not gonna stop me, because I got my mother. She's been my mother and my father."

Melvin didn't start playing football until he was twelve. That was around the same time the gangs had started showing interest in him. He needed an activity that would keep him busy and out of trouble. He chose football with his mother's blessing, and with a stern warning that if he didn't keep his grades up, he wouldn't be allowed to play.

"Actually, you have to put a lot of time into football," Melvin explained. "I go to practice. I get home about six. Everything is about football. I don't want to get into trouble. It keeps you out of gangs and street violence, because if you're doing football you have no time for anything else to do. And if you're not playing football, you're going to be on the streets. It really helps you out a lot. You don't get into trouble playing football."

Melvin's leadership skills extended from the football field to the classroom. He was a very good student taking a couple of honors classes. His intentions were to go to college and to continue playing football as long as possible. He was well grounded, focused, and determined to find a way out of Chelsea, and he had his mother to thank for that.

"My mother, she's really strict actually," Melvin said. "Before anything I have to do my homework. If my grades aren't good, I can't play football. She wants me to be somebody. That's why I am who I am today, and I gotta keep going."

On November 10, 2006, Melvin was the starting quarterback for the Red Devils against division rival North Shore. Today, he was nervous. It was Chelsea's last game of the year under the lights, and after one week of practice, Melvin would be making his first-ever start at quarterback. Atkins, disappointed that Melvin hadn't been his starting quarterback all season long, and even more disappointed that his season had come down to this, was excited to see what Melvin could do.

"Wait till you see him scramble," Atkins said while watching the pregame drills. "If they don't stay in their lanes, he might run for 700 yards. Jesus, what Melvin would be right now if he came to camp with us."

In the minutes leading up to most games, Atkins would be fixated on the game plan. He'd be observing the mood and behavior of his team. He'd look for players who might need encouragement. He'd look to the far sidelines and try to detect some little thing about the other team that might help his Red Devils. But tonight, Atkins was relaxed. He was jovial. He found his new goals to be less constraining than the old ones. More than thinking about winning, he wanted his seniors to have fun, to go out in style. He knew the end of their high school careers was fast approaching, and that many of them would never play football again. He had talked to his seniors about that at the Thursday night dinner.

"Any other sport you can play," he began. "You can't play football again. This is it. These are your last two shots. Make the best of it. Be animals. If you make a mistake, as long as you're killing someone, I won't yell at you. I want you to have a good game. I want you to remember the last two games of the year we kicked the shit out of those teams."

He was trying to prepare his seniors for potentially the final two games of their lives and prepare them for the rest of their lives. It always seemed to be that way. There was a natural intersection between his efforts to teach and to motivate them as football players with more valuable life lessons, and Atkins saw that as an opportunity to simultaneously build football players and men. How many times had he told them "Football is life"? It was a theme he returned to often.

"Guys, you're missing an opportunity," Atkins began when he had gathered the kids in his finished basement. "How quick did your high school career go by? Well, the next phase of your life will too. And the next phase of your life is starting right now, and you have to get goddamn ready! You guys could never get ready. No matter how hyped up I got. No matter what we talked about. No matter what drills we did. You need to know what it means to be ready. Life happens fast, fellas."

Atkins looked over the field and wondered if his team would be ready that night. He wondered why they had failed to recognize urgency throughout the season, and he wondered if that failure was his own. It was hard for him not to equate wins and losses with success and failure. After all, he was a football coach, and to this point in the season, he had a losing record. He was especially despondent about that as he sat in his kitchen the previous night talking to his wife and coaches. The seniors were in the dining room laughing and shouting. Atkins noticed Kenzi leaning back in his chair. Kenzi's mouth was wide open as he let out an effusive laugh. Even from another room, Kenzi's happiness was contagious. Atkins began laughing, and it brought upon a kind of epiphany. Atkins was able to shed new light on his losing season.

"For a couple of weeks, when we lost our first game and when we got knocked out, I took it hard," Atkins admitted. "I was thinking about it, talking about it with my wife. I was talking about it with the coaches, and then last night, I was sitting there looking at Kenzi. Okay, his sister is his cousin. His father had a baby with his mother and his aunt. I see the family, and I see when his aunt died and I went by the house. And his sister's always getting locked up. His mother is a goddamn mess. The whole family's a goddamn mess, and if I can get this kid thinking about college, then it was well worth it. I'm waiting for these kids, ten years from now, and hopefully I'm still here coaching, that these kids will come back with their college degrees, out of Chelsea."

Kenzi, the one with "no shot," was thinking about going to college and majoring in hotel management. He said he'd like to own his own business someday, and he frequently talked about being a role model to the underclassmen. Atkins gave him football. And football gave him his shot.

"Football is my life," Kenzi stated. "Without football I don't know what I'd be doing. The reason I'm staying out of trouble is all because of football. Football kept me going the right way. It kept me on the right track. If there was no football, I probably would be on the street doing something bad."

That evening Kenzi and the rest of the seniors would be playing their second to last high school football game. After the game against North Shore, all that would remain was the Thanksgiving Day game against Pope John. From the outside, two meaningless games may have seemed like an anticlimactic finish, but the seniors knew how far they'd come. As freshmen, they were part of the football program that was temporarily discontinued. They had run for miles every practice under Coach O'Brien, and they had been humiliated. They became familiar with losing, and they became known as the Red Devil team that was so bad and so much in danger of being hurt, the administration thought it prudent to quit. Then Coach Atkins came on board and made football cool again. He taught them how to play, how to win, and how to try. Sure, these were meaningless games, but they would play for Atkins and for the pride he had instilled in each one of them.

"Who remembers the Whittier game here?" Atkins asked his team in the locker room before the game. "Remember how close the Whittier game was? We're coming off the field and that fat fuck with the beard grabbed one of the Whittier coaches and started telling him what he needed to do. This is how bad people want to see us lose, fellas. The coach from North Shore was trying to coach another team, to the point where I almost got into a fucking fistfight with the guy. That's the honest to God's truth. The security guard had to come and throw the guy out. Now is the time for revenge. Lay the beating on them, fellas. Guys, let's start from the second half of last week. Come out and put the beating to them. Put the goddamn beating to them right from the beginning. We're gonna come out like we're the goddamn San Francisco 49ers, and we're gonna pass the shit all over these bastards. Understand? They're not gonna know what hit 'em. We're gonna go out and we're gonna kick the living shit out of them. Do you understand me?"

"Yes, Coach!"

"Do you understand me?!"

"Yes, Coach!"

"Every play, you remember what that guy did to us. If you're starting to fade away, you think about what that asshole did to us and you take it out on the next player you see. Understand me, fellas?"

"Yes, Coach!"

"Breakdown!"

"Red!"

"Breakdown!"

"Red!"

"Breakdown!"

"Chelsea!"

"Breakdown!"

"Devils!"

It was game on! The Red Devils raced out on to the field like this was their Super Bowl. They were smashing into each other, pounding their fists on each other's shoulder pads, and crashing their helmets together. The Red Devils bounced up and down on the sidelines, and rushed out to receive the kickoff.

On the second play of the game, Melvin scrambled for a 25-yard gain. After the drive stalled and Chelsea punted, North Shore moved the ball well until Orlando rushed in untouched and sacked the quarterback.

The two teams traded possessions again. First, Chelsea was forced to punt, then Kenzi forced a turnover when he flattened the running back. Ato fell on the loose ball. But Chelsea's offense looked disorganized. The offensive line was blocking poorly, and Melvin was being pressured from all sides. Atkins called time-out.

"Hey guys, I hate to say it, but right now they're out-toughing us. You're letting them out-tough us? Are you shitting me? Remember, if you make a mistake I won't yell at you, but if you get outtoughed, that's hard for me to swallow. Make a goddamn play. Get the ball and make a play."

North Shore put together its best drive of the game in the closing minutes of the first half.

"Kenzi," Atkins called out. "Seventy-four just kicked your ass. He just kicked your ass again. How can that be happening?"

North Shore moved the ball all the way down to the Chelsea 6-yard line with two minutes remaining in the half. Atkins continued shouting from the sidelines.

"They're just tougher than you!"

Frankie stuffed the run on 1st and goal. An incomplete pass made it 3rd and goal from the 7. Then North Shore looked like they might score, but Joey Barbosa came flying in from the side. Barbosa was playing with three torn ligaments in his left ankle. He'd been playing with the injury since before the Georgetown game. But he was able to move well enough to lay out the ball carrier and force another North Shore fumble. Miguel fell on top of it in the end zone, and Chelsea got the ball on their own 20. Only ninety seconds remained in the half.

The Red Devils didn't run out the clock. They wanted to see what their sophomore quarterback could do. So, Melvin stepped into the pocket and fired deep down the field. Kenzi hauled it in and ran all the way down to the North Shore 30-yard line. It was a 50-yard bomb!

"Double slot. All go!" Atkins said when Melvin raced to him on the sideline. "I want you rolling right. One-two-three, throw it. One-two-three, throw it. All go. Look where they're playing again. Throw it to the outside, not to the inside. Let's go."

Melvin was sacked.

"Four curl, two hook, X go. You're gonna sprint left."

Another busted play.

"Get over here," Atkins called to Melvin. "It's open. You gotta stay on him. Geez, you can't give me sorry. We're going in for a goddamn touchdown! All right, regular offense. Kenzi! I want the bootleg pass. Forty-nine left bootleg pass. Everybody know what they're doing? Roll right. Let's go."

This time Melvin completed the pass to his tight end, Carrington Guillaume. Frankie followed with a short run, and then Melvin had to hurry up and spike the ball. There were only ten seconds remaining in the half, and the ball was on the North Shore 13-yard line.

"Field goal! Field goal!" Atkins screamed for the first time as head coach of the Red Devils.

Junior Cesar Camacho raced on to the field and kicked the first field goal for Chelsea High School in forty years. The Red Devils reacted as if it were the most exciting play they had ever seen. They were deliriously happy as they bounded toward the locker room leading 3–0.

"It feels freaking good," Camacho shouted. "I didn't expect it. I never thought Coach was going to give me that responsibility."

Atkins primarily focused on blocking schemes during his half-time chat. North Shore had been blitzing more than he expected, and his offensive line wasn't adjusting to pick it up. With a few changes, Atkins hoped to still get Melvin out in the open in the second half.

Chelsea's first possession of the second half came after Kenzi stripped the ball away again and Miguel recovered his second fumble of the game. The defense was swarming to the ball and pushing North Shore back on its heels, but Melvin and the offense couldn't move the ball much at all. In fact, with penalties and sacks, they actually lost 32 yards on their first drive.

"Listen up, we've got 2nd and 70,000 yards," Atkins exaggerated. "Let's run it down their throats. Here we go. Sprint right pass. Orlando, you do a 5-yard out. Kenzi, you're doing a post. Melvin, you're taking your time. When I say it's a bootleg, it's a goddamn bootleg. You have to sprint. How many times have I told you that in practice?"

"All the time, Coach."

"Well, then you've got to goddamn sprint."

Melvin was sacked in the end zone for a safety on the next play. Chelsea led 3–2 with ten minutes to play. Chelsea returned to its regular running offense, allowing Frankie and Alex to take turns chewing up yardage. Alex finally scored, and Frankie went in on the 2-point conversion. That made it 11–2, and that's how it ended. Chelsea finished with a 3–2 record in their division, which was tied for second behind Manchester. They were 5–5 overall with a chance to finish with a winning record for a third straight season.

"All right guys, you made it tough, but a win's a goddamn win," Atkins said while the Red Devils cheered. "The toughness came toward the end, and the tougher team won the game. Ivan, it took you three quarters to get fired up, but once you did, you were a beast. I keep telling you guys, you've got to start earlier."

He praised the defense. He complimented Melvin and Cody. And he reminded them all to head straight home and stay out of trouble. Then he released them with one other useful tip.

"Nobody leaves the locker room until everything is cleaned. Sweep the floor, and get all your clothes home. Take all your clothes home, and clean your asses. You stink!"

CHAPTER THIRTEEN

The Dirty Dozen

Losing six seniors is completely and totally unacceptable. Somewhere along the lines we failed as coaches. Coming from a teaching background, if a kid fails a test, you didn't teach it well enough, because he didn't learn it. Y'know, it's all about the struggle, but if you give up the struggle, the battle is lost.
— Dennis O'Neil, Chelsea High School assistant coach

The posting of the first-quarter grades, always the week before the Thanksgiving Day game, was an anxious day for Coach Atkins and his assistant coaches. Which kids would be ineligible to play? Who would flunk off the team? The answer was that twelve kids, including six seniors, had failed their way to the sidelines. They would be watching the final game of the year in dress shirts and ties. The list included Miguel, Midnight, Carrington Guillaume, Jonathan Santiago, and Kenzi. And these weren't simply students who were victims of the "1-F" rule. Several other players had one F on their report cards, but because they weren't disciplinary problems, Principal Orlov was willing to let them play. Only players with two Fs were ineligible.

"I'm pissed," Frankie said angrily about his teammates who flunked off. "I don't understand. Coach says this is your last chance to make a name for yourself. It's the last time you'll put on the helmet, for most of us at least, because most of us aren't going to play college football. It's the last time you're going to do it, so why not want to play? I think if we won some of the games we needed to win to go to the playoffs, people would have worked harder. Especially if we were going to the playoffs, they'd say they have to

215

sit their ass down and get into the books, do my work, so I can stay on the team. Once we lost, I noticed people slacking off."

Coach O'Neil was also pissed, but mostly he felt disappointed and partially responsible. He and Atkins had spent so much time at those Thursday night dinners, and so much more time talking with the teachers, doing whatever they could to encourage the players to do their homework and pass their classes. Twelve kids with two Fs and many more with one F was, according to O'Neil, a reflection of his effectiveness as a teacher and motivator. He was not at the point where he was willing to say the kids were accountable for themselves.

"I will reach that point when I'm the best coach I can be," O'Neil said humbly. "I continually want to be a better and better coach. As I grow more familiar with these kids, I'll have more tools in my toolbox to recognize and implement. My brother's a colonel in the army, and the army has a way of making people accountable. Football and teaching are like that, too. It's unacceptable. I think there are other things we could have done as a staff."

O'Neil spoke somberly about several players. Santiago, he said, was too blasé about life. Orlando was a challenge, a prima donna who was not good enough to be one. Miguel wasn't coming close to reaching his potential. And Kenzi was an especially disappointing personal failure.

"He shouldn't have flunked off because he's a Special Ed. kid. I can't believe two teachers would flunk him, because being a Special Ed. kid you almost receive a mandate from the principal not to flunk these kids. And he had really come a long way. I kind of thought I reached him, kind of surprised he flunked off."

And while O'Neil may have wanted to give himself an F for failing to reach so many of the players, Atkins believed there might be some truth to the notion that less is more. Instead of offering more help or doing more for the kids, there may come a time when coaches and teachers and parents need to do less, so that these kids will stand up on their own and accept some personal responsibility. However, the risk may be too great. If the kids don't stand up, they could fall, and in Chelsea, sometimes they fall hard.

"In my opinion," Atkins began, "it's the culture of today. Everything is given to them. Everything is expected, even from the fucking parents. They'll come down to the police station and say, 'Why was my kid arrested?' Well, he was in a gang fight. 'Well, what about the other boys?' I just told you your son was arrested because he was in a gang fight. What do you give a shit about the other kid for? There's always an excuse. It's an entitlement society. Today, there's no self-denial. We can talk about it until we're blue in the face."

Atkins thought about the boy who went to school, then to football practice, and then to work at Logan Airport. That boy got home at ten at night and started his homework, and then got up and did it all over again the next day. That boy was Atkins. He learned to do for himself. But he was self-motivated. Something inside him told him what needed to be done, and he did it. Now, he told other kids what they needed to do, but if they were missing that certain something inside of them, the message had a hard time getting through.

"Kids don't understand," Atkins said. "Monday watching films I talked about all the things that are done for them, and they won't even do for themselves. I told them they're setting themselves up for failure, not only in football, but in life. They can't even work for themselves when somebody else is doing half the work for them."

That included Kenzi, the popular kid, the funny one, the kid Atkins believed in. Atkins thought Kenzi was a good kid stuck in the middle of a bad situation. He explained that Kenzi lived with his cousins, Jessica and Jose. Jessica was a tough girl who had beaten up a boy in the high school the previous year. Jose was not only his cousin, but also his half-brother because they had the same father and their mothers were sisters.

"It's a big tough family," Atkins concluded. "You just look at him, you can tell he's just lost a lot of the times."

Kenzi was not alone in that regard. In fact, a big part of Chelsea's problems on the football field that year was that many of its seniors were *lost* to some degree. Who were the younger kids supposed to follow into battle? Orlando, who quit sporadically? Kenzi and Miguel, two key starters who allowed themselves to fail two classes? Jonathan Luna, who was injured most of the year? Frankie, who skipped school in the middle of the season and didn't understand what he had done wrong? Certainly, there were Danny Cortez and Richie Oliveras, two good hard-working students who never caused Atkins any problems. And there was Mario, a quiet kid who led by example. But considering Chelsea had sixteen seniors on the team, and six of them failed off, it's easy to see there was an extreme lack of senior leadership. It didn't go unnoticed by some of the underclassmen.

"Dont'e Wilson, a junior, came up to me a while ago," O'Neil recalled. "He was confused about the general feel of the team. He looked at the leadership, the captains. We have poor captains, and he feels obliged to follow their example, but the example that he sees isn't how he feels himself. So, he was confused. I told him to just keep doing that Dont'e thing and you'll be fine. He gets Bs and Cs. He's got a nose for the ball, he's always aggressive. He's a great kid. The gist of that conversation was that he was feeling dragged down by the examples of the supposed leadership."

It was a problem the Red Devils might not have to face the following year when Dont'e, Alex, and Cody took over as captains, but that was a year away. The Red Devils still had one more game to play. All the players who had failed off the team continued coming to practice, because they knew if they didn't, they wouldn't be part of the team at all anymore. They posed for the team picture, and they stood quietly on the sidelines while the rest of the team prepared for Pope John. It would be the last time Chelsea would square off against the Tigers on Thanksgiving Day. Next year, Chelsea would begin a Thanksgiving tradition against Saugus High School.

Chelsea had played their neighbors from Everett on Thanksgiving for ninety-five years, but after Everett moved up to Division 1 and Chelsea temporarily moved down to Division 5, the rivalry ended. Since 1990, Chelsea had been playing Pope John, and while they weren't natural or division rivals, the games had proven to be competitive and spirited. For instance, last year the Tigers scored a touchdown on the last play of the game to beat Chelsea, 28–27. But this year's game wouldn't be about revenge. It would be about the seniors. Atkins made sure of that.

"Seniors, this is it," he began his pregame speech. "Like I said, it's been a goddamn pleasure. Go out there today and make a name for yourself. It's gonna be something that you guys are going to remember forever. I'm telling ya. I can remember almost every single play of my Thanksgiving Day game. I remember every mistake I made, and I remember every play I made. And I think about it. And it gets emotional. Mario, this is it for you, son. You may never wear a uniform again. You'll never wear a Chelsea football uniform again. This is it. You have to be proud of it. Orlando, you have to be proud. We've all made mistakes, including myself, this year. But let's let today make up for it. You have a chance today, Orlando. YOU have a chance today. Danny, you have a chance to make up for all the mistakes we made. Go out winners. If we win today, fellas, we'll have three seasons in a row with a winning record. It hasn't been done in about fifty years. Fifty years! You guys have a chance to make a legacy. We didn't make it to the playoffs that year, but we finished our senior year with a winning record three years in a row for the first time in fifty goddamn years."

Atkins was speaking from the heart. He remembered how much playing on Thanksgiving as a senior had meant to him, and he assumed his seniors felt the same way. Maybe they did. Maybe they didn't.

"Frankie, you have one day to make a highlight film, and it's gonna start in about fifteen minutes. Orlando, you have one day, one game to make a highlight film. We need, on both sides of the ball, balls to the wall on every play. You can't take any plays off. None. This is it, fellas. Seniors, you'll never be in this locker room having me talk to you about going out on the field and kicking someone's ass ever again. This is it, Orlando. This is goddamn it. Don't do it to yourself. Don't go out on that field and wind up saying, 'I should have done this.' Don't leave any 'I should haves' on that field today, fellas. No goddamn 'I should haves.' Just go out and do it. There's no time. You either do it or you don't. What are we gonna be? Are we gonna be the doers today? I have no doubt if you play like you practiced this week we're gonna kick some goddamn ass."

At this point, Atkins gave three of his seniors an opportunity to speak. Orlando, who looked hung over from a long night of drinking, talked despondently about not making the playoffs his senior year. Frankie admitted he didn't run as hard as he could have all year, but promised he'd be at his best today. And Mario asked for something from his teammates.

"I want you to put your heart and soul into it one more time," he said. "Give me all you got. I'm proud of all you guys."

Atkins wrapped things up by telling his team they could leave this high school as champions today, and then he sent them out into the pouring rain. After a season of sensational football weather, the 5–5 Red Devils and the 6–3 Tigers would close out the year in an ice cold downpour. The Red Devils hadn't even come outside for warm-ups, opting instead to get ready in the warm, dry gymnasium. The team had gotten together for a big breakfast of eggs and pancakes cooked by the coaches, and they had stayed together for the next couple of hours. They were warm and well fed, but when they stepped outside, they were stung by the cold, wet rain and sleet. Chelsea's field turf would prevent the game from getting muddy and sloppy, but it was an uncomfortable day to play, and especially, to watch football. There weren't two dozen people in the Chelsea stands when the game started. About forty people were on hand to support Pope John.

"Does it ever rain in goddamn Chelsea, fellas?" Coach asked with a huge grin. "This isn't rain. You understand? It's beautiful out here. I know and you know you guys are physically superior to this team. You just can't think it. Walking on that field isn't going to do it, fellas. Walking on that field and putting your foot up someone's ass is gonna do it."

The Red Devils, known for their slow starts, came out inspired. On a 4th down play, Frankie picked up 25 yards, more than enough for the 1st down. Then Richie sprinted for an 18-yard touchdown that gave Chelsea a 6–0 lead. The 2-point conversion was successful, but was negated by an illegal motion penalty. And on the second attempt, Melvin fumbled the snap.

Moments later, Orlando was thrown out of the game. A small skirmish erupted when a Pope John player hit Orlando after the whistle. Orlando responded by throwing two elbows at him. The referee, who was standing right next to the action, backed away and blew his whistle. Somehow he didn't see Cody racing in and punching the offending Pope John player. Cody's aggressiveness escalated the situation, but since the referee didn't notice it, he threw Orlando out of the game, but only for the rest of the first half.

"I was lucky I got out with my life," the referee exaggerated to Atkins. "I had so many guys around me."

Atkins fumed for the rest of the half. He screamed at Cody and then watched Pope John score the game-tying touchdown thirty seconds before the end of the half. The turn of events did nothing to assuage Atkins' mood.

"This is their senior game," he screamed at Cody as soon as they were behind closed doors. "You've just gotta sit there and take it. What the fuck did you do, Cody? What did you do?! You're acting like that after it was all over, because you're a PUNK! Stop being a goddamn punk! Jesus Christ, you're supposed to be our leader, and you're the biggest punk on the fucking team!"

Atkins paused momentarily and took a deep breath. He reminded himself that this day was about the seniors. He couldn't let it break down into something between him and Cody. He brought his focus back to trying to get the seniors a win in their final game.

"Guys, you let this goddamn team hang around. Now, it's a goddamn ballgame! Dont'e, what happened to you? You're getting your ass kicked out there! Can you play or not!"

"Yes, Coach."

"Just be tough, guys. That's all it is. C'mon. They get the ball at the start of the second half. Three plays and out. Three goddamn plays and out. Anybody have any questions about their assignments on offense? Pop Warner, if you're in there, you have to block, son. Would you fucking play off the ball? Fire off the goddamn ball. Simple stuff. We should be burying this goddamn team."

When the coaches left the room to talk more about their second-half strategy, several players went up to Cody and shook his hand for standing up and fighting for Orlando. Cody kept his helmet on and seemed to begrudgingly accept their support. Perhaps, he knew better than they did that taking a swing at another player was not something to be congratulated for.

Pope John began the second half by marching down the field and pushing the ball over the goal line, but the touchdown was called back because of a holding penalty. Chelsea's defense held its ground and took the ball over on downs.

The game remained tied until Alex took off down the sideline for an explosive 80-yard touchdown run. The 2-point conversion failed again, and the Red Devils' lead was 12–6.

Pope John held the ball for several minutes. There was a hard-hitting battle going on between the Tigers' offensive line and the Red Devils' defensive line. Chelsea was firing off the ball and hitting hard, but the Tigers were still able to pick up 3 and 4 yards at a time. By doing so, they converted several 3rd and 4th downs for 1st downs, and finally scored with under three minutes to play. Atkins called a time-out before what he expected to be a 2-point conversion attempt.

"This is the game, fellas," he said. "This is it."

But Pope John didn't come out and try to bull their way to victory. Instead, with the rain no longer pouring down, and the expensive field turf holding up well, the Tigers kicked the extra point and took a 13–12 lead.

"Guys, go out there and make a goddamn play," Atkins said with surprising calm.

Chelsea's final drive of the season would begin at their own 40-yard line with two and a half minutes left to play. It was the last 150 seconds many of them would ever play. Frankie began with a hard 5-yard run. Alex added 15, bringing the ball to the Pope John 40.

The Chelsea sideline came alive. All the kids were on their feet and cheering. Alex broke a tackle and picked up another 1st down. Then another. Finally, Alex took a toss to the left sideline and found a lane. There was still 1:10 left to go in the game as he crossed the goal line. Chelsea failed again on the 2-point conversion, but they had the lead, 18–13. Now, they just had to hold on to it for seventy seconds. And they did.

"Seniors, you did it," Atkins said when the applause died down. "Three years in a row, a winning season. It hasn't been done in almost fifty years. You should be proud of yourselves. That was a great goddamn job, guys. Another thing, we had two rushers that went over a thousand yards. Frankie went over a thousand today, and Alex had over a thousand, too. I don't know if that's ever been done before."

Again, Atkins waited for the cheers to subside.

"It's Thanksgiving, enjoy yourselves. I'm very proud of you. Seniors, where are you? Like I said last night, we have to get you into college. Where are you going, Orlando? If you're not going to college, you're going to the Army, the Navy or somewhere. You're not hanging out on the streets of goddamn Chelsea. You're going to make something of yourself, fellas, every goddamn one of you. I'm going to make sure of that."

After reminding the kids about the upcoming fashion show fund-raiser, and the football banquet the following month, Atkins looked up and saw a dozen parents standing nearby, waiting to take their sons home.

"Parents, I have forty kids here, which means we should have eighty parents here, or a minimum of sixty parents. So, we don't have enough, because we have a lot of work to do between now and next year. We got to get your kids on the right track for next year. We had twelve kids flunk off. It's unacceptable, and I need the parents' help. And I'll tell you right now, I'm not getting enough of it. I need your help. It's more than just about football. It's about your kids' futures. You understand that, parents? So you need to help me help the kids. You understand?"

The parents nodded dutifully. All that was missing was a resounding, "Yes, Coach," and they would have looked and sounded just like their kids.

Atkins concluded by giving out three game balls to Orlando, Frankie, and Danny. He pronounced Alex the star of the game, and then chose to single out Mario again for his incredible toughness.

"You know I work the Gang Unit, and I see all those guys who think they're tough guys. They bully people when they're with four or five guys. But here's Mario, broken foot, broken hand, broken finger, twisted knee, and he's probably got five other things wrong with him. But when you heard those pops today, they were coming from this man right there, fellas."

The players and parents erupted in applause one last time, and then the group slowly broke up. With rain still dripping off his Chelsea baseball cap, Atkins watched his team walk away and let a satisfied smile spread across his face. He knew these kids didn't have a lot, and he was happy they had a little something they could hold on to forever. They were winners.

CHAPTER FOURTEEN
Where Did the Money Go?

When the football season ended, players and coaches went their
separate ways only to reconvene at the annual fashion show on
the first Friday night in December. The players arrived in casual
clothes and spoke briefly to Coach Atkins, who was sweeping a
big pile of clothes, papers, and dust into the center of the varsity
locker room. Atkins was in a good mood, intermittently yapping
on his cellphone and redirecting the players to the auditorium to
get ready for the show.

"I'm excited to see all the girls," Frankie said while throwing
on his all-white tuxedo and shiny white shoes.

"I'm waiting to see if I get bought," Danny Cortez added.

The football players' fashion show was a fund-raising event
put on by the Booster Club. Each of the players walked out on
stage in a stylish tuxedo accompanied by a Chelsea High School
girl, and then the bidding would begin. The players were auc-
tioned off with the high bidder buying the rights to go out on a
date with the player of her choice. Seventeen players made their
way on to the stage that night. It would have been eighteen, but

Kenzi was sent home as soon as he arrived "as high as a kite," according to Atkins.

Hamza was almost sent home because Atkins was upset with him for sending his teenage daughter a message through the MySpace Web site.

"I told you if you ever do that again, I'll kill you," Atkins barked at Hamza. "Do you understand? I'll knock you out."

The evening began with loud rap and dance music playing in the small, dark auditorium. The high school dance club performed while about a hundred people took their seats. Dozens of red and black balloons formed a crescent around a disc jockey in the back of the stage. Then Atkins walked out in jeans, a T-shirt, and white sneakers.

Danny was the first to join him on stage and the crowd went wild. The bidding began at $5 and didn't stop until some lucky girl had pledged $45. Jose Ponce came out dressed all in black. He was wearing sunglasses and played to the crowd. Dont'e was in all white with a long jacket, black sunglasses, and his collar up. He was living the dream. Alex seemed very popular with the ladies, but the star of the evening was Orlando. He was dressed in bright, bright red: The Red Devil. He was both cool and a bit uncomfortable. One of the cheerleaders on stage pleaded with her mother in the audience to continue bidding until she had won a night with Orlando. She got him for a hundred bucks.

"We're gonna talk about what we need to do to help these kids succeed after high school," Atkins bellowed into the microphone, addressing his comments to the parents. "What's happening is we're losing them, and we don't need to be losing them. They need to be home. I check on them, but I need the parents at home checking on them at home as much as I do. I'm in their classes and in their lunch room every day. Hey guys, they're in high school, if they don't come home with a book, something's wrong. Look at their work and check it. Football gives them skills to get through hard times, but we need your help. It can be much better than it is."

The evening ended with a big round of applause. The rap music returned as the crowd filtered out into the hallway for refreshments. Shane Verge and Rich Oliveras stayed back to count the money. They had raised $950. It was a good night. But there would not be many more good nights for Atkins and the Chelsea High School football team. The problem was money. And the question was: "Where did it go?"

Shane was the first to ask the question. He had been keeping a close eye on the Booster Club account for several months. He watched the account balance grow, and he was stunned when he discovered nearly every dime was missing. His concerns launched an investigation in the early months of 2007.

"A good deal of money was raised," Shane said, referring to the many fund-raising events in 2006. "But when I went to the bank, there was nothing."

The Chelsea Booster Club account had been opened by Atkins in December of 2004 with a $250 deposit. Atkins and former Chelsea city councilor Paul Nowicki were named to the account, but Atkins was in charge. He made all the deposits and all the withdrawals for the first two years. After all, he initially did all the fund-raising and made all the purchases. But over time, Rich and Shane began raising thousands of dollars through various raffles and events. They would usually wrap a wad of cash in a rubber band and hand it to the coach. They'd watch him place the money in his pocket, but they had no way of knowing what happened to it after that. As the money and their discomfort grew, they asked Atkins several times for a greater role in the Booster Club. Finally, in September of 2006, Atkins acquiesced and added Shane to the account.

For the next two months, there were no withdrawals, only deposits. And by the end of November, there was more than $8,500 in the account. By late December, the account was empty.

There was an ATM withdrawal for $502 at 1:45 in the morning from 91 Squire Road in Revere, which was right across the street from a strip club. There were hundred-dollar withdrawals from ATMs in Mashantucket, Connecticut, where Foxwoods Casino is located. Another withdrawal in Seabrook, New Hampshire, where Atkins had participated in a Texas Hold 'Em poker tournament. In all, $5,400 was withdrawn in the month from Thanksgiving to Christmas.

"Go fuck yourself!" Atkins bellowed when Shane confronted him at a basketball tournament on December 26, 2006. "Who the fuck do you think you're talking to? I've been running this program for three years, and I'm gonna sit here and answer to you?"

Atkins stormed off, but Shane and Rich took their story to athletic director Frank DePatto. Jimmy, Shane, Rich, and Frank had a meeting in early January 2007. Shane produced the bank documents that not only showed the withdrawals unrelated to football expenses, but that also showed there was now a negative balance in the account, and that over the last two years there were overdraft fees totaling $979.44.

"All we want you to do is pay it back," Shane said.

"I'm not paying anything back," Atkins protested. "I'll do the fund-raising after the fact like I've always done. That money is mine. I've put in a shitload more than I've ever taken out."

Shane wasn't buying it. When his name was added to the account, he asked Atkins directly if there were any outstanding debts. Atkins said "no" and never mentioned he was owed any money. So, in that first meeting with Frank DePatto, Rich, and Shane, Atkins was pressured to sign a document that called for him to pay back $8,500. There was a payment schedule of $500 a month. If Atkins agreed, the whole mess would be forgotten.

Atkins didn't agree at that time, but another meeting was held on January 29. This time, Frank pulled Jimmy aside and tried to convince him to sign the document.

"These parents have bank statements, Jimmy. I'm telling you, if you don't sign, you're not going to be coaching in Chelsea anymore."

Atkins signed. Even though he didn't have the money, even though he had just borrowed $3,200 from Frank a few months earlier, even though he claimed he didn't actually owe the money, he signed. He walked into the junior varsity football locker room and signed a document in which he promised to pay back $8,500 because he was afraid of losing a job that paid $7,000. His righteous indignation was gone. And he signed.

Then he went out and solicited a $1,000 check from local businessman Lester Morovitz and deposited that money into the Booster Club account on March 19 as part of his restitution. That didn't fly with Shane and the others. Atkins wasn't supposed to pay what he owed with other people's money.

Dissatisfied, Shane and Rich once again brought their concerns to Frank, who in turn took them to the Chelsea High School principal, Morton Orlov. He determined the evidence was strong enough to put the matter in the hands of the superintendent, Thomas Kingston. Atkins was called in to meet with Kingston. As he'd done with the Boosters and with DePatto, Atkins was again asked to defend himself against the accusations. His meeting with Kingston occurred in mid-March of 2007. A few weeks later, he recalled the story this way.

"When we went to camp, I bought a piece of equipment. Frank DePatto knew all about this. I haven't heard from him yet. There is no relationship with him right now, not by my choice. We had about $4,500 for camp, but we needed another $3,500, so I put that on my credit card. And the reason I put that on my credit card was because we do the fund-raising after. So, the previous year when we went to camp we got a bill that was sent to school, and the principal broke my balls about the bill not being paid on time. So, this year, I put it on my credit card.

"So when I got called up to the superintendent's office, I brought all the receipts from my credit card. I gave them to the superintendent and then he went off on, 'You do too much on your own. You're like a rogue coach. You need to reel yourself in.'

"I was fucking furious, because just the word of that getting out there was horrible. Are you fucking kidding me? You can't say something like that. I paid for this stuff. That stuff was like $7,500 worth of bills. That doesn't include the thousands of other dollars I pay out of my own pocket as I go along. Each week with the team dinners that cost $200. But these were big hits, so I said, 'I'm not taking these hits, but I will pay for camp, because I can still go out and get the money from people.'"

According to Atkins, Kingston seemed satisfied with his version of the story. However, in that initial meeting, Kingston also expressed some concerns about the upcoming football banquet he believed Atkins had been planning without permission. Kingston cautioned Atkins about that kind of autocratic behavior, and told him to make sure to check with the AD and the principal before he did things like that. Atkins left that meeting thinking everything was fine. So, he was surprised when he got called back to Kingston's office two weeks later.

"First of all, I don't think you did anything illegal or immoral," Kingston began, according to Atkins. "As a matter of fact, I do not care about the Booster Club."

But the meeting quickly deteriorated into a litany of other problems and accusations.

"The meeting didn't go well," Atkins explained. "He was pissed!"

Kingston never broached the subject of embezzlement. Instead, he talked about Atkins' penchant for doing things on his own, like planning the football banquet and purchasing equipment, and then Kingston surprised Atkins by asking about newly surfacing allegations that he helped his players obtain muscle-building supplements. Someone had told Kingston that Atkins had arranged through a friend to get his players a discount on various muscle-building pills and powders—which Atkins admitted to doing.

"He brought all this stuff up about the American Nutrition Center in Everett," Atkins explained. "A former player, Larry Gregory, asked me about creatine once, and I said, 'No, you can't take creatine. That stuff is bad for your liver. You can't take any of that stuff for muscle growth other than protein. If you want to take protein, go ahead.'"

Atkins knew his players didn't have healthy diets and ate too much fast food, so he figured some additional protein would do them some good.

"I think it was, like, $20 of weight protein, and $10 of glutamine which helped us out when we were lifting, so we could get bigger and faster and stronger," Danny Cortez said. "It was all voluntary anyway. I used it. It definitely helped. I gained about 20 pounds in two months. You don't need a doctor's prescription. It's all legal stuff. It's actually recommended for all kinds of sports, not just football, if you're lifting weights."

But Kingston maintained that Atkins should have gotten permission from the kids' parents.

"This is just another example of you making decisions without going through the proper channels," he told Atkins. "You have no right to do what you do. Your problem is your ego. Your ego is too big for your job."

That made Atkins chuckle. When he stopped, he decided to stop defending his immediate supervisor.

"Listen, everything I've done, I've told Frank DePatto. Whether he told you or not is another issue. And I've never said that before, because I didn't want to put Frank in the middle. Even the banquet, I did tell Frank. And when I bought the equipment, I told

Frank. Even going back to 2004 when I bought the jackets, I told Frank DePatto."

The two men went back and forth for several minutes before Kingston finally said what he'd intended to say all along, what he'd been planning to say ever since the Booster Club allegations were brought to his attention.

"I'd like your resignation."

"You're not getting my resignation. If you want to fire me, you're gonna have to fire me. I'll start the process with my attorney. Let me tell you something, I'm not going quietly into that good night."

It was announced at the end of March in 2007 that Atkins would not be returning to coach the Red Devils. He wasn't officially fired, but his contract wasn't being renewed. Kingston gave no public reason why Atkins would not be retained.

"I think it is important to change these positions from time to time," Kingston told the *Chelsea Record*. "Coach Atkins had been with the team for three seasons, and I felt it was time to see what other candidates may be available."

Atkins' labor lawyer from the Massachusetts Police Association, Doug Louison, called Kingston's statement "disingenuous." Louison added that when he spoke with Kingston about Atkins' dismissal, Kingston characterized it simply as "a disagreement over leadership styles."

Atkins immediately threatened to file a lawsuit. The grounds, he believed, could have included discrimination, because there were nine varsity coaches at Chelsea High School, and all of them were white. Atkins was the only minority varsity coach in a predominantly black and Hispanic school. DePatto, Orlov, and Kingston were all white as well.

Defamation of character was another possible avenue to pursue. Kingston had been careful not to accuse Atkins of embezzlement in their second meeting, but that was almost exclusively what his first meeting with Atkins was about. If Atkins could prove the accusation was false, his case could be strengthened.

"To falsely accuse someone of a criminal behavior is defamation per se," Louison explained. "You don't have to prove damages or anything else."

Atkins further claimed that his discharge was unlawful because he didn't receive his due process. And Louison also considered using the Whistle Blower's Act, arguing that Atkins' public criticisms of B.U. could be construed as blowing the whistle on them.

Atkins didn't want to go through the ordeal of a lawsuit. He just wanted his job back, and he hoped that if he shouted "discrimination" loudly enough, Kingston would back down. Kingston never did, in large part, because he was well protected by contract law and semantics. He probably couldn't be found guilty of wrongfully firing Atkins, because he didn't fire him. He simply didn't renew his contract. Kingston's vague responses and nonspecific reasons for opening up a search for a new head football coach were frustrating, but legal.

Word of Atkins' dismissal spilled out into the school and community in drips and drabs. It was hard to keep something like that a secret in a city of less than 2 square miles. By the time Atkins called his captains to his office to let them know he would no longer be their coach, they had already heard the rumors. Still, they took the news hard. Alex, Pop Warner, Jose Ponce, Cody, and Dont'e Wilson all listened in stunned silence. They were captains of a rudderless, sinking ship. Their leader, their inspiration, was gone. Dont'e openly cried. Alex was also very emotional, and he was with Frankie later that day when they came upon Frank DePatto in the hallways.

"This is bullshit," Alex shouted unabashedly as he approached the sixty-eight-year-old athletic director. "He's my hero!"

"Well, maybe you should pick your heroes more carefully," DePatto said unsympathetically.

"This doesn't make any sense," Frankie chimed in. "He came in here and turned our football team around. Now, he's going to go somewhere else and bring some other team to a Super Bowl."

"He's done," DePatto said flatly. "He'll never coach again."

Undeterred, the Red Devils took their fight to the school committee. On a cool, clear night on the second Friday in May 2007, nearly three dozen Red Devils met at the high school football field. Wearing white shirts and ties, they marched together the mile or so down the street to City Hall. Patiently, quietly, they waited outside as the school committee members took their places along the semicircular dais. As the meeting was called to order, the Red Devils took their places, filling up several rows. The players were mostly underclassmen, guys who had hoped to play for Atkins again next season, but there were a few seniors, including Frankie and Danny. Richie Oliveras and Orlando were notably absent. There were a half dozen parents also in attendance.

The Red Devils were not surprise visitors, nor were they the first order of business. They were forced to sit through a lengthy presentation regarding a new housing project, and a few other minor issues until finally school committee chairman James Dwyer addressed the players. Dwyer, a heavyset man wearing a blue shirt with a button-down collar, told the players the committee would not address personnel matters in a public forum. There would be no question and answer period, but the committee would listen to what they had to say. Several players rose and walked over to the microphone.

Ironically, it was Cody Verge who was the first to speak. Certainly, he had overheard conversations in his own home. He must have known more details about why Atkins was really let go than any of his teammates. And while he didn't have his father's support on this matter, he knew his father would always stand by him. So, the kid who wanted to play quarterback, and who wanted his coach back, stepped up to the mike.

"We are here today to represent the confusion of the Chelsea High School football team. The reason we are here is not because of a football coach, because they come and go, but we are here for a teacher and friend who has taught us how we can succeed in life. He provided a goal for us, to be something in life. We come to you, the school committee, to speak out in the hopes that you will revise your decision and give us back the leader, mentor, and friend that made us believe we can be something in life."

Sirens blared from the street below as Cody delivered those eloquent opening remarks. Outside on the Chelsea city streets there was trouble. Inside City Hall, there were dozens of teenagers who believed their former football coach was a man who could lead them away from that trouble. He fought for them. So, they would fight for him.

"Kids in Chelsea are in gangs," Alex reminded the committee. "Coach calls our homes to make sure we're there. He's a big help to single parents."

More sirens interrupted the kids as they spoke.

"He's more than a coach," Melvin Ramirez declared. It was Melvin, "Pop Warner," who had organized the march on City Hall. "He makes sure we're safe, and he told us we can be somebody in life."

Dont'e Wilson and Jose Ponce made short statements as well. The sirens finally had stopped by the time Cody returned to the microphone.

"As you can see we are a united front," he said. "And we are willing to fight the release of our coach. I believe when the coach came to this school, he changed the way kids looked at life, because I know personally many kids who were good with just getting Ds on their report cards, but Coach Atkins changed that. Kids had a reason to want to get good grades and they actually wanted to go to college. I believe if the coach were to come back, he would show you, the school committee, that Chelsea High School is a great place, and that the football team is not only looking to get Ds on their report card. They are looking to go to college and looking to succeed in life and be somebody."

There was no discernible reaction from the members of the committee. Dwyer looked on attentively, but appeared unmoved. Gerald Lewis, the vice chairman from the B.U. management team, sat motionless. Morry Siegal and Michael Caulfield, two committee members who had supported Atkins in the past, nodded their heads and occasionally smiled, but they seemed more impressed with the kids' overall presentation than by anything they had to say.

Dwyer invited anyone else who wanted to speak to step up and be heard.

"We want our coach back," Dont'e's mother, Seneeca, began, and then she read from a petition. "In support of Chelsea High School football coach, Jimmy Atkins, we sign an agreement as a petition, a testament. We are all against allegations of any malpractice in his coaching position. We appreciate his firmness and his way of thinking. It encourages our children to stay off the streets and strive for academic success. Coach Atkins is a great positive to our community. He is a coach all year long, staying in close contact with our children and making sure they are performing academically and exhibiting sportsmanlike behavior. Coach Atkins is as much a part of our lives as he is our children's, serving as an extended parent. We have been lucky to have someone as kind-hearted and as strict as Jimmy Atkins coach our children. We attest at no time in our relationship with Coach Atkins has there ever been any sign of negligence to our children. We can attest to the fact that our children are taught to stay fit through regular exercise and they were told it is NOT okay to consume illegal substances. We the parents of the Chelsea High School football team sign as an extended part of the team in support of Jimmy Atkins. Without him, there is no team. We need and love our coach."

Melvin's mother, Janet, a patient services coordinator at Massachusetts General Hospital, told the committee that she'd known Coach Atkins for more than three years. She told the members about Atkins' impact on two of her children.

"He's not only my high school son's coach, he's also been the Pop Warner coach for my youngest child. I really appreciate his way of conduct toward the kids, because he shows the kids to be somebody in life, they need to be respectful and to have a goal in life. Not only that, he has always been a friend to our kids. The coach has been a teacher, and a parent. Anything these kids have needed, he has been there for them. I have seen him carefully watch over these kids like they were his own. I have seen him not giving up on these kids, and that makes them want to go on and do good for themselves. Coach Atkins has been such a great person, and a teacher, and a role model to his kids, that these kids have decided that, 'yes,' they want to be somebody in life. And I think they would not be a team without Coach Atkins. I've known him for a lot of years, and he has shown my kids a lot. I can say he has almost been like a parent to my kids, because I am a single mother, and anything I have needed from him as to speak to my children as to advice, he has always been there."

There was more from Alex's mom, Eve Alvarez.

"I am a single mother. My son, Alexander, you have no idea how hard I have worked to raise a good boy, and since my son went to high school and joined the team, my job has been so easy, because Coach Atkins has been there to help him and to help me. So, personally for me, Coach Atkins is not only the coach, he is the male role model that my son needed in life. You have no idea living in Chelsea, people say it is so dangerous, you have no idea how much peace of mind I have knowing that Coach Atkins belongs to the police department, and he said to me, 'Don't worry, Mrs. Alvarez, the whole police department is watching out for these boys.' And that makes me feel that my son is safe."

Finally, there was an unexpected speaker. Bob Hinkley, a tall middle-age man with a deep voice, bent low at the waist to speak into the microphone.

"I don't even have a son in high school. I have a son who's in seventh grade. I've had the pleasure of being with Coach Atkins since Pop Warner. I'm looking forward and looking for my son's future. I've seen what I can't do sometimes with my son. I've seen Coach Atkins help build my son into a little man, a twelve-year-old man. There must be some other alternative that might be overlooked at the present time as to Coach Atkins' tenure. He's coaching the team. The team has been successful. You've heard the student body talk about his fulfillment to help them get better. We all make mistakes. Being a football coach sometimes does not mean that you are exactly a mother's favorite coach. It's hard. But we're trying to build men. Being a graduate of 1974, I've experienced some of the thrills and some of the bad times in this city. I love the city of Chelsea. I love the people here. Coach Atkins is definitely a little man builder in the city of Chelsea. And me, being a parent, looking for my son's high school education as well as his athletic performance, I oppose the recommendations of the body concerning Coach Atkins not being reassigned as the coach."

When Hinkley concluded, there was a sudden outburst of applause from all the students and parents. It lasted for several seconds before Dwyer gestured he was ready to speak. He told the Red Devils how "dapper" they looked, and that they had made an excellent presentation. He asked to see the petition, but made it clear that the committee had no power to reinstate Atkins, and that it was unlikely to make such a recommendation to the superintendent. The pleas and protestations of the Red Devils and their parents were, at times, emotional and powerful, but they had fallen on deaf ears. There was no hope of Atkins ever coaching again in Chelsea, but hope could be found just a few miles down the road.

CHAPTER FIFTEEN
Kenzi Doesn't Graduate

If I had known there was another world on the other side of that
bridge, I probably wouldn't be so scared to try to go over that bridge
and try to see what's out there for me. Chelsea's just Chelsea. You
can make it beyond. You can cross that bridge and find a whole
new world out there. You don't have to be stuck here.
— Vivian Quiles, mother of Chelsea High
School quarterback, Miguel Medina

While the players who looked up to him were trying to save his job, Atkins was out looking for another one. It didn't take him long to find a school willing to overlook the fact that he didn't receive recommendations from his athletic director, principal, or the school superintendent. Certainly, that should have raised a red flag or two. He was a coach who had immediate and stunning success resurrecting a program and producing three straight winning seasons, yet he was let go. Why? Any school would have to wonder why a popular winning coach, a police officer, and a well-respected man in the community would be sent packing. But located just five miles down the road was Medford High School, and they needed a football coach more than they needed their curiosity satisfied.

"His track record in Chelsea spoke for itself," Medford athletic director Paul Mattatall said. "That was the kind of guy we needed, someone with the presence to recruit kids to play. His experience turning that program around, that's what impressed us."

Just a few days after the players had descended upon the school committee, Atkins interviewed for the recently vacated head coaching job at Medford. The school's football team was in much the same predicament that Chelsea had been in when

Atkins took over three years ago. Their numbers were down, and their record was terrible. In the previous year, the Mustangs were shut out in six straight games, and finished with a record of 1–9. They had won just four games in the past three seasons. They were desperate.

During an extensive interview process with Medford's headmaster, superintendent, and athletic director, Atkins was asked to explain what happened at Chelsea. Why, after posting a 22–11 record in three years, was he not welcomed back? Atkins never mentioned the Booster Club's allegations. Instead, he told them what Kingston had told him—that he had a tendency to do things first and ask permission later. Atkins admitted his aggressive style didn't sit well with the suits at Boston University. It was an accurate, though incomplete, assessment of what had transpired at Chelsea, and it was verified by Chelsea's city manager, Jay Ash, who just happened to be Mattatall's cousin.

"I used that connection," Mattatall explained. "That was obviously a cause for concern. Jay said to me, 'I just gave you fifteen minutes of how great this guy is, and now your next question is going to be, well, if he's so great, why isn't he being rehired?' But we understand the situation over there with Boston University. It was looked into and it wasn't anything that would discourage us from going forward with him. We all agreed we found our man."

So, Atkins was hired. Medford never got wind of the embezzlement allegations, because Kingston didn't want to publicly accuse Atkins of something without sufficient proof, and because Ash also didn't disclose the allegations to his cousin. Both men skirted the issue and, in effect, dumped their problem on an unsuspecting school. In their hearts and minds, Ash and Kingston believed Atkins was guilty of stealing money, but they couldn't tell Medford that without getting into a legal skirmish they weren't guaranteed to win. So, they kept their mouths shut, and let Medford hire a man they didn't trust.

"I wanted a face for Medford High School, and to me, that's what Jimmy brings to the table," Mattatall said.

The Mustangs quickly learned the new face of their program could be a volatile and angry face. When Atkins met with his new team a few days after being hired, he immediately threw a kid out of the meeting for talking in the back of the room. It was important to Atkins that none of the kids thought he was soft, so he flexed some muscle and set the tone right away. Ten minutes later, the evicted student reappeared and apologized to Atkins in front of the rest of the team. Atkins welcomed him back and moved on as if it had never happened. The Mustangs knew exactly how their new coach operated. Dozens of players stayed long after Atkins had wrapped up his opening speech. They welcomed him with smiles and enthusiasm and promises that they would follow his direction on the football field and in the classroom.

"That made it a lot easier for me to leave Chelsea," Atkins said. "I hate saying that, because if a Chelsea kid heard me say that, he'd be like 'Geez, Coach, you forgot us already?' And that's not my point at all. I'll never forget these kids, and if I didn't have to leave, I would have never left. I have to keep that balance that now that I'm gone, I got that response from the kids that I was looking for, and it was exactly like Chelsea."

Like Chelsea, Medford has a large minority population. And like Chelsea, it would be a significant challenge to turn the program around. The Mustangs played in the Greater Boston League against perennial powerhouses like Everett, B.C. High, Malden, and Arlington Catholic. But Atkins saw the tougher league as a potential advantage. He believed Medford had the same type of kids as those schools. He just needed to do a good job of recruiting and coaching. He told the kids they could win seven or eight games next year. It was a lofty goal that the players might have scoffed at if they didn't already know that their new coach had done exactly that in Chelsea. After being defunct for half a year, the Red Devils won eight games in Atkins' first year. Atkins walked through the doors of Medford High School with instant credibility. And though he still walked the streets of Chelsea as a police officer, and he was committed to coaching Pop Warner football for two more years in Chelsea, he belonged to Medford now.

"I still feel wronged, very wronged by Chelsea," Atkins said. "But it is what it is."

And it was difficult for the Red Devils to understand what had happened. Their lives, which so frequently seemed unfair anyway, just exploded once again. Sometimes it was an uncle dying of a drug overdose. Other times it was a brother going to jail, or an altercation with a rival gang, or a teacher presuming they were the cause of some trouble. Still other times they simply watched their father or mother being taken away to jail or driving away on their own.

Jonathan Luna's home had just burned down. Police believe that on April 16, an arsonist threw gasoline up the stairway of his home and lit a match while Jonathan's parents were sleeping on the third floor. Jonathan was at his sister's house at the time, and firefighters were able to get his parents safely out through a window. Jonathan told the story with a shrug of his shoulders, adding that his brother, Pascual, had been out of jail for less than a week.

"He has a lot of enemies," Jonathan said.

But Pascual wasn't home at the time of the fire, unless as some investigators believe, he was the one who set it.

Clearly, these were kids who struggled. They struggled at home, on the streets, and at school. They struggled to find hope, and they struggled to find fairness. These were kids who didn't have much, but they had Coach. He was their hope. He was their fairness. And now he was gone. It hurt to see him go. But it hurt even more to see him go without more of a fight.

"They feel betrayed," Seneeca Wilson said flatly. "He went and took care of himself. He's only thinking of himself at this point.

He gave up. I was totally shocked. I thought Coach was gonna give this a fight, but he might not have a leg to stand on."

It was going to be difficult to stand and fight, because Atkins had kept such poor records. He had receipts in his nightstand. He had receipts in his desk drawer in the football office. And he had receipts in the glove compartment of his Navigator that was costing him $891 a month in a car loan. But he didn't have all the receipts going back three years. And he certainly didn't save the receipts for all the pizzas, dinners, Gatorade, footballs, cleats, and other items for which he estimated he spent over $8,000 in cash since taking over the football program. No, it was easier to leave and hang his shingle in Medford.

There was plenty of anger among the players. They were angry that their coach was being treated unfairly. They were angry that he left so willingly. And they were upset about how they were being treated since Coach had been fired. They felt like they were being picked on even more than usual. They had even been prohibited from using the school's weight room.

"That school has really been treating those boys bad," Seneeca said sadly. "They locked them out of the weight room. Told them they couldn't be there. They haven't heard the end of this. I'm not a racist person at all, but these children are all minorities. These children don't have the resources that other cities have for their children. When it comes down to character and respect for the individual person, they don't have it for the children. They don't have it for the young boys growing up in Chelsea."

The players never received a satisfactory explanation about what happened, not even from Atkins. He spoke to the captains, but because he was ostracized so quickly, he was never able to call a team meeting. He was, however, still a Chelsea cop, so he could walk into the school whenever he wanted, and he made that point clear to the principal, Morton Orlov, one May afternoon in the cafeteria.

Orlov heard that Atkins was in the lunchroom casually conversing with several of the players. It was an informal and impromptu meeting between a coach and his former players, but Orlov thought it was inappropriate since Atkins had recently been let go. Orlov approached Atkins and suggested it might be better if he left.

"Hey, I'm a sergeant in the Chelsea Police Department, and I'll go wherever I damn well please," Atkins told Orlov. "I have every right to be here."

Orlov knew his authority was being challenged, but he also knew there wasn't anything he could do about it, at least not at that moment. He yielded to the larger man with the badge, and the kids loved Atkins all the more for it. As Orlov walked away, Atkins continued his conversation with the boys.

"No matter how upset you guys are," Atkins said, "You have to promise me you'll give the new coach a fair shot. He didn't have anything to do with this. So, give him a chance, and play just as hard for him as you did for me."

The new head coach was Mike Stellato, and it didn't take long for Chelsea to hire him. Stellato was already working in the Chelsea school system. He was the dean of students at the Clark Avenue School, and he had a Super Bowl championship on his résumé. He had coached football at Salem High School, St. Mary's of Lynn, and Danvers High School. It was in 2005 that he led the St. Mary's team to the Division 3A Super Bowl. He moved on the next year to coach at Danvers, where he would likely have stayed except that Danvers wanted him to teach in the high school. He couldn't afford the pay cut from his job as dean of students, so he stayed at Clark Avenue. Stellato didn't expect to be coaching in 2007, but the Chelsea job opened up suddenly. Two weeks after Atkins was fired, Stellato, a white man, was hired. There really wasn't much Atkins could do at that point. Chelsea was moving on without him. So, he moved on as well.

"All I can say is I think he was the best thing that ever happened to these kids in Chelsea High School," Miguel's mother, Vivian Quiles said. She was a product of the Chelsea school system herself. She graduated from the high school and attended college for one year. She now worked with children with multiple disabilities in the North Suffolk Mental Health facility. She was raising Miguel and her fifteen-year-old daughter, Stephanie, alone. The children's father had been out of Miguel's life since he was ten. That's why Vivian appreciated Atkins' strong male personality as a role model for her son.

"Miguel's never had that male figure at home on a constant basis," she explained. "It's hard, because it doesn't matter, a woman can only do so much. We cannot ever fill the space of a father in the household."

Yet, she believed Atkins came close.

"They saw him not only as a coach, but they saw him as a friend and a father. He was great. There wasn't a time when I called him and I said, 'Look, I'm really worried about Miguel. He's slacking.' And he could have been anywhere, on duty, off duty, he would make his way to the high school to sit with Miguel and talk to him. He was incredible. I really don't know how they would let someone like that go."

However, the firing of James Atkins as the head football coach of the Chelsea Red Devils was not enough for Rich Oliveras and Shane Verge. They wanted justice, and they wanted the money back. More than $8,000 was missing from an account that was supposed to support the football team. It was not James Atkins' personal account. They had brought their case to Frank DePatto and Thomas Kingston, and then they brought it to the state's district attorney's office. Investigations were launched by the D.A. and by the Chelsea Police Department. Under normal circumstances a police officer is placed on paid administrative leave as soon as he is officially under investigation. That didn't happen to Atkins.

He continued walking the beat, working the Gang Unit, and chatting up citizens on the street. It was an inexplicably obvious act of favoritism to allow Atkins to continue working, and it rankled several of the other officers in the department.

The investigation went on for several months. In the interim, all of the seniors on the football team graduated—except for Kenzi.

"I failed chemistry and something else," Kenzi said somewhat apathetically. "My fucking ADD. I couldn't do that stuff."

So, on a cool, overcast day in the middle of May, Kenzi sat in the audience and watched his teammates and classmates graduate. The girls wore red robes. The boys wore black. And they all walked slowly in a procession from the back of the basketball gym to the front. Parents and friends filled the bleachers. Thirty-two men and women from the school committee, the B.U. Management Team, the city council, and the high school administration sat on the stage looking out at 221 success stories. James Atkins had played a big role in a small percentage of those tales, but he was not present. Six other police officers were there, but Atkins chose to stay away. His absence was noted by his onetime friend Frank DePatto.

"There was $8,500 in that account," DePatto said while watching the graduates accept their diplomas. "Now, it's down to nothing. Three or four checks a day for non-football-related expenses. You tell me."

Atkins wasn't there to see Orlando, who looked even taller than usual in his shiny new dress shoes. When his row was called, Orlando stood and followed three girls to the stage. There was a big smile on his face and a little hop in his step as he reached for his diploma and swung the tassel on his cap from his right to his left. A loud roar went up from the crowd.

Atkins didn't see Danny Cortez in his well-groomed beard and mustache. He didn't see Ato and Joey Barbosa stand and cheer as each football player's name was called. He missed David Flores holding his face in disbelief, walking on air, and unable to sit still, buzzing with an abundance of energy. Atkins would have been proud to see Miguel and Frankie walking up the steps to the stage, soaking in the applause, and embracing one another as high school graduates. It would have bothered Atkins to see Kingston and Orlov on the stage shaking the hands of each of the players and wishing them well.

"Orlov is a B.U. hack," Atkins was fond of saying. "When B.U. goes, so goes Orlov. The powers to be aren't going to let some guy . . . who the fuck are you coming in and making decisions that you know nothing about these kids?"

Atkins most certainly would have had mixed feelings watching Richie Oliveras receive the Citizenship Award voted on by the faculty and given to the student who best exemplifies kindness and values. Atkins' relationship with Richie wasn't the same as it was with most of his football players. Richie didn't need Atkins like they did. He didn't react to him the same way, and never got as close. Plus, Richie's father was one of the two men who accused Atkins of embezzling and cost him his job. Still, Richie was a football player, and the fact that he received $5,000 in scholarships was a point of pride for the entire team.

This could have been a very special day for Atkins, but he missed it. Either he was embarrassed, or he didn't want to steal the attention away from the kids. Whatever the reason, Atkins didn't get to enjoy the sight of Orlando standing on top of a cafeteria table posing for pictures, looking over the milling crowd for friends, and shouting, "It's true! It's true! I graduated!"

Three years ago, that didn't seem possible. Orlando was in a gang and looking to earn the respect of his fellow gang members, no matter what it took to get it. Then Atkins came into his life. He walked right into his cell and offered him a chance to play football. He got inside Orlando's head and got him to think about things differently.

"I cared about school," Orlando reflected. "I wanted my diploma. I wanted all that, but there's two sides. I've seen the whole gangbanging side and the whole thing at school. I wanted to go to school, but at the same time I want to hang with my boys and just chill when school was over."

Orlando was being pulled in two directions, and then he got pushed by Atkins. Shoved, really. Orlando could be considered Atkins' crowning achievement. In his three years as Chelsea's head football coach, Atkins won twenty-one games and restored the program's credibility, but his greatest victories were the kids who held their diplomas so tightly and so close to their hearts.

"Ten years from now?" Orlando asked aloud. "I want to be a policeman. I should be with my family, having a family and having a good job. Enjoying life. Three years ago I would have said I'd be dead . . . or in jail."

Who knows, maybe if Atkins had arrived on the scene a little sooner, he could have helped keep Pascual Luna out of jail as well, and then P could have attended his brother's graduation. He could have seen Jonathan in his bright, white sneakers raising two fists over his head when he heard his name and rushed to the stage. Instead, P was back in jail being held on $100,000 bail.

Pascual had violated his parole and was supposed to appear in court, but didn't. So, a warrant was issued for his arrest. On May 1, P was one of four hundred protestors marching through Chelsea in an immigration rally. When the police spotted him, he ran. According to the official report, when the police caught up to him at the intersection of Congress Avenue and Division Street, P pulled out a .38-caliber Smith & Wesson revolver and fired. The bullet narrowly missed the three pursuing officers, but a fragment deflected off something and hit Sergeant Dan Delaney, leaving a bee sting welt on his chest. P was eventually wrestled to the ground and taken away.

"We will work very hard to hold Pascual Luna accountable," the Suffolk County district attorney, Daniel Conley, told the *Chelsea Record*. "This is a very, very dangerous man."

There were plenty of dangerous young men in Chelsea. Some of them played for the Red Devils. Orlando had as much bad potential as good. Black Josh was slipping through the cracks. There were reports that Josh had robbed a Taunton gang kid who had passed out from drinking. And that may be why that kid came back on May 15 and fired six shots into the wall, the door, and the air conditioner of Josh's house.

Luis Verde was a gang kid who, Atkins said, "had so much anger in him, I could see him killing somebody." But Luis graduated and went off to college in Minnesota. Orlando graduated and planned on taking classes at Bunker Hill Community College in Chelsea. Ato would be there, too.

Mario and Frankie were on their way to Bridgton Academy in Maine. It was a one-year prep school that could help them get into a better school. They hoped to eventually graduate from Florida State.

Jonathan Luna was going to Suffolk University in Boston. Miguel opted for Fisher College. Danny Cortez enrolled at Bay State College. And Richie was going to Virginia Tech. Almost everyone was moving on, including Atkins.

Chelsea was sure to be a very different place next year, and very much the same.

CHAPTER SIXTEEN

The Trial of James Atkins

*The first time coach came, he always used to say "football is life,"
and I guess that stuck in my head. I'd be home and I'd be like,
"Damn, you have to work so hard for everything you want. You
have to go to school. You have to wake up early. You've got football.
You have to go home and do homework. It's not easy. You have
to work hard for what you want. Football is life. It goes hand in
hand. Most likely, the person who works hard is going to win."*
—FRANKIE QUILES, CHELSEA HIGH SCHOOL RUNNING BACK

James Atkins left his mark on the Red Devils. He was called a savior
by some, and properly so. After all, no matter how his story ends,
he was the man who resurrected a defunct football program, who
restored pride in a school and a city. Where would the team be
without him? And more to the point, where would several of the
individual players be without him?

But his message became murky. Football is life, he'd say. He
preached hard work. No shortcuts. He lectured them about doing
the right things. He talked to them about personal responsibility
and integrity. He looked them in the eye. Promised them things.
And James Atkins, the coach and the cop, represented something to
the young men of Chelsea. He was hope. He was a way out. A path.
He was like them, only better. And if they aspired to be better themselves, they could end up like him. Successful. Respected. Happy.

In a city that fell from the weight of corruption, James Atkins
was a pillar. In a world where too many dads were absent, he was
omnipresent. Then he was gone. He didn't walk into a bright sun-
set. He walked under a cloud. What were the boys to think? What
if the best thing in their lives turned out to be a lie?

It would take nearly two years for the truth to even begin to make an appearance. Atkins had been fired because of a mere allegation. There were no criminal charges, nor had any evidence of wrongdoing been publicly revealed. He was then hired at Medford, and that's when the timeline for all of this became frustratingly slow for all involved. The Booster Club had brought its suspicions to the high school and the superintendent in January of 2007. Atkins was fired in March. But it wasn't until mid-August that Atkins was placed on paid administrative leave from the police department. Nearly eight months after the allegations first surfaced, the Suffolk County District Attorney's office and the Chelsea Police Internal Affairs Unit decided to launch an official investigation. Three days later, Medford High School also put him on paid suspension. Atkins had two jobs, but was prevented from doing either one.

His suspension from coaching at Medford occurred just four days before the Mustangs were scheduled to leave for a four-day training camp in New Hampshire. Atkins was not permitted to travel with his new team. He couldn't attend practices, and he wasn't supposed to interact with the players at school, though he frequently did. He was allowed to watch practice and game film, but he was relegated to bystander as the Mustangs went 4–7 under interim head coach Jon Wilson.

The Mustangs lost their first five games by an aggregate score of 159–20 before finally pulling off an upset against Austin Prep. Medford stumbled to a losing season, and Atkins never got a chance to coach. His case remained open for another full year before he was finally indicted on October 1, 2008. That's when he stopped receiving paychecks from the Chelsea Police Department. And it was just a few weeks later that his marriage officially ended. After twenty-one years as husband and wife, James and Julie Atkins divorced due to irreconcilable differences. Those differences were well-known to the residents of Chelsea for several years, but they remained a secret to Julie until the district attorney's investigation dug deeply enough into Atkins' finances and personal life that he finally had to reveal the skeleton in his closet. That skeleton had a name: Widalys Acevedo.

She was the secretary to city manager Jay Ash. She had two sons, Marcus and James. Atkins was their father.

While married to Julie and raising two beautiful girls, Atkins was also romantically involved with Widalys and was helping to raise two boys. By the time Atkins' trial began in May of 2009, those boys were ten and thirteen years old. James and Julie were divorced. And James and Widalys were engaged and living together. Of all the evidence that would come out during the trial, the scandalous fourteen-year affair may have been the most damaging. It told the jury that Atkins was dishonest, and it gave him motivation to steal. With the Booster Club account at his disposal, he could financially support Widalys and the boys without Julie ever finding out. But of course, everyone else knew. Parents, players, school and city administrators. And nobody seemed to care.

"We're all human," Widalys's boss, Jay Ash said. "We have our strong points and our weak points. Jimmy presents himself as a father figure to a lot of these kids, and his personal life doesn't affect the kids directly. You have to take the good with the bad. It's also not unusual for police officers to be in these situations, and it's not unusual for kids growing up in the rough-and-tumble world of the inner city to be in these situations."

Ash had recommended Atkins twice, once for the Chelsea coaching job and again in Medford. He, along with Kingston, DePatto, and presumably officials at Boston University were willing to overlook the infidelity in Atkins' personal life. Widalys even testified that Atkins was a "great father." Julie may have agreed. He certainly was devoted to all his children. He put in the time. Unlike many Chelsea fathers, he was present. So, even with his moral indiscretion and the mixed message it sent, he remained a better role model than most.

"They hired him knowing he had a double life, and it's nobody's business," Miguel Medina's mom, Vivian Quiles, said. "Yeah, he had some issues in his private life, but what did I care? He's there for my son. That's his life. Nobody can tell him what to do with his life. And the guy, even though, it can seem not being honest, that's his life. We have nothing to do with it. If he chooses to do it, it doesn't mean we're going to do the same thing. I truly believe that what you instill in your home, it will stay with your kids forever. And if they choose when they grow older and go that path, they're not going to be the first man or the last to have a double life, or to have two women at the same time. The kids didn't want to talk about it. The important thing is that he's a really great coach. He's taught us a lot."

Atkins gave Widalys $200 every week to help with the boys, and he routinely picked them up after school and brought them to their activities. He was with them on their birthdays, and on Christmas Day. Occasionally, Atkins would bring Marcus and James to practice, in full view of his players. He even brought his second family on vacation every year: Mexico, Miami, cruises. His affair with Widalys was not humiliating or embarrassing. And it wasn't a secret, at least not in Chelsea. Atkins would arrive at the Credit Union at Chelsea City Hall every Wednesday for several years, smile at Laurie the teller, and transfer $200 directly into Widalys' checking account. Again, the affair was not a secret in Chelsea.

"This case is about arrogance," Assistant District Attorney Edward Beagan said in his opening statement. "It's about deceit. And it's about the compulsive behavior of the defendant, James Atkins."

Atkins' trial began on May 4, 2009, in courtroom 817 of the Suffolk Superior Courthouse, the honorable Judge Judith Fabricant presiding. It had taken almost two-and-a-half years since the allegations of embezzlement had surfaced to get there. And over the next ten days, six men and six women, ten white, one black and one Hispanic, would hear the details of Atkins' affair, his gambling tendencies, his trips to strip clubs and casinos, and his management of the Booster Club account. Through it all, Atkins sat and listened. He wore an assortment of bright ties and dark suits that accentuated his broad shoulders and muscular build. He appeared relaxed at all times, smiling frequently, and offering help to his counsel. The jurors did not see an angry or nervous defendant.

And what they heard were a lot of numbers. They heard about the weekly payments to Widalys, and the many other times he gave her money. They heard about the shared vacations they took each year, and the $891-a-month car payments he made on two Ford Navigators. They heard about Atkins' income, approximately $125,000 a year, and Julie's income, about $240,000 a year after bonuses. And it may have seemed implausible that with that kind of income Atkins would bother to steal ten grand over three years. After all, if the motivation to steal was to hide the affair, as the prosecution contended, the jury had to consider that the affair was ongoing for ten years before the Booster Club account was created.

The scope of the investigation went from the day Atkins opened the Booster Club account with his own $250 deposit to the day he was forced to hand over his ATM card to Shane Verge. From December of 2005 to January of 2007, there was a total of $75,133 deposited into the account. Half of that was from third-party deposits. The rest came from Atkins' Credit Union account, one deposit from Julie Atkins, and various cash deposits.

Both the prosecution and the defense tried to convince the jury the case was about math and intent. The prosecution's math showed a shortfall in the account of nearly $10,000, and it was their contention that Atkins opened the Booster Club account with the intention of using it as his own personal slush fund. The defense tried to prove that Atkins consistently put his own money into the account, and that he had personally supported the football team with thousands of dollars of contributions during the 2004 season, before the Booster Club account was opened.

"They owe me $17,000," Jimmy said during a break in the trial. "And I'm gonna ask for it."

Both sides agreed, and there was no disputing, that Atkins used the Booster Club account for his own personal use. He paid a $634 bar bill at the Boston Marriott Hotel that covered more than fifty alcoholic beverages and appetizers on Super Bowl Sunday, 2006. He used the account to make travel reservations to Birmingham, Alabama, to visit relatives in April of 2005, and used the ATM card to withdraw $204.50 while he was there. He traveled with his daughter, Lauren, to Orlando, Florida, and paid for the trip with funds from the Booster Club account. In December of 2006, he took out another $502 from an ATM machine on Squire Road in Revere which is conspicuously close to a strip club. There were a series of withdrawals at Connecticut casinos and New Hampshire poker tournaments. There were hundreds of ATM withdrawals totaling more than $28,000 in two years.

"Isn't that what this case is all about?" Beagan questioned Atkins on the stand. "Money for the football team is money for you?"

"I was taking my money back when I needed it," Atkins stated unapologetically.

"Did you keep a running total of money going in and out?"

"No."

"Why not?"

"Because I knew the money I put in far exceeded what I took out."

But in the end, the jury may have disregarded the confusing money trail. There were two years of deposits and withdrawals, some football related, some not. Some receipts were provided.

Others were not. There were two versions of the same story being told. Which tale was more believable really came down to which person was more believable: Shane Verge or James Atkins.

According to Shane, he and Richard Oliveras tried several times during the 2005 season to help Atkins run the Booster Club. Each offer was rejected. That alone confused the two dads. The coach was always in a hurry, always talking about how busy he was, yet he was unwilling to have part of his burden alleviated. Maybe Atkins was just a control freak. What else could it be?

But Shane grew frustrated. He devoted a lot of time to raising money with the raffles, concession stands, fashion shows, and various other enterprises, but he couldn't get a handle on exactly how much money was raised, or how the money was being spent. Time after time, Shane would hand Atkins a wad of cash wrapped with a rubber band, and watch Atkins put the money in his pocket. Money raised. Money gone. No accounting. No accountability.

So, at the start of the 2006 season, Shane invited Atkins over to his house. There he showed him a ledger his wife had purchased at Office Max that could be used to keep track of funds. Atkins brushed it off as unnecessary. He assured Shane that the account was in good shape, and that there was zero debt coming out of the previous season. There was nothing to worry about. However, in a later conversation, Atkins told Shane that money still needed to be raised to pay for the $1,900 professional-style headphones that were purchased the previous year.

"You told me those were already paid for," Shane responded. And it was at this point that Shane became suspicious. He expressed his concerns to Richie, who brought them to the athletic director, Frank DePatto.

"How could you do this to me?" Atkins asked Shane after practice one day. "After everything I've done for this team."

Atkins was genuinely hurt, but Shane said flatly, "We just wanted to know where the money went."

Soon Shane would find out. He and Atkins went to the bank on September 28, 2006, to have Shane's name added to the account. At that time the account balance was $4.78. Atkins reiterated that there was no outstanding debt, and they agreed to move forward with Shane in charge of the account. Atkins, however, retained the ATM card associated with the account.

Over the next few months, Shane tracked every dollar that went in or out of the account. If coach needed money for a football-related expense, he simply provided Shane with a receipt, and Shane cut him a check. There were no ATM withdrawals from September to early December, and according to Shane's ledger, by Christmas there should have been $8,062.13. In actuality, there was 102 bucks left.

That led to the showdown between Shane, Richie, and Atkins. With DePatto present, Atkins signed the document agreeing to pay back $8,500 in $500 installments every month for the next year and a half. It could have ended there. Everyone agreed to keep the matter among themselves, but when Atkins tried to make his first payment with a third-party check from Lester Morovitz, Shane and Richie went to the district attorney, and Atkins' life began to unravel. He lost two jobs and one wife, and sat in a court-room with the potential of also losing his freedom.

"I never thought I'd be sitting here defending what I was doing," Atkins testified. "Everything I was doing I did for the high school team and those kids of Chelsea, so they could have an opportunity."

The jury heard Shane's and the prosecution's version of what happened. They were presented with a lot of bank and credit card statements. Totals and subtotals were shown on whiteboards, flip-charts and in PowerPoint summations. The defense had different numbers, and theirs went back to Coach's inaugural season of 2004, before there was a Booster Club account, before there was any fund-raising at all, and when Atkins paid for things out of his own pocket.

"You never started a ledger of any kind?" Beagan asked. "You never tracked the tens of thousands of dollars of donations? You never tracked your own monies put into the account?"

"No, I did not," Atkins responded to each question.

The case would hinge on Atkins' credibility. And Beagan was able to successfully chip away at it. The fourteen-year affair and double life suggested that Atkins was a liar and a cheat. And his insistence that he run the account without supervision for over a year made it look like he had something to hide, perhaps his payments to Acevedo and his expenses at bars, strip clubs, and casinos.

"There was no level of competence managing this account," Beagan told the jury. "His refusal repeatedly to accept help on this, and his refusal to listen to the superintendent about keeping records goes to his intent. He wanted exclusive control over this account to perpetuate his scheme to slowly and methodically embezzle from this account."

That may have been more speculative than convincing, but when Beagan produced three different obviously fraudulent receipts, the jury took notice. Each year, Atkins bought hats, sweatshirts, and caps at an embroidery shop known as Krazy Kats. It was run out of the home of a kindly, white-haired woman named Katherine Webber.

Beagan showed Atkins and the jury three receipts from September and November of 2005 totaling $1,502. Then he produced three more receipts from September and November of 2006 for the exact same amounts and on the exact same dates. The orders and the handwriting were identical. The only difference was that one indicated '05 and the other '06. And Beagan was more than happy to point out to the jury that there was a smudge and shadow on the 2006 receipts clearly suggesting that a copy had been made and the year had been changed. Webber, who smiled at Atkins as she entered the witness stand, admitted she couldn't find the invoice for the 2006 receipts, though she had them for 2005.

"After seeing all three of these documents, are you still asserting that you're owed reimbursement for the total of $1,500?" Beagan had asked Atkins aggressively when he was on the stand.

"For the total of $1,500? No," Atkins replied. His credibility had taken a bigger hit than he'd ever received on the football field. And Beagan pounded it home in his closing.

"Credibility is a big part of this case," he said. "At the close of this case, you saw some compelling evidence about the credibility of the defendant. Take a look at those documents. Compare '05 to '06. You'll see these documents are exactly similar. The handwriting on those receipts, every element of it is exactly the same. They're exactly the same because the defendant falsified them. He was trying to gather receipts to demonstrate why he had withdrawn all this money. So, the defendant came across 2005 versions, and he doctored them. He changed them to 2006. But he forgot something. He forgot to prove that he had paid the 2006 receipts."

To a jury inundated with numbers and looking for the truth between two vastly different stories, the adulterer who had successfully hidden his mistress and two children from his wife for over a decade had just been caught in another lie. Atkins needed the jury to believe the money he took from the account was reimbursement for money he had spent to help the football team. But he didn't have receipts or records to verify his contention, and his credibility was bleeding on the floor of the courtroom.

And there was the agreement with Frank and Shane to pay the money back. This was another area where Atkins' obvious intelligence weakened his case. The jury already wondered why someone who consistently finished at the top of his class on promotions exams could so badly mismanage the Booster Club account. He had failed to keep receipts. He paid no attention to the perception of misappropriations of funds, and his failure to keep good records had resulted in over a dozen bounced checks and nearly $1,000 in overdraft fees charged to the Booster Club account. When Beagan pointed this out to him, Atkins' attempt at humility came off as smug.

"Yeah, I wasn't very good at it," he said with a smile.

Now, the jury was left to consider why a veteran police officer with a master's degree in criminal justice would sign a document agreeing to pay back $8,500 if he didn't actually take the money in the first place.

"I signed this document to keep my football job," Atkins explained in court. "I showed Frank DePatto receipts that proved I didn't owe the money. But it was my belief that if I didn't sign this document that I would lose my coaching job."

"You were afraid of losing your job, but you signed a document that called for you to pay back $8,500?" Beagan asked incredulously. "You thought Frank was gonna sit on this?"

"He sat on it for a month prior. So, yes."

"You're familiar with a confession. You've listened to a lot of confessions. This was a confession, wasn't it, Sergeant?"

"No, it was not."

"I have no further questions, your honor."

It was a strong close to the cross-examination. Beagan knew he wouldn't be able to get Atkins to admit the signed document was an admission of guilt, but he had put the idea in the minds of the jurors, and he re-emphasized it during his closing argument.

"He wants you to believe this was an agreement to fund-raise," Beagan said holding up the document. "It's simply a confession. The document was placed before the defendant. He read it. There were bank statements in front of him. There was nothing he could do but sign the document. After he signed it he knew he was in trouble. He went to Lester Morovitz, and then he went to Shane Verge and said he had a thousand-dollar payment. He tried to pass off a thousand-dollar check from a senior citizen in Chelsea as his own money. That's the depth to which he went to conceal his scheme."

He was a bad guy. He took from old people. He stole from the kids he was entrusted to protect. He gambled and went to strip clubs. He forged receipts. And he had two children from an extramarital affair. Shame on him! That's how the prosecution tried to frame it. But that picture was incomplete. The coach was also a good guy. Through the sheer force of his personality and the strength of his convictions, he saved the troubled kids of Chelsea. He pulled them off the streets and pushed them toward a better life. And the defense wanted to make sure Atkins was painted with that brush as well.

"The defense calls Orlando Echevarria to the stand."

The irony was conspicuous. Orlando, the one-time gang-banger who met Atkins while sitting in jail, was now a young man with a bright future, and Atkins was the one in trouble with the law. Orlando strode confidently through the courtroom past his former coach and on to the witness stand. He appeared to have grown at least three inches taller from his graduation day two years earlier. His shoulders were broader, and his face was much older. He was an imposing, but nonthreatening figure. He wore a dark red dress shirt pulled out of his baggy blue jeans, and he carried his Chelsea High School varsity football jacket by his side.

Orlando leaned toward the microphone and told the jury he was now a twenty-year-old freshman at Bunker Hill Community College who spent his summers working with kids. Five years earlier he had swung a baseball bat in a gang fight.

"Somehow I got locked up," he said. "And Coach came down to my cell and talked to me. The deal was 'play football and you'll get out.' That was the summer going into my sophomore year."

Orlando was the essence of Atkins' life's work, and while that may have been immaterial to the case, it might have helped make Atkins a more sympathetic character if the jury came to fully appreciate what Atkins had done for some of the most hard-core kids of Chelsea. Orlando said he was in a gang fight, but never mentioned the bat or the machete. There was no mention of the Bloods or Tiny Rascal Gang. The violent difference between what the jury thought of as 'some kids getting into a fight' and a potentially deadly gang fight was never spelled out. Orlando sat there looking like a fine upstanding young man. How could the jury know who he was or where he was headed before Atkins entered his life and changed it? Would it have helped if Orlando had testified to what happened in the hallways of Chelsea High School a month after Atkins led Orlando out of that jail cell?

"There was this MS-13 kid," Orlando recalled once. "I was walking through the hallway. And he was talking shit. I thought about fucking him up right there, but then I thought it was just the beginning of football season, and I was just starting to like it. And the kid had a cane with a flag wrapped around it. In the school, you can't have that. He was just walking around chilling with his flag. He tried to put it on me that I was around saying something. So, I said, 'You know what? Why don't you meet me outside after school and I'll fuck you up?' That's the only thing I said to the kid. I didn't want no drama. I didn't bother making a scene, because then I'd go down to the office, and they'd say I couldn't play. So, I said one thing and then I kept walking. So, the kid comes after me again. So, he's grilling me, and I say, 'What the fuck are you looking at?' I just couldn't take it anymore, and I thought, 'I'm just gonna have to fuck him up right now.'"

Orlando never told that story in court, nor did he ever fight the MS-13 kid. And the jury never heard that Atkins' influence was the reason why. The jury didn't see the process. They only saw the finished product. They saw a cooperative, polite, and intelligent man, and they listened to him swear under oath that Atkins paid for all the football-related expenses. Orlando verified that Coach paid for the senior dinners, the Friday afternoon pizza, the extra balls, Gatorade for the games, and various other things. Orlando and his seventy teammates didn't pay for anything.

"Cleats and socks? Did you pay for any of those?"

"No."

"Did you attend a football banquet?"

"Yes."

"Were you presented with a jacket?"

"Yes."

"Did you pay for that jacket?"

"No."

Orlando held up the jacket, no doubt, as instructed beforehand, then he left without looking at his former coach. Jonathan Luna was also called to testify on Atkins' behalf. Jonathan had gained some weight since high school. He wore glasses that aged him a bit. Like Orlando, he was now a college kid. He was doing well right next door at Suffolk University. He was another tough kid that Atkins had helped fight past his troubled environment. In fact, two weeks after this court appearance, Jonathan would be in another court watching his brother, Pascual, be convicted by a federal jury. Pascual would serve twenty-five years to life for shooting at police officers at the immigration rally.

Orlando and Jonathan had arrived at the courthouse separately, and they would leave the same way. Once outside, Jonathan turned left, crossed the street and entered Suffolk University where he was finishing up his spring term. Orlando went right. Still clinging to his varsity football jacket as if clinging to the past, Orlando could see one possible future. There before him was the Tobin Bridge rising up off the highway and then down into Chelsea. It was the bridge to nowhere, and Orlando took a moment to think about his boys, especially Black Josh.

"I always try to help him," he thought. "But it's the gang thing. He couldn't make it. School and the street thing just fucked him all up. I have to work more than him. I need a future for myself."

That determination was why he was enrolled at Bunker Hill Community College even though he never believed he was college material. Orlando had been placed in the Special Education classes in high school, and he was smart enough to know that was because teachers thought he was stupid. But when Coach started believing in him, he started believing in himself. He stopped "chilling" and fighting, and started thinking about a future way beyond the Tobin Bridge.

"After high school, I'm leaving here," Orlando used to say. "I just gotta get out of here and start all over. When I accomplish my goals, it's gonna be somewhere I want to be. I can get a job here. I understand the city, but it all depends on where I want to go."

It's impossible to know where Orlando will end up. His loyalty to his boys is deeply ingrained. While he recognizes the dangers of a gang life, he still respects that life and understands why others would choose it. He no longer carries weapons, or hangs out on the streets, but that's because he's been keeping himself busy. Things could definitely break down in a hurry. He was, after all, getting on the bus headed back to Chelsea. He'd find out the very next day the fate of his former coach.

"That dog don't hunt," Louison closed in his best folksy manner. "The commonwealth wants to steer you, and not allow you to consider all of the money that Jim Atkins put into the program. And they did a whole lot of work to distract you from that fact. They're going to ask you not to add up the money that Jim Atkins put into the program. But it was his money that he put in. It was his money that he took out."

That was Atkins' whole case. There was plenty of evidence that he put his own money into the account, that he paid for things long before the account was created, and that he had deposited thousands of dollars of donors' checks that were made out to him.

"It doesn't add up," Louison continued. "When actual checks were sent to him and made out to him, what did he do? He deposited them. Why would a man financially pressured to steal take cash and put it in, and then take it out?"

It was not a strong closing. Without the help of supportive facts, Louison relied on common sense. He argued that Atkins didn't need to steal, because he and his wife made so much money. He also wondered aloud why someone who had finally gotten the head coaching job he coveted would put that at risk "in order to palm a few thousand dollars." Further, he tried to persuade the jury that Atkins was merely a sloppy record keeper. Louison ignored the forged receipts to Krazy Kats, and called the ATM withdrawals at strip clubs and casinos a red herring.

"In this case, the red herring is these ATM locations. They've got blow-ups of aerials of the North Shore, and they've got dollar signs all over the North Shore. That's a distraction to make you think he's a bad guy, but these were places where he accessed his own money with the ATM card. Don't go in there and say all the good that you've done, Jim Atkins, for these kids, we're going to call you a criminal for taking out that money that you honestly believed you put in."

Louison sat down and received a reassuring nod from Atkins. He had listened intently to Louison's closing remarks while simultaneously trying to read the jury. Whatever it was he saw on the jurors' faces had made him appear even more confident. Now, it was Beagan's turn.

"His status in the community led him to believe that he was untouchable. Unquestionable," Beagan began. "And he treated this account as his own personal property. He used the account to fund gas for his Navigator, for personal travel, to make calls from Mexico, to have his car detailed. The fact that there was no level of competence managing the account goes to his motive. He wanted exclusive control over this account to perpetuate his scheme to slowly and methodically embezzle from this account."

Beagan never referenced Widalys Acevedo. That damage had already been done. Instead, he focused on the thousands of dollars Atkins claimed he was owed, but the prosecution had successfully shown that he wasn't. The Krazy Kats receipts, along with Atkins' classification of his Super Bowl party as a high school banquet showed Atkins to be dishonest, and it proved his math regarding money in and money out was less reliable than the prosecution's math.

Guilty. It only took a few hours of deliberation for the jury to come back with guilty verdicts on five of the six counts of larceny. Judge Fabricant ordered Atkins to repay $12,900 in restitution to the Chelsea football team. Ironically, Atkins was required to make restitution in $500-a-month payments. If he had simply lived up to that same arrangement with Shane, Richie, and Frank, he would still be a cop and a coach. Now he was neither. Atkins was also sentenced to ninety days home confinement. He would remain on probation for an additional five years.

"James Atkins was once a police sergeant, a football coach, and a mentor to so many students," Beagan's boss, Suffolk County district attorney Daniel F. Conley said. "Not anymore. Through his own greed and selfishness, he threw it all away."

It's hard to see it any other way. James Atkins used to say, "Football is life." And he had just been taken down in the open field. The end zone was right there in front of him. He could see Orlando and Jonathan. Frankie and Miguel. Midnight. Kenzi and Luis Verde. Danny, Fatty, Mario, and all the rest. Even Cody and Richie. He had delivered a powerful message to all of them. He had exerted his influence. He had come to symbolize success after struggle. He was one of them. And they were standing at the goal line waiting for him to lead them even further, to push them in new directions. Higher and higher. Hope had come to Chelsea, and it had no limits. Then, Atkins got tripped up. All he had to do was stay on his feet. Be a stand-up guy. Instead, those kids who had found a man they could respect, who had seen the cop and the coach police the streets and patrol the sidelines, who watched the father figure bring discipline to their lives, and who listened to him preach and scream and curse, had just been exposed to the bitter chill of another hard fall in Chelsea.

CHELSEA RED DEVILS 2006 RESULTS

09/08	at	East Boston	(L)	56–20
09/15	vs	Madison Park	(W)	22–16
09/22	vs	Minuteman Regional	(W)	61–12
09/29	vs	Tyngsboro	(L)	41–22
10/06	at	Lynn Tech	(W)	8–6
10/13	vs	Whittier Tech	(L)	36–22
10/21	at	Northeast Tech	(W)	30–18
10/27	vs	Manchester	(L)	33–22
11/04	at	Georgetown	(L)	25–16
11/10	vs	North Shore	(W)	11–2
11/23	vs	Pope John	(W)	18–13

EPILOGUE

In late fall of 2009, Orlando Echevarria walked briskly between classes on the campus of Bunker Hill Community College in Charlestown, Massachusetts. He was only a few miles from home, but he had distanced himself from the confused, angry boy who had been sitting in a jail cell five years earlier.

"I hated cops," Orlando recalled. "I still hate 'em."

Yes, even though it was a police officer named James Atkins who had offered Orlando his "get out of jail free" card, and pushed him toward high school graduation and beyond, Orlando still hated cops. Orlando's hatred may have run so deep that he couldn't even see the irony in his stated goal.

"I'm studying criminal justice," he said. "I'm gonna be a police officer. It's good money, and I can provide for my family someday."

James Atkins once thought the same thing. But while Orlando now walked among other students like himself, the ones with dreams as big as their potential, Atkins stepped out into a new and uncertain future. He had served his time under house arrest and had started an executive protection company in Lynn. He was going to be a bodyguard for businessmen. He was also working on an appeal of his conviction and continued to maintain his innocence.

"I'm bitter," he said. "I still have my same cocky attitude. I still crack jokes and shit on everybody. But those motherfuckers tortured my life. And I will never admit I did anything wrong."

Atkins was engaged now to Widalys and was especially pleased that his boys and girls from both relationships got along very well.

The police department Atkins left behind had seen a 10 percent increase in the number of officers patrolling the streets, but because of the historic economic downturn, Chelsea's budget was cut by $1.5 million in 2009, and was going to drop another $3 million the next year.

"It was a quiet summer for us," said Jay Ash, now in his ninth year as city manager. "We were able to have police officers standing on street corners for visibility, introducing themselves in the neighborhood. But the success is being threatened by budget realities that all cities are facing."

But Ash and the city of Chelsea still had Molly Baldwin and ROCA on their side. Baldwin, now in her twenty-first year of getting in the faces of high-risk youth, spoke proudly of the progress ROCA had made over the past three years.

"The quality of the work has just gone through the roof," she said. "We've gotten much better at what we're doing. We can see that in the changes young people are making in their lives."

For instance, 111 people were placed in jobs in 2008 through ROCA's transition employment model that had just been introduced in 2006. But Chelsea continued to have a high violent crime rate, and residents like City Red, Big J, and Angel Acavedo all continued to struggle and wander aimlessly. Dana Betts regularly checked in on them.

"We're into outreach, transformational relationships, life skills, education, and employment," Baldwin explained. "Whatever else we use doesn't really matter. It's really about the relationships."

That's true for ROCA as well as Atkins, other coaches, educators, and the city's leaders. The relationships they build, and the trust they earn, is what can lead directionless and uninspired kids out of Chelsea. And it worked for many of the Chelsea Red Devils.

Orlando was a college sophomore now. Football was behind him, but he hoped to earn a basketball scholarship to a four-year college. He said a few small schools in Florida were looking at him. If nothing came of that, Orlando would probably transfer to the University of Massachusetts in Dartmouth. He still believed Atkins saved his life.

"I don't see it being his fault," Orlando said, regarding the Booster Club account. "He helped me out, and I have nothing against him. He got me off the street. I wasn't planning to go to college, but he got me focused. He got me here."

Not far away from Orlando, his former teammate Jonathan Luna shared a similar dream. Jonathan was a junior at Suffolk University, also studying to become a police officer. He lived at home with his parents and worked part-time at a Rent-A-Center. His brother, Pascual, was serving his time in a federal prison in Kentucky. Jonathan had no plans to go see him.

And the Chelsea High School graduation class of 2007 could have at least one more alumnus who becomes a police officer. Danny Cortez was at Bay State College studying criminal justice. He had recently taken the police exam and was waiting to hear back from the only police department to which he applied—Chelsea.

"I know it's a huge goal," he said. "But I eventually want to be the police chief of the city."

After high school, Danny also coached Pop Warner football with Coach Atkins, but because of his growing responsibilities at home, Danny couldn't accept Atkins' offer to coach the Medford High School freshman team. Danny's mother remained completely out of the picture, and Danny said he would "like to keep it that way." His two younger brothers were playing football at Chelsea High, one of whom had just made Danny an uncle for the first time. His older sister, Yvette, suffering from Engelmann's syndrome, continued to need around-the-clock care.

Meanwhile, Danny said that Fatty was kicked out of his house after coming home "high and drunk" and throwing up all over the place. Fatty spent a year at Miguel Medina's home before moving back in with his mother.

"As for the situation with Coach Atkins," Danny said, "What really gets to me is that I really thought Coach was going to bring the city back to the days of glory where everyone can walk around proud of Chelsea. I thought he was going to do it through football, and he was gonna end up being some sort of Messiah. Other than that, I don't feel I'm the one to be commenting on the matter."

Frankie Quiles earned a 3.42 GPA at Bridgton Academy before transferring to Florida International University where he expected to play Division I football.

"It was the hardest, but best decision I have ever made," Frankie said. "It made me more of a man and showed me how much work you have to put in to play in the big times."

Richie Oliveras was a junior at Virginia Tech majoring in urban affairs and planning. His parents and younger sister remained in Chelsea, unable to get a good price for their home and move to Virginia as planned.

Alex Caraballo tore his ACL during his senior year at Chelsea, thus ending his football career. He was married now with a baby girl on the way and was going to school to become a barber.

Mario Hernandez attempted to join the Marines after high school, but was rejected due to his allergy to bees. He was working in the health care industry, helping his mother with the bills, and considering college.

Ivan Romero graduated from Chelsea High School in 2008. He was a part-time student at Bunker Hill Community College, working at a liquor store in Medford and as a bouncer at a bar in Revere on the weekends.

Saba Omeragic still went by the nickname "Alphabet." He was at the University of Massachusetts in Amherst majoring in finance.

Hamza Abdul was an assistant coach for the Chelsea High School football and track teams. He currently had a 4.0 grade point average at North Shore Community College and would be transferring to U-Mass Boston the next spring.

Josh Rubiera said that while playing football for Coach Atkins, he was also inspired to pursue a career in law enforcement. He was attending Bunker Hill Community College, pursuing an associate's degree in business. He plans to attempt to get his bachelor's degree at U-Mass Boston.

Austin Hightower graduated from Chelsea High School in 2009 and was studying political science at Regis College. He was interested in getting an internship with a lobbyist firm in either Boston or Washington, D.C.

Cody Verge was the Red Devils' starting quarterback in 2007, graduated on time, and went into the Air Force. He was a wide receiver now for the Air Force Academy. His father, Shane, was now a coach for the freshman football team at Chelsea under the direct supervision of head coach, Mike Stellato, and still athletic director, Frank DePatto.

After taking over for Atkins in 2007, Stellato led the Red Devils to a 3–8 record, then 4–7 in 2008. But in a remarkable turnaround, the Red Devils reeled off six straight wins to start the 2009 season, lost to Whittier, and then beat North Shore. With two regular-season games remaining, the Red Devils were on the inside track to the Division 4 Super Bowl, but they would miss by a few inches. Their game against Northeast Tech would decide which team would make the playoffs, and with less than a minute remaining in the game, Chelsea had a chance to tie it up with a 2-point conversion. The pass fell to the ground, and Chelsea lost 14–12, finishing the season 8–2.

Pride had returned to Chelsea. A successful football team can do that for a city. With three consecutive winning seasons, Coach Atkins was able to help restore that pride. It may have been lost in the confusion of his departure and the two losing seasons that followed, but Stellato and the Red Devils, along with Ash, Baldwin, police chief Brian Kyes, and many others, were bringing back Chelsea pride. Through the power of football, the power of relationships, and the power of positive influences, there was tremendous hope for kids growing up in Chelsea, kids like Dont'e Wilson. His Facebook reply to my queries, printed here exactly as he wrote it, shows both intelligence and an expressiveness about how a young person sees the hand they're dealt and the help they receive. Adults who teach can also learn that even though they're with a child for a relatively short time, the impact can be felt for a lifetime.

Dont'e Wilson September 29 at 1:17 pm

> *Hay um sence the thing with coach atkins things feel a lot different for me personaly I fell like my senior year was a waist I've spent three years tryna prove to not only the team but to myself and aktins who was my only farther figure at that time I had and still have respect for himm I just feel like my lifes ben cut short and I was paralyzed of my dreams everything just seems so dead and hopless .yes I stay in touch with him we are all humen no ones perfect but what he's done for me is the most anyones done for me and I just wake up everyday with this same chip on my shoulder with shattered dream.but I do live I have a job I was going to school but outside I live but inside I feel numb going from a kid the doctor told me I wouldn't be able to make it I was over weight 230 with horrible asma I cried and beged that doctor to let me play I said this is my calling on to my senior year was my peek I was only 170 man what a change I've grown from the kid who had all black everyday and hid myself cuzz ppl making fun of me to a man and I thank him I was in college and I wanna be a cop but I can't styll help but to roll over and feel empty . . . . I just wish I can have my wings back and play ball.*

SOURCES

The information in this book is predominantly from firsthand accounts and taped interviews. Any time there are quotation marks, the statement is verbatim. The interviews were conducted by either Drew Crea or myself. Between us we were at nearly every game walking the sidelines, in the locker rooms, in the press boxes, and mingling with the fans. One or both of us were also at Coach's house for Senior Dinner, in the audience for the fashion show, at Chelsea High School's graduation, and we also visited several players in their homes.

The accounts of criminal behavior by certain individuals were told to me by one or more of the police officers interviewed and then, where possible, confirmed by police records and/or newspaper accounts from the *Boston Globe* and the *Chelsea Record*.

The trial of James Atkins, of course, was public. I attended three days of the trial and took detailed notes of what was said by the lawyers, witnesses, and the judge. I was not present for the testimonies of Cody Verge, Widalys Acevedo, or Julie Atkins, but the court reporter provided me with the official transcripts.

ACKNOWLEDGMENTS

As always, there are a number of people to thank and credit for this book coming to fruition, and like the best things in life, it starts in the home. My wife, Eileen, has a demanding and stressful job. And I know there has to be at least a moment when she hears I'm going to start on another book when she thinks: "Great, so while you're off writing, who's going to help me with the kids, and the shopping, and the cleaning, and everything else?"

But she doesn't say that. Instead she says, "That sounds like a great idea. How can I help?"

And I think, "Well, first of all, you just did."

Then, as a journalist herself, she helps by listening to frequent updates on the story and asking a lot of questions for which I don't have the answers. That's when I realize I need to go back out there and ask those same questions and get the answers. And of course, to show my appreciation to her for filling in potential blanks, I occasionally do the dishes. Everybody wins.

For this book, in particular, I not only had tremendous support at home, I had a lot of help from eight houses down the street. Without my neighbor and good friend, Jill DiCarlo, I couldn't have done the necessary research or put in a sufficient amount of time to meet the demands of a project like this. Several times a week, I headed into Chelsea to conduct interviews, attend practices, or simply walk the streets to observe and to learn, and each time I needed her to, Jill took care of my daughter, Grace, who had just turned five years old when I started to follow the Red Devils.

Jill was much more than a reliable babysitter. She also listened attentively as I told her the story and updated her on what was happening with the kids and the coach. I could tell she was genuinely fascinated, and that encouraged me to keep digging, and to follow through to the end.

ACKNOWLEDGMENTS

As mentioned in the preface, I had the assistance of a college intern named Drew Crea. I'm especially grateful to him for doing so much more than I asked him to do. He brought a real passion and aggression to this project that produced several unexpected details and insights. The information he provided sent me in new directions that made the story either more emotional, shocking, or funny. Drew's enthusiasm was matched by his intelligence and instincts, and I'm sure he'll carry those attributes with him into a bright future.

There certainly would have been a lot of empty pages if it weren't for James Atkins. I hope his infectious personality, charm, and charisma aren't overshadowed by his crudeness, his toughness, and his ultimate downfall. He is truly a likable and kind man. Flaws aside for the moment, he absolutely had the kids' best interests at heart. He worked extremely hard to keep them moving in the right direction.

I thank him for his openness and his accessibility, and yes, his honesty. Granted, I knew about Widalys and his sons for a long time before I confronted him about it. Obviously, he wanted to keep that a secret, but he was forthright with his responses.

As for the embezzlement charges, I don't know if he told me the truth, his version of the truth, or if he lied. I know he put a lot of his own money into the account, and I know he took a lot of money out. The math is fuzzy, but I like to think we became friends, and I still have a lot of respect for him for what he did for those kids. Thank you, Jimmy.

Each of the players deserves credit and gratitude. They didn't have to cooperate, and they certainly didn't have to open up old wounds with a total stranger, but they did. Their stories of hardships and hopes give us all a better understanding of the struggles many people are going through. I thank them for letting me into their world and letting me share it with the rest of the world.

I thank everyone who gave up their valuable time to sit and talk to me. Jay Ash was especially helpful as he detailed the history of Chelsea and the changes taking place in the city's government, culture, population, and attitude.

Detectives Dan Delaney and Scott Conley, Sergeant David Batchelor and police chief Frank Garvin were nice enough to regale me with war stories and to offer background information about the extent of the gang problem in Chelsea.

Mary Baldwin opened the doors of ROCA to me and approved my night out with caseworker Dana Betts. Thank you both.

I'd like to thank Rich Oliveras, Shane Verge, and Frank DePatto for the tremendous amount of time and cooperation they gave me. They are good men doing good things in Chelsea.

Special thanks to my editor Keith Wallman who trimmed the fat and cleaned up the prose. I trusted him implicitly, which I know made me a better writer and this a better book.

And to whomever it was at Globe Pequot that came up with the title *Breakdown,* thank you. I love it.

INDEX

About the Author

Bob Halloran is the author of *Irish Thunder* (Lyons Press) and a well-known and well-respected television journalist in Boston. He is currently the weekend news and sports anchor at WCVB-TV, Channel 5 in Boston. He is also a former ESPN anchor and columnist for espn.com. He has been working as a news and sports anchor in New England for over twenty years, and he writes a weekly column for *The Metro* newspaper in Boston, where he lives.